PAUL G. HOFFMAN

Discovery Hall Archival Collections

Paul G. Hoffman *Architect of Foreign Aid*

ALAN R. RAUCHER

THE UNIVERSITY PRESS OF KENTUCKY

Scholarly publisher for the Commonwealth, serving
Bellarmine College, Berea College, Centre College of
Kentucky, Eastern Kentucky University, The Filson Club,
Georgetown College, Kentucky Historical Society, Kentucky
State University, Morehead State University, Murray State
University, Northern Kentucky University, Transylvania
University, University of Kentucky, University of Louisville,
and Western Kentucky University.

Editorial and Sales Offices: Lexington, Kentucky 40506-0024

Library of Congress Cataloging-in-Publication Data

Raucher, Alan R.
  Paul G. Hoffman, architect of foreign aid.

  Bibliography: p.
  Includes index.
  1. Hoffman, Paul G. (Paul Gary), 1891–1974—
Biography. 2. Businessmen—United States—Biography.
3. Government executives—United States—Biography.
4. Automobile industry and trade—United States.
I. Title.
HC102.5.H63R38   1985   973.9'092'4 [B]   81-13406

ISBN: 978-0-8131-5626-2

For Margaret and Adam

Contents

Preface

Into a long life of eighty-three years, Paul G. Hoffman crowded many notable successes and achievements. By 1948, when President Truman appointed him to administer the multibillion-dollar Marshall Plan, he had already earned fame and fortune as the president of the Studebaker Corporation and as an articulate spokesman for business progressivism. After he left the Marshall Plan, he went on to a series of important positions, culminating with his direction of the United Nations development programs, from which he finally retired at the end of 1971.

As a businessman and as a public figure, Hoffman understood well the importance of public opinion and mass communications in the modern world. He became an adept publicist who knew how to communicate with the public and how to cultivate journalists. With the help of assistants and public relations advisors, he delivered hundreds of speeches and published hundreds of articles, as well as several books. He engaged in those activities not simply because he craved the limelight; more important, he sought to publicize himself in order to personalize the otherwise impersonal institutions he led. It is not unfair to say that he created his own public image.

Nonetheless, he was genuinely modest. He felt that a biography about him would not be worthwhile or interesting. To a magazine editor seeking information, he wrote, "There are altogether too many biographies kicking about for the good of the world."[1] When a writer decided to include him among six individuals whose lives revealed the nature of American culture in the modern industrial age, he expressed surprise: "Perhaps I should add that I haven't the remotest idea why you chose to honor me."[2] That modesty did scant justice to his accomplishments.

Although he won praise and honors from contemporaries, Hoffman now seems in danger of slipping into historical obscurity. Occasionally he is remembered in connection with particular incidents or organizations, and Theodore H. White's recent autobiography includes a sentimental sketch of Hoffman, one of his few heroes in modern history. But until now no full biography of him has appeared.[3] In textbooks on American history since World War II, he barely gets noticed and is often unmentioned by authors who manage to take note of radical activist Abbie Hoffman and his adversary Julius Hoffman. To put the case simply, Paul Hoffman was too important to be forgotten in that way.

Perhaps he has not received the attention he deserves because he followed two careers: one in the automotive industry and the other in public affairs. Those interested in one rarely care about the other. In the specialized world of automotive history, the story ends with his departure from Studebaker. Conversely, those who focus on his role with the Marshall Plan, the Ford Foundation, the Eisenhower administration, and the United Nations tend to regard his business career as mere prologue to the main events.

Of course, many other successful businessmen, out of a sense of social responsibility or a desire for the challenge of power, also made that transition to public affairs. Men like Bernard Baruch, Averell Harriman, and later Robert McNamara often served as members of presidential Cabinets, government commissions, and other institutions that allowed them to exert influence on public policies. Most commonly for such men, their public roles overshadowed their business activities. With Hoffman, however, the business career itself was noteworthy; in addition, the core of values that formed during his business career had direct bearing on his other activities.

Some may regard him as a shallow booster for free enterprise and the American Way of Life, but it is a mistake to dismiss Hoffman as an administrator-bureaucrat lacking vision or imagination. Without brilliance or originality, he grew intellectually and acquired interest in some of the most important issues of public policy. Because of his network of influential associations and his standing within the so-called Establishment, what he did and what he said are significant. This biography seeks to examine those aspects of his career in order to shed light on how the national leadership confronted the modern world.

To understand how Hoffman impressed his contemporaries, it is necessary to take note, however superficially, of his personality and his character. All the evidence reveals a man of remarkably sunny disposition. His optimism and confidence may not always have been warranted by the circumstances, but they made him a doer, not a brooder. Moreover, his natural decency, courtesy, sincerity, and good humor inspired others. He possessed the ability to persuade and to motivate without a touch of slickness. Widely different types of people—subordinates, peers, men of power, and cynical observers—recognized and felt moved by him.

Among the many contemporaries who admired him, Walter Lippmann paid special homage to his character. Not one to mince words when judging leaders on the national or international level, Lippmann declared that with Hoffman, "the outside and the inside are all the same stuff"; he did not scheme, or play a game, or hide his meaning. Instinctively and intuitively, according to Lippmann, he possessed the gift of leadership within American democracy.[4]

The exercise of that gift sometimes required courage. It should go without saying that he was no radical; on domestic and foreign affairs he sought to preserve the fundamental features of the American democratic and capitalist system. As an advocate of progressivism and internationalism, however, he aroused particularly vicious personal attacks from right-wing extremists. Yet even when those attacks made life difficult for him, he did not back down.

Fortunately, he also retained the confidence and support of powerful friends. With their help he continued to pursue his public career long after the common age of retirement. In very real ways, his last positions at the U.N. were successful extensions of the internationalism to which he had committed himself during the previous decades. Thus he was able to feel, quite legitimately, that he had used his life in a worthwhile way.

Acknowledgments

I am indebted to the Harry S. Truman Library Institute, the American Philosophical Society, and Wayne State University for awarding me grants to conduct the research for this book. A sabbatical leave made it possible for me to devote an academic year to research and writing. The research fund of the Department of History at Wayne State helped to pay for the photographs and other materials.

I could not have written this book without the assistance of the staffs of many libraries and archives. In particular, I want to thank Benedict K. Zobrist and his highly competent staff at the Truman Library for making so valuable the weeks I spent there. Marsha Mullin of Discovery Hall Museum in South Bend provided help under difficult conditions.

For encouragement and support I want to thank colleagues and friends. Loren Pennington of Emporia State University made available his thorough transcripts of oral interviews with Studebaker's union officials. Robert Zieger of Wayne State University and Morrell Heald of Case-Western Reserve University each read a chapter of work in progress, offering valuable criticism. I also benefited from the extraordinarily thorough criticism provided by the evaluators for the University Press of Kentucky. Of course, I remain responsible for all errors and flaws.

This entire manuscript and all its revisions were expertly typed by Ginny Corbin.

1 Making
A Million
Selling Cars

When he attracted national attention as a public figure, journalistic profiles sometimes suggested that Paul G. Hoffman (1891–1974) fit the much admired model of the self-made American businessman. But, a stickler for accuracy, he eventually set the record straight. He certainly did not start from humble origins in rural or small-town America to become a millionaire by his own efforts. More typical of successful businessmen of his time, he came from a background that gave him distinct advantages, both material and cultural.

Paul Hoffman was born in Chicago, the boom city of late-nineteenth-century America. Rebuilt and still growing after its terrible fire, the city of new skyscrapers was the intellectual and cultural capital of the Midwest, attracting to it professionals, writers, social crusaders, and other talented and ambitious individuals. With money from John D. Rockefeller, the University of Chicago rose to challenge the leading eastern universities. The Columbian Exposition, the World's Fair hosted by the city in 1893, gave proof of its dynamism.

There was, of course, an underside to Chicago. Probably more than any other American city of that era, it was the site of often violent labor strife. Its rapid industrialization and modernization, plus large-scale immigration, seemed to exaggerate the conflict between labor and capital. Five years before Hoffman was born, Chicago won notoriety with the Haymarket riot and the conspiracy trial that followed. When he was three, the strike that began in nearby Pullman spread into a national railway strike, with Chicago the hub of the labor effort. A few years after that, the squalor and brutality of the city's meatpacking industry became the focal point of exposés and public revulsion.

None of those seamy aspects of the city touched Paul Hoffman, however. He came from one of the city's prosperous and prominent pioneer families, and from such origins he acquired the values and the self-confidence that always impressed those who knew him.

Paul's grandfather, William Delos Hoffman, achieved success as the Illinois agent for a sewing machine company. He married the daughter of John Gray, wealthy and civic-minded developer of the Grayland subdivision, who served on Chicago's first school board and then as sheriff of Cook County. By the 1880s Paul's grandparents lived on the South Side of Chicago as one of the city's wealthiest families. Mrs. Hoffman considered herself a great society lady and raised her son, George Delos Hoffman, without regard to expense. After he graduated from high school and learned German, he was sent not to college but to Germany to study the flute. But when he returned after a few years and married against his mother's wishes, she disinherited him.[1]

Nevertheless, George Delos Hoffman, Paul's father, himself became quite well off as an inventor and businessman. Tinkering with steam engines and heating equipment, he invented an important control valve that was named after him. Around the turn of the century he organized and ran the Norwall Valve Company, though owning only a minority share. Early in 1907, when Norwall sold out to the American Radiator Company, one of the newly integrated corporations, he became a department head for that larger concern.[2]

As he prospered and Chicago changed, George Hoffman moved his family in 1892 to Western Springs. Paul, then a year old, grew up in that Chicago suburb in surroundings he described as "upper middle class." The Hoffmans' house, the biggest in town, even had its own ballroom. George Hoffman, a natural spender who could not resist new inventions, bought one of the first automobiles in town as well as the first washing machine and the first dishwasher—neither of which worked. His success, however, was not unmixed. George Hoffman's income varied enormously, and the family did know the value of frugality and the need for saving.[3]

Serious-minded and usually preoccupied with his job and inventions, George Hoffman spent much time in his laboratory and traveling on business. He had no interest in trivial conversation or sociability, and when his children were young, he remained a remote figure with little time or affection for them. Yet he set an example that won their respect and instilled strong values. His son remembered him as a mild-mannered and patient perfectionist who never said anything derogatory about any individual. Without religion himself, he adhered to a personal code that forbade drinking, smoking, gambling, profanity, and gossip. He remained true to his solidly Republican family tradition and proud enough of his ancestry to join the Sons of the American Revolution, but George Hoffman always tolerated different and opposing views, even within his own family. Most important, he imparted to his children a respect for independent thought, progressive ideas, technological innovation, and modernity.[4]

Paul's mother, Eleanor Lott Hoffman, a lighthearted woman with a good sense of humor, provided her children with maternal warmth, fun, and a cultured environment. A native of a small Illinois town, she had graduated from a private high school for girls, where she studied painting. She also shared with her husband a love of music, sometimes accompanying him on the piano when he played the flute. Although the family roles were fairly conventional, Mrs. Hoffman was not the silent and subservient wife; with a mind of her own and contrary to her husband's practices, she was a devout Christian Scientist and a nonvoting supporter of the Democrats.[5]

As his mother's favorite, Paul received both affection and encouragement to work hard in school. Her ambition for him and reassurance that he was bright no doubt accounted for some of his unbridled self-confidence. In any case, his teachers in public school found him a good student, especially in mathematics, history, and composition. To his mother's delight, they skipped him two grades.[6]

The early independence encouraged by his family environment was tested during Paul's last year in high school when American Radiator transferred his father to New York: Paul decided to finish school where he had started and stayed behind. Lonely but self-confident and adaptable, he moved from the family home in Western Springs to a boardinghouse in nearby La Grange until he graduated in 1907 from what became Lyons Township High School. Then sixteen years old, he rejoined the family in New York and worked that summer for $5 a week as an office boy for American Radiator.[7]

In 1908, when the family returned to Chicago, Paul entered the University of Chicago intending to become a lawyer. In what he recalled as a glorious time, he joined the Delta Tau Delta fraternity, where, thoroughly sociable, he enjoyed the friendships and give-and-take of living within a large group. That little dream world, where serious discussion about classes or public affairs never intruded, also gave him a smug sense of social superiority. Academically, however, his experience at the university proved disappointing. First of all, his pride was deflated when he failed the entrance examination in composition and had to take a noncredit course in writing. His other classes bored him, and at the end of the year his professors did not encourage him to return. Therefore, at the age of eighteen, eager to earn money, Paul Hoffman ended his formal education and found a job in Chicago.[8]

The very year that he made that decision, a completely unrelated development provided him with an important lesson that he carried the rest of his life: Architect and urban planner Daniel Burnham made public his *Plan of Chicago,* an elaborate scheme for building streets and parks. Besides the fact that the plan tacitly encouraged the use of automobiles, Hoffman may have seen in it a similarity to the efforts of his great-grandfather, John Gray, to have the city buy valuable land for Chicago's public schools. In any case, from the 1930s on, he quoted Daniel Burnham's credo: "Make no small plans, for they have no magic to stir the imagination of men. Make big plans."[9]

A few years later, Paul's father made his own big plans. The American Radiator Company provided the stimulus in 1911 by demoting him to district branch manager in southern California at about half his previous salary.[10] Amid the shabbiness, instability, and unrestrained commercialism of that area, George Hoffman settled his family in the town that best suited his tastes and aspirations: Pasadena. Founded during the 1870s by middle-class residents of Indianapolis as an orange-growing area, Pasadena reflected the civic consciousness that midwesterners had carried from their distant New England roots. With many churches, good schools, libraries, associations for music and debate, and blue laws, this model of rectitude was already the place for the emerging elite when Hoffman arrived.[11] Understandably, he liked what he found there and decided to stay permanently, but not with American Radiator.

Ever an optimist, he borrowed a few thousand dollars from his friends, acquired a substantial credit line, and launched his own business in 1913. Drawing on his previous technical experience and familiarity with modern industrial enterprise, he founded a company to produce heating and plumbing parts. The Hoffman Specialty Manufacturing Corporation, located in Waterbury, Connecticut, the principal home of the brass industry, became a leader in a field where no big firms dominated and enabled its founder to earn as much as $250,000 a year. The success of that business, which later provided income for his children and grandchildren, also permitted George Hoffman to pursue from his home in Pasadena an avocation of avocado growing and marketing, and a successful experiment with dairy farming.[12]

By his willingness to take risks and back new ideas, by augmenting traditional nineteenth-century business values with his experience in the bureaucratic administration of a modern, integrated corporation, George Hoffman taught his son the spirit of entrepreneurship. For Paul, who had become at twenty a close business confidant of his father, that background provided skills and an outlook that served him well in his own business career. By personality and training, then, he was prepared to deal with a changing economy and a changing world.

Paul Hoffman started his own career at the bottom of the automobile business. The choice reflected his early fascination with cars and the personal experience that began when his father bought a used Pope-Toledo, one of the most expensive American makes. For $1,500 the family had acquired a small, open, unreliable vehicle for travel on unpaved and thoroughly inadequate roads. Because he had done all the driving for the family and made the frequently needed repairs, Paul developed skills that proved especially valuable when he dropped out of the university in 1909. Despite the fact that he had to start in a menial position, he began working for a car dealer in Chicago, eventually becoming a salesman.[13]

Even as a young salesman not yet earning full commission, he demonstrated qualities of the traditional success formula: a friendly personality, a willingness to work hard, and an ability to recognize new opportunities. Assigned a rural territory around Chicago, he sold "on the hoof," driving a car until he found a buyer and then returning to the dealership for another car. By offering free rides to bankers and physicians in nearby small towns, he discovered prospective buyers. Once he had demonstrated success in selling to prosperous farmers, he moved to a better-established dealership for cars manufactured in nearby South Bend, Indiana, by the Studebakers, a family his father knew. By 1911, when he decided to follow his family to California, he was earning $300 to $400 a month selling Studebakers.[14]

The move to California opened new opportunities. First, he learned about the country by traveling alone from Chicago, paying his way by selling car parts. When he arrived in Pasadena, he moved into his father's home and got a job selling Studebakers in downtown Los Angeles. Not yet a car owner himself, he commuted to work by motorcycle and trolley. In Los Angeles he enjoyed instant and phenomenal success; during one month in 1912, he set a sales record and earned $1,250.[15] Then, perhaps demonstrating that the year of remedial composition at the university had not been wasted, he also won the grand prize in the Studebaker national sales contest. For his essay on how to sell cars, he received $100, a cup, and a trip back to corporation headquarters in South Bend, where he met J. B. Studebaker and other top executives.

In southern California, where the population swelled with the steady tide of fellow midwesterners, his success as a salesman enabled Hoffman to climb rapidly up the organizational ladder. He knew how to get the most out of a demonstration drive, how to convey his enthusiasm, and how to gain trust from prospective buyers. Studebaker rewarded him with a promotion to sales manager for Los Angeles and Orange Counties in 1915 and for the entire southern California district two years later. In those positions he not only remained his own best salesman but also showed leadership skills in motivating his subordinates: besides selling cars, he sold salesmanship. Self-assured but never arrogant, most of all he sold himself.

World War I proved only a minor interruption in Hoffman's business career. Already married and a father, he enlisted in the army and rose from private to lieutenant without leaving the country. Then, in 1919, a veteran not yet thirty years old, he decided to plunge into business for himself. He no longer wanted to remain a mere employee, even if well paid. Just as his father had successfully left a managerial position with a major corporation to establish his own business, he too had bigger ambitions.

Hoffman's ambitions posed a difficult decision for the top management of the Studebaker Corporation. The company offered to make him manager of the New York City distributorship, its largest, and a member of the board of directors at a salary of $50,000. But rather than accept that position, he told Studebaker president Albert

·Erskine that he wanted to own a distributorship for all of Los Angeles and Orange Counties. Erskine decided that Hoffman was so valuable to the organization that it could not risk losing him and therefore agreed to sell the southern California distributorship for $60,000, provided he took on a partner.[16]

Thus, with capital borrowed from relatives and friends, Hoffman acquired his own business. By choosing the independence and uncertainties of the small businessman, he took a calculated risk: he thought that he could make a lot more money working for himself than for a Studebaker salary, and he was right. Of course, the fact that the distributorship received 3 percent from the sale of every Studebaker it supplied to dealers in southern California virtually guaranteed profits. Within a year he was able to buy out his partner and establish the Paul G. Hoffman Company, which eventually operated stores in six locations.[17]

Hoffman brought to his own business not only knowledge of the Los Angeles market and a willingness to take risks but also a thoroughly modern, pragmatic outlook. He had already absorbed the ethos of rational, bureaucratic management. Other people considered personality a key to success in sales, but he minimized its importance. He felt that salesmanship, like other aspects of modern business, required systematic and even scientific methods with policies based on knowledge of the facts. That lesson, he often said, he learned from Ray Wilbur, president of Stanford University and later Secretary of the Interior under Herbert Hoover. Hoffman remembered hearing Wilbur tell listeners that if they did not get the facts, the facts would get them.[18]

The success of the Paul G. Hoffman Company seemed to bear out the soundness of that advice. Hoffman set policy only after studying the product, consumer desires, and market conditions. He watched inventories and costs carefully to maximize profits. Employing a body shop where Harley J. Earl, the future chief designer of General Motors, was applying his skills, he customized factory models to suit often flamboyant local tastes.[19] Always ready to use the best and latest advertising methods, in 1921 he invested $35,000 to help launch KNX radio, one of the nation's pioneering stations, which for several years broadcast from his showroom on Hollywood Boulevard.[20]

Part of Hoffman's success was undoubtedly due to the rapid growth of population and even more rapid growth of automobile ownership in southern California. But while car sales boomed, chaotic traffic congestion led city officials to ban downtown parking briefly during the early 1920s, and questions of automobile safety threatened future sales. As a businessman and local booster, Hoffman responded to that situation in a manner common among contemporary progressives. He insisted that sound public policies had to be based on a scientific study of the facts. Maximum efficiency called for a nonpartisan fact-finding commission. Therefore, he became chairman of the Los Angeles Chamber of Commerce's roads committee and helped to organize the Traffic Commission of Los Angeles, a nongovernmental body on which he served as president.[21]

Hoffman believed that the Los Angeles area needed to plan its street arrangement and land use. Accordingly, the Traffic Commission hired the well-known firm of planning experts headed by Frederick Law Olmsted, Jr. That firm's report, which Hoffman delivered to city officials, claimed that traffic safety in Los Angeles could be improved by properly designed streets. It urged the city to widen existing streets, to separate some intersections by grade, and to expand construction into outlying areas for future needs.[22]

The report of the experts served Hoffman's purposes quite well. Under the banner of traffic safety and commercial development, he used it to promote the kind of street and highway construction that encouraged horizontal urban growth and expanded dependence on the private car for transportation. Thus he allied himself with other powerful forces shaping public policy in southern California. Harry Chandler, for example, publisher of the *Los Angeles Times* and a heavy investor in local real estate, ardently promoted the automobile and highway construction as a way to enhance the value of his holdings. Little wonder, then, that his newspaper regarded Hoffman as a "merchandizing genius."[23]

By 1925, at the age of thirty-four, Paul Hoffman had made himself a success. His distributorship was Studebaker's second largest, with annual sales of 4,000 vehicles worth several million dollars and assets of $1.5 million. Profits were so large that he had saved and invested $1 million of his own money, mainly in blue chip stocks. He came in contact with important people who thrust other money-making opportunities before him: he served as a director of three corporations, including a bank and an oil company. His investment in KNX, made primarily to advertise his car dealership, proved highly lucrative when CBS bought the station in 1936 for $1 million.[24]

While achieving that success in business, Hoffman had also gained prominence in local politics. He had made the right connections and impressed the right people; he socialized with the city's political leaders. Active in promoting road construction, he had been elected to the Republican Central Committee of Los Angeles County when the party was dominated by Harry Chandler. He had business ties with the owner of another local newspaper. The Non-Partisan Committee had named Hoffman to receive nominations for the coming mayoralty election.[25] His future in Los Angeles looked bright.

At that point in his career, when he was financially secure and emerging as a public figure in southern California, he confronted a new challenge: the president of Studebaker insisted that he join the company in South Bend as vice-president in charge of sales and as a member of the board of directors. From the time he had negotiated in 1919 to buy his distributorship, Hoffman had met Erskine often and felt obligated to him. Also seeing in Erskine's offer the chance to shape the policies of a major corporation with assets of $75 million, he agreed to take the position for at least two years. Ownership of the Paul G. Hoffman Company—with Hoffman as chairman of the board—transferred to his wife; Earl Carpenter, his competent aide and minority partner, became president; and Paul Hoffman was off to South Bend and a new career as a corporate executive.[26]

2 Apprenticeship in Corporate Management 1925-33

Hoffman accepted his new position at Studebaker with at least mixed emotions. He was uncertain about forsaking the role of independent entrepreneur to become a corporate executive; furthermore, he regarded southern California as his real home and did not want to leave. Neither did his wife.

Dorothy Brown Hoffman seems to have resembled Paul's mother in many ways. She was also a midwesterner with roots in New England, a dedicated Christian Scientist, and a woman of strong character. Originally from Michigan, she had moved with her family to southern California and met Paul there while home for vacation from Wellesley. They married in 1915 after she graduated.[1]

Far from being the ambitious wife of a mobile organization man, Mrs. Hoffman was an unpretentious, informal, and family-oriented woman. Lively and opinionated, she nevertheless avoided the limelight sought by her husband. Although she preferred that they stay in southern California, she did not strenuously resist the move in 1925.

South Bend, the Hoffmans' new home, was unlike Los Angeles but not exactly a sleepy small town either. By the mid-1920s this old industrial city had a growing population of nearly 100,000. Besides Studebaker, two other large and nationally prominent institutions— the Bendix Corporation and the University of Notre Dame—made their homes there. (After careful consideration, sociologist Robert Lynd concluded that South Bend was too large and too ethnically diverse for his famous Small City Study and instead chose Muncie, Indiana, as "Middletown.")[2]

In South Bend the Hoffmans lived very well. They bought several acres and built a handsome three-story house that Dorothy designed. Comfortable rather than opulent, it suited the needs of a family with seven children and provided an excellent setting for entertaining. When the Hoffmans moved out in the mid-1940s, the house was converted into a school.

Although the Hoffmans tried to retain their informal lifestyle in their new setting, the move to South Bend necessitated substantial changes. Becoming a vice-president and director of Studebaker meant a big step up in the business world for Paul Hoffman. He took on new responsibilities and often had to travel on business. In an industry facing difficult new challenges he began to acquire national prominence.

By joining Studebaker in 1925 as a top executive, Paul Hoffman appeared to have hitched his star to the right wagonmaker. The oldest company manufacturing automobiles, Studebaker started making wagons and carriages in South Bend during the 1850s and grew as a conservative family firm that tried to operate on the principle of giving buyers more than it promised. During the early twentieth century it modernized its product line to include automobiles and trucks, soon to the exclusion of its older products. It also bought additional plant facilities in Detroit and modernized its administrative structure, turning over management to a non–family member.[3]

During the early 1920s, Studebaker continued to prosper. By joining Ford and a few other automakers in cutting prices, it did well even during the recession of 1920–21. Its rugged cars sold in the middle price range ($750–$1,000) that suggested future growth, and its trucks benefited from the reputation of Studebaker wagons in rural areas. At its peak, Studebaker sold 145,000 units, ranking sixth in volume of sales.[4]

In assets, though far behind General Motors and Ford, Studebaker ranked third within the industry. In 1919 it announced a $15 million expansion program and other efforts intended to make it among the most progressive and modern automakers. In addition to its large administration building, its South Bend facilities included a new six-story body plant designed by Albert Kahn, Detroit's foremost factory architect. The company also boasted about the skill and loyalty of its workforce, which reached a peak of about 15,000, and about its strong engineering department.[5]

But all was not well within the automotive industry; the economics of manufacturing quickly altered its structure and Studebaker's position within it. During the first postwar recession, trade journals began to discuss possible saturation of the market. The large volume of used cars already available and new low-priced cars entering the market created intense competition, especially in the middle price range that had been so profitable for Studebaker. With another recession in 1924, manufacturers frequently forced their dealers to accept surplus production, which could be sold only at low retail prices that wiped out dealers' profit margins.[6]

During the mid-1920s the market leveled off when some automakers adopted a new strategy: instead of avoiding or minimizing design changes in order to hold down costs and offer buyers basic transportation at a low price, they began to offer better cars. The success of the new models, especially all-weather closed bodies, while the rest of the industry declined proved the profitability of the approach. Automakers found that success in the new "mass-class" market required changes that appealed to consumers' desires for social prestige. Soon competitors were emphasizing styling aesthetics with annual or biennial model changes, heavier bodies, and more powerful engines to accommodate them.

The new strategy of offering more car, comfort, and trade-in value was most successfully exploited by General Motors under the direction of Alfred P. Sloan. With a model for every taste and every income, GM sought to educate consumers to expect higher quality, even though it meant higher prices. Those who could not afford such new cars could buy used cars. That market, by absorbing cars traded in by high-income consumers, gave further encouragement to superficial style changes.

The enormous costs of shifting to the production of closed bodies and frequent model changes greatly increased the minimum corporate size needed for survival within the now highly competitive automotive industry. Product innovation required expensive innovation in production techniques that only corporations with very large capital resources could afford; among those, the new strategy required that more attention be given to the problems of management and marketing. Nevertheless, despite his preference for price reductions and his belief that annual model changes were "the curse of the industry," even Henry Ford stopped production of the Model T and adapted to the new market conditions.[7]

The main burden for leading Studebaker through the changing market fell on Albert Russel Erskine, its president since 1915. A bold risk-taker whose motto was "We eat obstacles for Breakfast," Erskine completely dominated the corporation. His policies of high dividends and expansion had made Studebaker a stock-market sensation during the early 1920s. Stockholders considered him a miracle man. His compliant board of directors rewarded him with a large salary and generous stock options, enabling him to accumulate a personal fortune estimated at $12 to $15 million. His palatial estate, Twyckenham Manor, was the equal of any of the residences of the Detroit automobile tycoons.[8]

Erskine responded to the challenges of the 1920s with a broadly conceived plan to have Studebaker join GM and Ford as one of the industry's giants. In his effort to expand quickly, however, he tried and failed to buy out the Maxwell Motor Company, and Walter P. Chrysler then used Maxwell as the base for creating the Chrysler Corporation, which became the third big automaker. Despite that setback, Studebaker still held a solid position within the industry, and Erskine was determined to strengthen it.

Realizing that the corporation was bigger than any individual, he upgraded his management team. Thus he brought in Paul Hoffman as a vice-president and also promoted to vice-president his sales manager, Harold S. Vance. So confident was Erskine about these two young executives that he said he would match them against any in the industry.[9] Further stressing the importance of teamwork, Studebaker hired Notre Dame football coach Knute Rockne as a personnel consultant. With Vance supervising the arrangements, Studebaker then disposed of inadequate plants in the Detroit area, consolidated production in South Bend, and spent $1 million on a new proving ground.

Although Albert Erskine made the major decisions, especially regarding finances, from the mid-1920s on Paul G. Hoffman and Harold S. Vance emerged as highly valued members of Studebaker's leadership team. The young vice-presidents, heirs apparent to Erskine, never became close personal friends, but their relationship grew into mutual respect rather than rivalry. While Vance generally supervised the production side of the business, Hoffman showed acute sensitivity to what was coming to be called public relations in the broadest sense and influenced the entire range of corporate activities. With Erskine—whom he regarded as kindly, generous, and courageous as well as forceful—Hoffman had learned from previous experience to use tact and to avoid face-to-face challenges.[10]

His main responsibility required the maintenance, in the face of threatened defections, of a strong dealer organization. Having been a dealer himself, he was uniquely qualified for that task and tried to apply to the entire sales organization the lessons he had learned in Los Angeles. He communicated directly with dealers and sales managers through extensive and frequent speaking tours. He also wrote often for trade journals and coauthored a book of advice intended for Studebaker dealers.

Using the slogan "America's Friendliest Factory," he tried to show dealers that the Studebaker Corporation would treat them fairly. Over Albert Erskine's objection, he refused to ship cars without dealer orders and assured dealers that they would not be forced to accept surplus production. He sought to help them advertise, train service and sales personnel, and manage their affairs so that they operated profitably. To demonstrate his concern for their well-being, he invited disgruntled dealers to bring their complaints directly to him. When sales lagged, however, he did urge dealers to give overallowances on cars traded in, though he knew that such a policy was a "delicate subject" which—like the rebate policy adopted by a troubled industry of another generation—reduced dealers' profits.[11]

Although Hoffman added a personal touch and the "Friendliest Factory" slogan was distinctive, Studebaker was not alone in its efforts to control dealers. Automakers generally realized that it was dealers and salesmen who met the customers and shaped their opinions. In his own messages to dealers, Hoffman tried to impress upon them what other manufacturers were also trying to put into practice: through "clean" methods and efficient service, dealers needed to build good will, even at the sacrifice of immediate profits. "Chiseling" had to be avoided, because it created ill will that eventually hurt business. To assure satisfied customers who would buy again and help build the company's reputation, he wanted Studebaker's service department to lead the industry in the investigation of customer complaints. He pushed the concept of selling "certified" used cars on a five-day trial, with trade-in guaranteed to dissatisfied buyers.[12]

Through his efforts to maintain Studebaker's strong dealer organization, Hoffman became a recognized leader in modern sales management. In that capacity, he sought to boost the morale and upgrade the status of salesmen generally by emphasizing that they were involved in a career of great social and economic significance. He believed that if trained properly, paid well, and treated fairly, salesmen as merchandizers—rather than mere traders—would maintain high ethical standards and thus help build good will. Accordingly, he advocated special training, organizational teamwork, and scientific methods for sales comparable to progressive methods of production. Old-fashioned lone-wolf tactics and sales by hunches and "pep talks" would not bring satisfactory results. Hoffman spent $1 million during his first five years as vice-president to implement these ideas.[13]

Beyond that kind of sales management role, Hoffman addressed the broader issues of marketing strategy. He never doubted the benefits of "America's great personal transportation system." In his view, the automobile was and would always remain "America's greatest plaything and greatest necessity."[14] That belief did not, however, lead him to pursue the same marketing strategy as Alfred P. Sloan and GM.

According to Hoffman, Studebaker had to produce the kinds of cars Americans wanted and could use with practical economy. He did not know precisely what Americans wanted to buy, but he did know that engineering excellence alone did not sell cars. Automobile design had to reflect a compromise between technological excellence, economics, and consumer tastes. Having made his fortune selling cars in southern California, he understood well the importance of stylistic details (such as slanting windshield posts) to improve appearance and appeal. To take the guesswork out of such decisions, he wanted Studebaker to create a research department that would survey and evaluate the opinions—including complaints—of its engineers, its best salesmen, and its car owners.[15]

Even before moving to South Bend, Hoffman got Erskine to agree that Studebaker should stop announcing annual model changes, which by the mid-1920s had become a common feature of the industry. Hoffman believed, however, that the practice was illogical: although it did temporarily stimulate buyer interest, that benefit proved insignificant because such "artificial obsoletion" cost the buying public heavily and hurt dealers stuck with unsold inventories of previous models. By ending annual changes and introducing new models only when necessary, Studebaker could avoid needless production costs and could gain sales by emphasizing that its used cars retained higher values. He also wanted the entire Studebaker line simplified, with fewer body stampings and greater interchangeability of parts. When Erskine was willing to sell poorly made cars in 1925, Hoffman argued that the company's reputation required strict quality control; cars that did not measure up should not be shipped to dealers.[16]

Although it was Erskine who ultimately decided what kinds of cars Studebaker sold, Hoffman played a major role in shaping the company's advertising. As a dealer, he had become convinced that good advertising could promote acceptance of modern products and help overcome popular resistance to change. That conviction grew stronger when he worked closely with Albert Lasker and Claude Hopkins of Lord & Thomas, the Chicago agency directing Studebaker's advertising. Two of the shrewdest and most successful of advertising agents, Lasker and Hopkins impressed upon Hoffman that there was "no mystery to mastery" of the market: what was needed was "scientific advertising," salesmanship based on knowing what buyers want and what they were about to want. Market research and experimentation had to precede any large expenditure for advertising. The modern media, radio and—by the late 1920s—sound movies, should be used in sales promotion because they helped to associate the product with modern trends.[17]

During the 1920s, the automotive industry relied heavily on advertising and contributed mightily to the growth of that business. When advertisers discovered that mechanical features and price alone would not sell enough cars, they consistently associated the car with fashion, social status, speed, and sexuality. Critics then and since charged that the vast amounts spent on sales promotion made products more expensive to buyers and encouraged extravagance. They objected to the promotion of the automobile not as transportation but as the fulfillment of a desire for power.[18]

Despite Hoffman's preference for cars of "practical economy," however, Studebaker advertisements reflected the general trends within the industry; in fact, they stood out by emphasizing speed performance, including the success of Studebaker engines in racing cars. Hoffman insisted that the public demanded speed and that speed was one measure of civilization.[19] At the same time, he denied that money spent on advertisements featuring style and speed made cars more expensive to buyers; by increasing volume, such efforts reduced distribution costs and thereby allowed automakers to sell cars at prices affordable within the mass market.

What did make Hoffman's advertising unusual was his effort to link the sales pitch to Studebaker's labor relations. When he arrived at South Bend in 1925, Studebaker's cultivation of friendly relations with workers had already earned it a reputation as a good employer. Although Erskine inclined toward paternalism, Studebaker did not sponsor a company union, and the Cooperative Department it created in 1919 avoided much of the "welfare capitalism" in vogue among progressive business leaders. Instead, Studebaker offered a unique incentive pay system that gave workers higher wages, vacation pay, pensions, group health insurance, a stock purchase plan, and high annual bonuses based on length of service.[20] With his slogan "America's Friendliest Factory," Hoffman publicized those labor policies, asserting that they gave Studebaker an extraordinarily loyal, skilled, and experienced workforce with high morale and low turnover, and permitted Studebaker to build cars of better quality than the lower-priced Detroit products.

While he promoted Studebaker sales, Hoffman also continued his efforts to head off public complaints about traffic problems. In 1926, he persuaded Harvard to establish the Albert Russel Erskine Bureau for Street Traffic Research. Financed with $10,000 a year from the Studebaker Corporation, the bureau conducted its research and academic instruction free from direct interference by Hoffman or other automotive executives. Yet this typically progressive response to a public controversy never questioned the policies of the automakers themselves with regard to safety. Benefiting from the prestige of Harvard, the bureau did establish valuable connections with important organizations such as the National Safety Council. Hoffman himself participated in the National Conferences on Street and Highway Safety sponsored by the Commerce Department.[21]

The broad range of Hoffman's activities built up not only Studebaker's reputation but also his own. He recognized the importance of the media and knew how to deal with them. Again he impressed the right people—Henry Luce, for example. In 1930, Luce—cofounder of *Time* but not yet a great power in American journalism—launched *Fortune* and set out to tell the story of worthy, responsible businessmen. Perhaps because his brother-in-law, Maurice T. Moore, was Studebaker's lawyer, Luce went to South Bend to write about the automaker. Hoffman helped him gather his material and demonstrated just the qualities Luce aimed to encourage: intelligence, responsibility, a larger vision than profit at any human cost. Two years later, *Fortune* called Hoffman "one of the ablest of sales managers" in the industry. Other business-oriented journals agreed. *Business Week*, commenting that one of Studebaker's greatest assets was its attitude toward sales and service through dealers, attributed that policy, "naturally," to Hoffman.[22]

Within the corporation, Hoffman himself was well rewarded. While Erskine received a salary of $100,000 and chairman Frederick S. Fish (a Studebaker son-in-law) $50,000, Hoffman and Vance each received $75,000, until the 10 percent salary reductions implemented in the middle of 1931. In addition, although the terms proved to be unfavorable, a stock option plan in 1927 provided that he and Vance would each receive 20,000 shares. In 1931 Hoffman was named president of the Studebaker Sales Corporation, the manufacturer's marketing instrument.[23]

At the end of the prosperous, volatile, and competitive 1920s, Studebaker still appeared to have enjoyed considerable success, even while remaining a small automaker. What most observers did not realize was that the policies of Albert Erskine were leading Studebaker to disaster. While profits remained stable after 1924, Erskine, a gambler who speculated heavily in the stock market, increased dividends to boost stock prices. Capital reserves, so important in the industry because of the heavy costs of model changes, were dissipated; reinvestment for modernization declined and then disappeared entirely in 1928. By the end of the decade, Studebaker sales fell below 100,000 units and working capital to about half what it had been a few years earlier.[24]

When the Depression struck, the consequences of Erskine's errors of judgment became almost fatal. At the start of 1930, for example, he declared that Studebaker expected a good year that would improve its competitive position. In April, reports from his aides forced him to reverse himself and recommend to the directors a comprehensive program for retrenchment. Specifically, he proposed to eliminate anniversary checks for workers and his own profit-sharing; management bonuses would be reduced; even his salary would be renegotiated to be "more in keeping with existing conditions." Dividends would be cut from $5 to $4 a share, to be paid from the "Special Surplus" fund accumulated during the 1920s. Yet even that dividend policy was absurd and irresponsible, committing Studebaker in 1930 to pay out 506 percent of net profits.[25]

That the judgments of one man could prove so disastrous for the entire corporation revealed the deficiencies of Studebaker's managerial structure. Like Ford but unlike GM, the company concentrated too much power at the very top. One director, complaining that Studebaker's conduct raised "many perplexing questions," finally did resign, but most directors simply lacked critical perspective and accepted whatever Erskine told them. Vice-Presidents Hoffman and Vance could not, at least publicly, challenge Erskine; if they recognized what the policies were leading to, they kept their opinions to themselves. Albert Lasker, the head of Lord & Thomas, did not have to operate under such restraint, however. Appalled by Erskine's recklessness, Lasker gave up the Studebaker account rather than have his advertising agency tied to certain failure.[26]

Erskine did take steps to combat the problem of declining sales, but his decisions made matters worse. In 1926, the year that Studebaker sold its millionth car, his annual report blamed the decline on consumer preference for cheaper cars. To meet what he perceived as a shift in the market, he launched a new Studebaker model inspired by the small fuel-efficient cars he had seen in Europe. But the Erskine, a light, six-cylinder car, completely failed in the American market. Advertised as "The Little Aristocrat of Motordom," the new model was smaller, lighter, and more fuel-efficient than other Studebakers but sold for $800 to $900—not much less—and American car buyers found the Erskine less appealing than established low-priced models from other automakers. Its fuel economy just was not a strong selling point at a time when gasoline prices were actually declining.[27]

Production of the unsuccessful Erskine soon ceased, and Studebaker next tried to boost sales by entering the luxury field. In 1928 it acquired Pierce-Arrow, one of the grand automobiles of that era, after Erskine persuaded the board of directors that Studebaker management could reduce costs and prices while still making a good profit. And for a brief period the recent money loser did become profitable, and did give Erskine the kind of prestige he wanted. Soon however, the Pierce-Arrow proved as unprofitable for Studebaker as it had for its previous owner, and the acquisition ended up costing Studebaker almost $9 million.[28]

In 1931, to combat the continued erosion of sales, Erskine gambled once more on a new model. With newly acquired facilities in Detroit, he launched another light, six-cylinder car. Well engineered and better priced ($585 to $840 FOB Detroit) than the unsuccessful Erskine, the new Rockne suffered particularly bad timing:

before it could enter the market, Knute Rockne, for whom it was named, died in an airplane accident. When the car was finally introduced into a collapsing market, even worse than Hoffman's pessimistic forecast of early that year,[29] it could not compete with cars already established in the low price field. The gamble failed, and the capital lifeblood further drained away from the corporate body.

As the Depression reached its nadir, Studebaker maintained a deceptive facade. Its sales declined to less than 50,000 units, but its share of the market actually improved because the rest of the industry suffered worse. For outsiders looking at dividends and familiar with Studebaker's reputation, the corporation still appeared healthy. Too many people failed to note that Erskine's high dividend policy disbursed more than $11 million of unearned capital.[30]

Erskine himself, however, knew that the situation had become quite desperate. In frustration, he lashed out at government bureaucracy and excessive spending as the cause of the nation's economic problems.[31] Then, to get a quick transfusion of capital for his own company, he tried to engineer a merger with White Motors of Cleveland, Ohio. A manufacturer of trucks, White enjoyed a good share of urban markets, while Studebaker trucks sold better in rural markets. The merger, based on the exchange of Studebaker stock for White capital, offered promise of mutual benefits, but a minority of White stockholders opposed to the merger got a court order blocking it. Erskine's efforts to save Studebaker had failed.

In March of 1933 the collapse finally came. Short of cash to meet immediate obligations, Studebaker could not find banks willing to lend more. When creditors went to U.S. District Court, the company fell into receivership.

Albert Erskine became a tragic casualty of the folly he had created. His removal by the court from Studebaker's management left him humiliated and convinced that he had betrayed a trust. His personal fortune, based on Studebaker stock and South Bend real estate, had been squandered in speculation. In July he told Hoffman that he planned to commit suicide so that his family could collect his insurance money, and a few days later he shot himself in the heart. Hoffman, having failed to dissuade Erskine from that final act, made the public announcement.[32]

Although Erskine's reckless policies now can be seen as part of the excesses of that era, the collapse of the venerable Studebaker Corporation shocked contemporary industry observers. One prominent trade journal said it came with the suddenness of an earth-quake, and Wall Street experts were apparently taken by complete surprise.[33] Failure in the automotive industry during the 1920s was, to be sure, not at all unusual: during that decade the number of manufacturers declined by almost 80 percent.[34] The Depression further reduced the field. But unlike the other failures, Studebaker was not a small newcomer but an old and seemingly successful manufacturer.

For Hoffman, Studebaker's collapse meant the end of his apprenticeship. Since the mid-1920s, he and Harold Vance had been groomed by Albert Erskine to take over the company, and during his eight years as a vice-president, he had gained experience with the broadest aspects of the company and the automobile industry. Hoffman liked to say that one learns by recognizing mistakes. Beginning in March of 1933, he had a chance to show what he had learned. His abilities, his energies, and the breadth of his vision were to be tested to the full.

3 Bringing Studebaker Back, 1933-48

Paul Hoffman, who loved being a businessman, ran Studebaker for fifteen years, beginning in 1933. Compared with the three giants of the industry—GM, Ford, and Chrysler—which produced about 90 percent of American cars, Studebaker was always small; compared with other American businesses, however, it was not. With capital investments of tens of millions of dollars, it operated large plants employing several thousand workers. In an oligopolistic industry, Hoffman tried to prove that the right kind of management could achieve profitability for a company that was not gigantic.

Hoffman's achievements at Studebaker during the 1930s and 1940s established his reputation as a progressive business leader. Whatever else he became grew from his achievements at Studebaker. To understand Hoffman, one must understand those business experiences that shaped his views on broader public issues.

For the first two years, between March 1933 and March 1935, Hoffman barely kept the bankrupt Studebaker from the liquidation some bankers apparently would have preferred. Fortunately, U.S. District Judge Thomas W. Slick, who declared the company in receivership, cared about the adverse impact of the failure on South Bend. Therefore, he appointed as "friendly" receivers Hoffman, his fellow Studebaker vice-president Harold Vance, and Ashton G. Bean, the president of White Motors, with which Albert Erskine had unsuccessfully sought merger.[1]

With Hoffman the dominant figure, the three receivers immediately took steps to save the company. Two days after Judge Slick placed Studebaker in receivership, Hoffman launched a publicity campaign and other policies to stimulate sales and to reassure dealers. An audit in April of 1933 revealed that Studebaker was actually operating at a profit and appeared to be "fundamentally sound."[2] With that good news the receivers persuaded Judge Slick to release $700,000 of Studebaker funds so that the company could retool for new models. They raised additional cash by selling off the unprofitable Pierce-Arrow line and all the White Motors stock acquired by Erskine.

Like the Chrysler Corporation when it faced financial collapse during the late 1970s, Studebaker also turned to the federal government for relief, but unlike Chrysler it did not seek a "bail out" through loan guarantees. Rather, in June of 1934, Hoffman went to Washington to urge the Indiana congressional delegation to support Section 77B of the pending bankruptcy bill. What the passage of that law gave Studebaker and other companies in receivership was exclusion from restrictions imposed by the Securities Act on their ability to borrow capital. Without costing the government anything, the new provision opened the road for corporate reorganization.

That road led Hoffman and Vance to Wall Street. For months, while Studebaker operated at a loss, they commuted between South Bend and New York to consult with lawyers and bankers. Maurice "Tex" Moore, a partner in the prestigious Cravath law firm that already represented the corporation, helped to negotiate a new loan with a syndicate of investment bankers headed by Lehman Bros. Hoffman's energy and attractive personality greatly impressed the bankers.[3] Nevertheless, before they would agree to lend more money, they insisted that Studebaker submit to an outside appraisal by the management consulting firm Sanderson & Porter.

After studying the entire plant and operations in South Bend as well as the dealer network, the consultants issued a favorable report. They found that Studebaker, with an engineering staff among the best in the industry, could compete in any price field except the lowest. They estimated Studebaker's break-even point at about 65,000 units per year, while its plants had capacity for 150,000 units. The company needed to cut administrative overhead, increase sales volume, and perhaps merge with other small automakers. But its biggest problem was lack of cash.[4] The bankers responded by agreeing to lend another $6.8 million if the receivers could secure underwriting for half that amount.

In part by pleading the case of Studebaker's 7,000 workers in South Bend, Hoffman and Vance located underwriters and then had

Tex Moore draw up the reorganization plan, which was submitted to Judge Slick in December 1934. By that plan the Rockne Corporation, a wholly owned subsidiary, would disappear; holders of Studebaker common stock would lose their equity; and a new Studebaker Corporation would be created. When Judge Slick approved the plan in January 1935, Studebaker became one of the first important reorganizations affected under Section 77B.

Reorganization left Studebaker's management in the hands of Hoffman and Vance. In March 1935, Hoffman became president and Vance chairman of the new Studebaker Corporation at salaries of $50,000—less than they had received as vice-presidents of the displaced corporation.[5] From adjacent offices they operated as a team. Vance continued to concentrate on production and Hoffman on sales and public relations. Quite different in personality, temperament, and lifestyle, they rarely socialized. But on the job they got along well and agreed about basic policies.

As a cost-cutting measure, they launched a comprehensive program for expense and inventory control. Hoffman insisted that within a corporation, as within the national economy, the best organization rested on decentralized responsibility. Studebaker asked every executive at every level to consider costs for the entire corporation. It required department heads to control costs by keeping careful records. Periodically, it challenged all forms, reports, and other paperwork to eliminate excess. It centralized record-keeping with expensive office machines only when high volume yielded cost economies.[6]

Those organizational changes did not generally meet serious opposition. Executives throughout the corporation could understand that top management did not use decentralization to avoid responsibilities; as president, Hoffman was accessible, even answering his own phone. What the decentralization program did achieve, according to Hoffman, was significant reduction in managerial overhead, helping Studebaker to become more competitive within the industry.

Meanwhile, Hoffman and Vance also sought to generate the kind of publicity that would protect Studebaker's reputation. Henry Luce, now an old friend, proved most helpful by publishing in *Fortune* an article entitled "Studebaker Comes Back." Hoffman himself circulated a personally signed advertisement thanking competitors for giving Studebaker a square deal during its crisis and a chance to get back on its feet. That advertisement closed "So thanks—and look out." According to its chief executives, the new Studebaker Corporation was down to fighting trim. They wanted to prove, as Vance said, that the automotive industry had room for a "progressive, hard-hitting, compact" organization able to adjust quickly to market changes.[7]

To a great extent, Studebaker's corporate self-image as David fighting the Goliaths especially suited Hoffman's managerial style and his faith in capitalism. He understood well how to use the popular celebration of the "little guy" to promote Studebaker. Once he took over the leadership, his old slogan, "America's Friendliest Factory," gained even greater currency and acquired new relevance in the area of labor relations.

Within the automobile industry the Depression had produced massive reductions in employment and wages. Workers responded by seeking the protection of labor unions. Workers' desires then collided with managerial traditions and anti-union sentiments. The result was a dramatic and sometimes violent episode in American industrial relations.

At Studebaker, the Depression and the company's economic crisis threatened to undo its good record in labor relations. During his last years Albert Erskine had ended annual bonuses, vacation pay, and the stock purchase plan, and had sharply cut wages and the number of workers. In the crisis of 1933, Hoffman and Vance notified workers that they might have to eliminate the pension program as well. As Hoffman later admitted, Studebaker workers suffered very badly during that period.[8]

Facing the possibility that the company would try to save itself at their expense, some Studebaker workers set out to create a union. With a federal charter from the American Federation of Labor, a local union won the support of Studebaker workers. In February 1934, the union leaders met directly with Hoffman and Vance and achieved virtual recognition.

Partly because of the company's vulnerability and partly because they believed that the workers had legitimate grievances, Hoffman and Vance responded to unionization quite differently from leaders in the rest of the automotive industry. They refused to join a no-union pledge urged by other automakers. They sought to preserve good labor relations and refrained from any anti-union activities, though some lower echelon executives and supervisors may have tried intimidation. When they first met with union leaders, they opened sales records and explained the company's prospects. More important, because they believed that responsible unionism depended on union security, they encouraged Studebaker workers to join.[9]

Without struggle or bitterness, collective bargaining began at Studebaker. Offering easy access to union officials, Hoffman and Vance sought to settle disputes without the need for intervening lawyers. In 1935 they secretly arranged with local union leaders to exclude Studebaker from a threatened industry-wide strike. Hoffman personally reminded supervisors to see that fair play and teamwork prevailed without discrimination or favoritism. The company also assured workers that, within its economic ability, it would maximize its payroll and continue to produce as much as possible within its own plants, rather than "out-sourcing" with cheaper labor.[10]

The policies of Hoffman and Vance during the turbulent 1930s bought labor peace for Studebaker. The company did not face a single strike from the United Automobile Workers. In sharp contrast, the UAW conducted a sit-down strike in November 1936 against South Bend's other big employer, the Bendix Corporation. Of course, Studebaker workers realized that an interruption in production could push the automaker back into bankruptcy and could thus eliminate their jobs altogether, but they also responded to management's generous treatment.

Labor peace did not come cheaply; Hoffman admitted that Studebaker paid the highest wages while operating its production lines about 8 percent slower than was common within the industry. When the recession of 1937–38 reduced production, management accepted a union plan to spread work and avoid layoffs, even though the company incurred higher insurance costs.[11] In the long run, perhaps the most costly practice permitted by Hoffman and Vance established a virtually unlimited right for transfer. By this "bumping" system, workers with more seniority displaced those with less, regardless of training; as a result, some workers held jobs for which they were not trained, and production costs increased.

Studebaker's costly labor policies, strenuously resisted by other automakers, did not flow from any sense of paternalism, a concept Hoffman always distrusted. When he discussed the social responsibilities of corporations, he avoided the broad definitions associated with "welfare capitalism." Instead, he emphasized the need for enlightened self-interest within what one scholar has called a "functional approach to managerial obligations."[12] Profitability, not the image of benevolence, remained the ultimate goal.

Hoffman and Vance insisted that their decency in labor relations paid dividends. At Studebaker, management operated on the principle that to be humane was good business because workers usually responded by giving their best efforts. In articles, speeches, and signed advertisements, Hoffman used the "Friendly Factory" theme to show how the small but progressive and efficient automaker competed against the industry's giants. He claimed that Studebaker encouraged its unique force of mature craftsmen to maintain pride in good work. In return for higher production costs and higher car prices, Studebaker offered customers better-quality cars than those produced by the transient labor force working on Detroit's speeded-up production lines.

The test of such claims, Hoffman knew full well, came in the marketplace. Unfortunately for Studebaker, too few customers during the Depression bought its cars. From a peak of 145,000 vehicles in the early 1920s, sales fell to about 48,000 in 1933. Sales did rebound with the national economy in 1936 and 1937, exceeding 90,000 for each of those years, but with the recession of 1938 they fell to less than 53,000—below the break-even point—and the company lost $1.7 million. Unless they increased volume, Hoffman and Vance realized, Studebaker could not survive.

Following Hoffman's long-standing insistence that decisions had to be based on knowledge of the facts, Studebaker hired a market research organization. Facts, Inc., of New York discovered that the American car-buying public, even while cost-conscious, would not accept small, underpowered, and stripped-down cars that sacrificed comfort, ride, equipment, or quality. But the public would accept lighter-weight cars: a lighter and more fuel-efficient car in the low price field could find a profitable market.[13]

In 1935, with that report from market research, Hoffman and Vance laid out a three-year program for Studebaker to enter the big volume, low price field. But Studebaker faced enormous obstacles. Ford, Chevrolet, Plymouth, and Dodge already accounted for about 70 percent of the more than 20 million cars registered in the United States; customer brand loyalty alone created serious difficulties for newcomers. Furthermore, a huge number of used cars were clogging the distribution system and competing directly with low-priced new cars.

Studebaker could compete successfully with the Big Three, Hoffman and Vance believed, not by imitating them but by offering the public a distinctive and better product. Unencumbered by a large bureaucracy, a smaller company could actually become a leader in the industry. With that in mind, Hoffman and Vance gave free reign to Studebaker engineers to design a new car without using parts from existing models. They wanted a car lighter and more fuel-efficient but not smaller than competitors' cars. They decided that savings resulting from weight reduction were to be put into better trim, equipment, and quality control than usual in low-priced models.

By the spring of 1938, they had spent about $1 million for engineering the new model and building four test vehicles. Although they had hoped to accumulate more working capital before pushing ahead, the recession forced them to assume the "financial hazard" of introducing the new model as quickly as possible. Sanderson & Porter, their management consultants, agreed that Studebaker could not wait for a general economic recovery. Those arguments and the performance of the test cars convinced the board of directors to authorize production, allowing Hoffman and Vance to spend more than $3 million for retooling and plant modernization and another $1.5 million for advertising.[14]

The new cars, which carried the Champion nameplate, reflected Hoffman's efforts at innovation. With the size and power of other low-priced cars, they achieved 20 to 25 percent greater fuel efficiency with new and lighter engines and transmissions, enhanced by the only overdrive option among cars in that price category. Hoffman, the industry's "apostle of safety" and the founder and first president of the Automobile Safety Foundation, also emphasized its safety features. According to company publicity, the engineering department had built the car around the passenger compartment to provide greater protection. Its more rigid frame and lower body were designed to increase stability and ease of handling. Hoffman assumed that customers cared about the safety of cars they bought.[15]

Around the Champion's innovative engineering, Studebaker provided distinctive but not radical styling. As he had for the successful 1936 models, Hoffman hired on a fee basis flamboyant, Parisian-born designer Raymond Loewy. His sales promotion emphasized Loewy's reputation for the functional industrial design then much in vogue. But commentators called Loewy's design for the Champion conservative and almost conventional. With little chrome, no running boards, and headlights mounted within the fenders, it looked modern but not avant-garde. Studebaker hoped it would appeal to young car buyers.

Engineering and styling meant little, of course, without the right economics. Hoffman knew that because most car sales came from individuals in low income brackets, manufacturers had to offer less expensive cars that were more economical to operate. But competitors also recognized those facts and responded to the decline of car sales during the recession of 1937–38 by lowering the prices of their cheapest models. The Champion sold for $660 to $740, about the same price as Plymouth but slightly higher than Chevrolet. As he had done earlier, Hoffman justified the prices by emphasizing quality of production; dealers must sell Studebakers by convincing buyers to spend a little extra for better quality. With the Champion, he explained, Studebaker had taken great care in quality control and testing "to get the bugs out." In addition, dealers should emphasize the car's fuel economy, which had become an important consideration at a time when gasoline retail prices for motorists reached record peaks.[16]

Launched with fanfare, the Champion lived up to all its creators' hopes. Experts generally praised the new Studebaker. *Fortune* speculated that it might start a trend back to a real American "people's car," something that disappeared in the 1920s with the Model-T Ford. The Consumers Union rated the Champion with overdrive a "best buy" in its field and praised the simple design that would facilitate easy repair. Its automobile expert, usually a sharp critic of the industry, reported that the Champion had the best all-round characteristics in the low price field. He singled out for special praise its ability to provide both adequate performance and economy.[17]

More important than that praise was that the public responded by buying the new Studebaker in extraordinary numbers. Orders backlogged ahead of production, while plants operated five and a half days a week. Hoffman and Vance revised their sales forecasts upward, noting that the Champion brought more people into Studebaker dealerships and stimulated interest in the entire line.[18] When the 1939 model year ended, the company had sold over 114,000 cars, twice its sales for the previous year and its highest mark since 1928. During the next two years, with Champions leading the way, it sold even more.

That success cannot be explained simply by the national economic recovery; the increase in Studebaker sales outstripped the gains made throughout the industry. By modest innovation within the existing market pattern of the highly competitive low price field, Studebaker had found a profitable niche. According to one contemporary critic of the automotive industry, "Hoffman had done a good job at Studebaker, which was emerging as the most substantial survivor among the independent makers."[19]

The Champion's success brought immediate rewards for the entire Studebaker organization. Although no dividends were yet paid to stockholders, the directors restored the managerial salaries that Hoffman and Vance had cut during the recession of 1937–38. The president and chairman modestly announced that they preferred to wait for restoration of their own salaries until there was clearer proof that their efforts had brought real progress. The directors insisted, however, that Hoffman and Vance deserved a raise: from $42,500 in 1938, their salaries increased in 1939 to $50,000, and in 1940 to $60,000 plus bonuses of $21,000. Compared with the rest of the automotive industry, these were not high salaries: in 1938, thirty-two executives at other companies received over $75,000. But Hoffman told one interviewer that he had no great personal ambition; he just wanted to have Studebaker build good cars and sell them at a profit.[20]

When he testified before the Temporary National Economic Committee (TNEC) in December 1939, Hoffman had an opportunity to explain the philosophy that guided his management of Studebaker. Emphasizing his favorite economic theme, he argued that even with heavy concentration among the Big Three, the competitive system worked to produce better products at lower prices. The automobile was America's greatest industrial bargain.[21]

The small automakers, according to Hoffman, could compete successfully. To be sure, they faced disadvantages because the Big Three could spread over much larger volumes the high production costs of all-steel bodies and large annual expenditures for retooling new models. But the small automakers enjoyed compensating advantages. Excellence in engineering and design did not, he claimed, depend on the size of the staffs. The best and most innovative brains, because they wanted independence and the feeling that they counted, could not always be bought with the highest salaries. By maintaining closer and friendlier relations with engineers, production workers, and dealers, small companies could adapt more quickly than their larger competitors to meet market changes.

In the specific case of Studebaker, Hoffman claimed that it could compete successfully, given production over 100,000 units per year. With the introduction of the Champion, it surpassed that figure for the model year 1939 and continued to do so until car production was halted during World War II. Hoffman told the TNEC that Studebaker reached the volume needed for profitable economies of scale by building cars of better value at prices comparable to those of GM and Chrysler. But for the national economy and the automotive industry, the years just before the United States entered the war were unusual. It remained to be seen whether an automaker the size of Studebaker, guided by Hoffman's managerial philosophy, could indeed continue to achieve even its limited goals within a normal car market.

From its introduction in the fall of 1938, the Champion had sold well and made Studebaker profitable. But Hoffman and Vance did not rest there. They wanted to develop a boldly innovative new Champion that would firmly establish Studebaker in the low price market. Just when Studebaker seemed on the brink of even greater success, however, the war intervened.

During the more than two years between the outbreak of war in Europe and American belligerency, Hoffman and Vance tried to take advantage of the improving domestic economy. Like other leaders of the automotive industry, they wanted to expand car production and did not welcome suggestions that military needs required cutting back—perhaps even eliminating—car production. But with the plant operating below capacity, they went to Washington and personally offered Studebaker facilities for military production. By October 1939, they had negotiated a contract to produce trucks for France.[22]

Within Studebaker's executive offices Hoffman discussed how the automaker could best fit into the national defense program without sacrificing its car market. He thought that Harold Vance's selection in June 1940 to serve on the National Defense Advisory Commission gave Studebaker a significant advantage. By overseeing specialized military production, Vance could, he said, "render a service to the Corporation as well as to the Government." Vance's inside information would allow the company to plan without guessing. Thus, while its officials talked with Wright Aeronautical

Corporation about using the skilled workers of South Bend to produce airplane parts, Studebaker also increased production goals for cars and looked forward to strong sales for 1941.[23]

As a vice-president of the Automobile Manufacturers Association and a member of its Automotive Committee for Air Defense, Hoffman spoke out repeatedly against proposed government restrictions on car production. America did not have to choose between guns and butter, he said; it did not have to restrict car production to meet military needs, which had, of course, top priority. A premature cut in car production would, in fact, actually increase unemployment, hurt morale, and weaken the national economy just when it had to be strongest to pay for military needs. On a national radio broadcast in late 1940, Hoffman called impractical the proposals to have government take over the automotive industry and mobilize it to produce "500 Planes a Day." He pointed out that automotive plants could make engine parts but they could not be converted to make planes.[24]

The entry of the United States into the war, however, changed the whole situation. The day after Pearl Harbor, directors of the Automobile Manufacturers Association convened a special meeting, and Hoffman asked for permission to speak before the proceedings formally opened. He put his case very simply: "I think," he said, "the country expects an announcement of a cut in auto production from us this morning."[25] Like Hoffman, General Motors president Charles E. Wilson recognized the political realities of the defense program.

Yet though the bottlenecks and material shortages were quite obvious, Hoffman and other industry leaders still hoped that automaking would not be entirely eliminated. When that hope had to be scrapped by the Office of Production Management's order to end all car production by 31 January 1942, Hoffman and Vance rushed to Washington to find out how their organization could fit into the new defense production system. As a result, Studebaker soon sent to dealers instructions on how to convert for small-scale production of parts as well as service work on military vehicles. Thus Studebaker created the "first real bits and pieces manufacturing program" in the war effort.[26]

In March 1942, Hoffman became chairman of the Automotive Council for War Production, the three-month-old organization created by the Automobile Manufacturers Association. In that capacity he praised the head of the Office of Price Management, Leon Henderson. Many businessmen and politicians disliked the blunt New Deal economist, but Hoffman called him the kind of tough-minded realist America needed. He promised Henderson that the automotive industry, like the rest of the nation, would cooperate fully with the government if given adequate explanations.[27]

Instead of the uncertainties of competition, in the wartime economy the success of automakers depended upon complex dealings with a variety of government agencies. Early in the war, Studebaker became one of the first major defense contractors to be paid by the "cost plus a fixed fee" formula that predetermined profits. In all its contractual relations with the government, Studebaker avoided legal impasses and court action. The only blemish on its wartime record occurred in November 1942, when a Senate Committee headed by Harry Truman discovered that Studebaker had improperly sold the government obsolete machine tools. The incident led to the resignation of one company executive and the disciplining of a few others.[28]

On the whole, wartime production provided a magnificent record of what Studebaker could achieve. By the war's end it had built almost 65,000 airplane engines at one of the lowest unit costs of any supplier. It had designed and built tens of thousands of Weasels—amphibious personnel-cargo carriers—and about 200,000 heavy-duty, six-wheel trucks. It delivered all orders on schedule and even found ways to cut shipping costs for the government.

Studebaker benefited handsomely from those military contracts. Despite what one stock analyst called burdensome taxes, it enjoyed good earnings as net sales increased from $115 million in 1941 to $415 million in 1944. For the first time since the reorganization in 1935, it started to pay its stockholders dividends even while reducing its indebtedness.[29] Meanwhile, to handle the increased volume, Hoffman and Vance expanded Studebaker's existing facilities and acquired new plants as well for a workforce that grew from about 8,000 to a peak of about 24,000.

Regardless of those gains, Hoffman and Vance, like other leaders in the industry, realized that all-out military production would not continue indefinitely and therefore wanted to resume production for the civilian market. The war had retarded the momentum of Studebaker's image as an automaker on the way up; as a result, the trade-in value of its cars and the survival of its dealer network were seriously threatened. To combat those threats and also to whet the appetites of American consumers, Studebaker spent millions of dollars on advertising and publicity even before it had new cars to sell.[30]

The company also made what *Business Week* called a "big league move" to hold its dealers and attract new ones. Hoffman and Vance decided that Studebaker would become the first independent automaker to eliminate the payment to each regional distributor for every car sold in its region; in that way, Studebaker could offer discounts on car prices directly to the dealers. To set a good example, Hoffman applied the new policy first to his own distributorship in southern California. But some distributors resisted the change long after the policy announcement, because it reduced a lucrative part of their businesses.[31]

The reason Hoffman and Vance wanted to strengthen Studebaker's sales organization and speed its reconversion to a civilian market was a simple one. Unlike many economic forecasters, they correctly recognized that the nation stood at the brink of a great boom and that the car market would expand enormously. To take advantage of that postwar demand, Studebaker needed to organize for quick action.

One early step in reestablishing a civilian market was to terminate defense contracts. Studebaker's relatively small size and resolute management allowed it to achieve the fastest and smoothest termination among major defense contractors: within 105 days after V-J Day, it had settled terms to end all government defense contracts and, according to *Business Week*, had become the model and pride of contract termination officials.[32] By paying off subcontractors itself rather than waiting for government action, as was commonly done, it sometimes received only partial payment or nothing at all from the government. Those added costs proved insignificant, however, against the larger advantage of time gained for reconversion.

In mid-1945, while many defense contractors found themselves temporarily caught between cancellations of military orders and the resumption of civilian business, Hoffman and Vance started refinancing. With the sale of more stock and with conventional bank loans, they retired the remaining $12 million of loans acquired under a special wartime credit line and began costly retooling. Had they waited even a little longer, those changes would have cost perhaps 20 percent more. One cautious stock analyst concluded then that Studebaker had come out of the war with adequate working capital to meet its needs. According to a more recent judgment, Hoffman and Vance brought Studebaker out of the war "a healthy and prosperous company," seemingly on the verge of achieving a business miracle.[33]

The last step in Studebaker's reconversion came with the negotiation of a new union contract in December of 1945. The once self-proclaimed Friendly Factory had discovered during the war that its relations with labor were changing. Across the nation, industrial expansion eroded managerial authority over production standards and factory discipline, and workers displayed a truculent spirit of independence. Even in South Bend, short wildcat strikes interrupted war production. And for the first time, the National Labor Relations Board had accused Studebaker's management in 1943 of violating the Wagner Act.[34]

To negotiate the new labor contract, Hoffman and Vance took special care, meeting several times with union leaders in preparation. And when formal negotiations began, Hoffman declared that he would serve as a buffer between the union and the corporation's board, which wanted better performance. Sharing with labor leaders the company's plans for expansion, and promising policies that would give workers high weekly pay, he asked the union to make the contract work for mutual benefit. Otherwise, he warned, the board would demand a tougher contract at the next negotiations.[35]

Other automakers, determined to reestablish work rules that had eroded under wartime government contracts, bargained harder. GM endured a 113-day strike to preserve managerial prerogatives. Critics of Studebaker's management later charged that Hoffman and Vance should have reasserted efficiency as other automakers did, even at the risk of a strike. According to the critics, Studebaker failed to restore work standards because Hoffman and Vance wanted to preserve their company's image as America's Friendly Factory.[36]

There is some merit in that criticism, but it misses an important element. Hoffman preferred not to drive too hard a bargain because he believed that in the long run, fair dealing would do more for efficiency, quality, and productivity. Beyond any ethical or humane considerations, he based that policy on his practical judgment of Studebaker's competitive position. To compete against the Big Three, it had to exploit its own advantages of speedy conversion and superior human relations. In 1946, when he accepted the American Management Association's Henry Laurence Gantt Memorial Gold Medal "for providing an inspiring, practical example of successful management-labor relations," he emphasized the need for the "human relations approach" to strengthen the teamwork essential for the success of free enterprise.[37] Given the changes in the size, composition, and aspirations of the workforce, it still remained to be seen, however, whether Studebaker could continue to operate by that managerial philosophy in a competitive car market.

As the nation converted from a wartime to a new domestic economy, Paul Hoffman entered a new stage in both his business career and his personal life. He was then in his mid-fifties, full of vigor and still youthful in appearance. With most of their children grown, in 1946 he and Dorothy sold their big house in South Bend, using the proceeds to improve the family estate in Pasadena, which became their permanent home. For work in South Bend, Paul lived alone in their summer home at Union Pier, Michigan, commuting by car about twenty miles. Weekends he usually spent with the family in southern California, where Studebaker had operated an assembly plant since the mid-1930s and where his own dealership continued as a major retail outlet.

In those years after the war, the backlog of pentup savings and unfulfilled consumer demands fueled a sellers' market for cars. With GM leading the way, the Big Three continued to dominate the industry, but the independent automakers also discovered new life within the expanding market. From a prewar combined share of about 10 percent, by 1949 they reached a share of about 15 percent.[38]

During the boom they had correctly predicted, Hoffman and Vance showed special daring and vigor. They knew that the sellers' market would not last long, and they wanted to gain the maximum advantage by quickly retooling for an entirely new car. If Studebaker could be first with a distinctively modern car, the sellers' market would overcome possible resistance to new styling; then superior quality and service would win over customers who might continue their brand loyalty even when normal conditions returned. With that potential in mind, Studebaker was able to launch the entirely new 1947 Champion for only about $11 million.[39]

What emerged from its commitment to innovation was a car with modern engineering and distinctive styling. The 1947 Champion no longer had a small car appearance, yet even with a longer wheelbase than the 1939 model, it weighed 400 pounds less than the low-priced cars produced by the Big Three. Built lower and with a stiffer frame, it had the first self-centering, self-adjusting hydraulic brakes in an American production car and an instrument panel with ultraviolet light for greater visibility. Studebaker claimed that it offered greater comfort, more safety, and better economy than its competitors.

To achieve distinctive styling, Hoffman again hired outside designers. Raymond Loewy sought a design that would not sacrifice the car's efficient functionalism. As a reminder to his staff, he put up in his studios posters that proclaimed, "Weight is the enemy." That view was shared by Virgil Exner, who had headed Loewy's studio in South Bend during the early 1940s and who became an independent consultant on the new Champion. As a consultant for Studebaker, Exner declared that the average motorist did not want bulky, bulbous, ponderous, elephantine cars costly to buy and to operate. For the heavy city traffic where most driving was done, he thought motorists would prefer the ease of handling and fuel economy possible with lighter and sleeker cars.[41]

The design of the 1947 Champion was an amalgam of the ideas of both Loewy Associates and Exner, mostly Loewy's. Flat fenders integrated with the body; an elongated, tapered rear deck gave the car smooth, sleek contours. Its rear window wrapped around almost to a semicircle, providing greater visibility. Comedians joked that motorists would not know which end to drive forward, but the design made the car recognizably different.

The job of selling the new car fell to Hoffman, who set about making dealers and their sales personnel effective and enthusiastic spokesmen. Everywhere he could, he emphasized that the new car combined functionalism, beauty, and safety not previously possible. Built with production techniques developed during the war, the modern Studebaker, according to Hoffman, reached higher quality standards. Car buyers would not forget that Studebaker was the first to give buyers those benefits of progress.

With a network of personal contacts, Hoffman knew how to generate favorable publicity; journalists often referred to him as what one magazine called an "excellent national advertisement for Studebaker." Press reports usually reinforced common themes: Studebaker was a progressive organization run by an industrial statesman and producing modern cars with high-quality workmanship.[42]

A ten-page article in *Life* in the fall of 1946 illustrated this successful promotion. Still a close friend of publisher Henry Luce, Hoffman wrote to the magazine's editor to complain that the press was focusing too much on labor strife in the postwar era. *Life* responded, with help from Studebaker's public relations staff, by praising the spry, independent, and forward-looking company that maintained "glass-smooth labor relations." The article called the new Champion the "epitome of U.S. industrial accomplishment" and suggested that even more was promised because Studebaker had already gone far with development of a simplified automatic transmission and torsion suspension.[43]

Presumably less swayed by Studebaker publicity, even consumer-oriented automotive commentators generally gave the company high marks, too. They praised the Champion as a "car of the future," a spectacular achievement of modern design. They noted that besides its safety features the Champion offered savings in fuel economy without sacrificing durability, a common fault of cars with very small engines. However, *Consumer Reports* pointed out that while Studebaker advertising appealed to thriftiness, car buyers had little reason to seek economical cars because gasoline prices were now low. In contrast with Studebaker's emphasis on economy, for example, GM anticipated that car buyers would be most attracted by appearance, automatic transmissions, and powerful engines—in that order.[44]

Nevertheless, Studebaker sales after the war completely vindicated the decisions made by Hoffman and Vance to rush a new model into production. In 1948 the company sold 143,000 cars, more than in any year since its peak during the early 1920s, and two years later it sold a record 268,000 cars. Its market share, which before the war had topped 3 percent only in one year, climbed above 4 percent and stayed at that level for four straight years, placing it behind only the Big Three. With that expanded volume, in 1948 it earned $18 million in profit, compared with only $2 million in 1940. Those profits enabled Studebaker to reach the $50 million level in working capital and to pay stockholders extra dividends.

Hoffman must have felt gratified running Studebaker during the postwar boom he had forecast. Business was fun when customers clamored for new cars. Prominent individuals, even movie stars, wrote directly to him to place their orders and to express thanks for his help. He took pride in knowing that people like columnist Walter Lippmann and Dallas merchandizing magnate Stanley Marcus—no amateur when it came to style and salesmanship—appreciated Studebaker cars.

Yet even with success, Hoffman realized that Studebaker had to maintain its advantages in styling and engineering while reducing its retail prices. During the sellers' market, Studebaker was not hurt by the fact that its retail prices were substantially higher than those of the Big Three. But he told the board of directors that he preferred a deliberate policy of underpricing to win car buyers and to force internal efforts at efficiency; with the return of normal market conditions, Studebaker would have to reduce costs to make its car prices more competitive.[45]

Studebaker's long-term success, he knew, hinged on relations with its workers: the company had to lower its labor costs, which had become excessive, without sacrificing the superior quality of its workmanship. Plant managers, very competent but traditional, still often viewed the union with antagonism. On the other side, Local 5 was a well-managed union, better than average, but its leaders did not know enough about the economics of the industry.[46] Therefore, Hoffman and Vance tried to bring the two sides together.

Like many other corporate managers, Hoffman hoped to use the union to help maintain production standards. Periodically, he and Vance met with both supervisory and union personnel. During the 1947 contract negotiations, his last as president of Studebaker, Hoffman explained to labor leaders why costs had to be cut and why the workforce, then about 17,700, had to be reduced about 10 percent and had to become more efficient. In October, after strenuous negotiations and over the objections of many of its members, the union accepted a new contract that Hoffman said would help bring costs down.[47]

In April 1948, just when he and Studebaker were riding high, Paul Hoffman left the presidency to become the first administrator of the new Marshall Plan. From the unfamiliar perspective of a concerned outsider, he had nothing but praise for the way Harold Vance ran Studebaker during the late 1940s. Profits seemed "fantastic." Studebaker would become a "major league" operator. "I don't see what can stop us," he wrote to Vance, "from becoming the fourth big company in the field."[48]

When Vance testified before a congressional committee in December 1948, Studebaker's record seemed to vindicate the strategy he and Hoffman had outlined for the Temporary National Economic Committee eight years earlier. Vance said he still believed that the way to increase profits was to expand volume by offering car buyers better value for lower prices. With that strategy, the company had created a profitable niche within a highly concentrated industry. Even if its business were to fall off by more than 50 percent, Vance felt that Studebaker could still operate profitably.[49]

What now stands out most strikingly about Studebaker's postwar record is the disparity between contemporary and subsequent assessments. Perhaps because of Hoffman's deft handling of public relations, the contemporary press widely praised Studebaker; only after it had suffered from irreversible setbacks did critics point to long-term deficiencies that went right to the top executive offices.

Automotive historian Richard M. Langworth, while commending Studebaker cars, has summarized the most thorough indictment of the leadership of Hoffman and Vance. According to him, during the postwar era they "generally failed to understand the changing nature of the automobile industry and plan accordingly." Like other critics, he charges that they failed to resist union pressures as fully as Studebaker's financial resources would have allowed. With excessive labor costs, the company's competitive position worsened. But even a tougher labor policy would not have solved the problems that resulted from small size. Hoffman and Vance failed to recognize that survival in the automobile business required a larger scale of operation possible only with merger.[50]

The case for a merger of small automakers found strong support even during the boom of the late 1940s. Among the independents, George Mason of Nash most vigorously urged them to consolidate while they enjoyed the sellers' market; merger would allow them to compete against the Big Three when the market declined.[51] Before 1953, however, the clash of executive egos and corporate rivalries prevented any such move.

For Studebaker, Hoffman opposed merger. Optimistic about his company's prospects for growth, he preferred going it alone. He was relieved that a rumored merger with the new but financially weak Kaiser-Frazer organization failed to materialize. He also felt that Studebaker should consider buying out Packard only at a bargain price, because that automaker would not likely regain its once lofty position in the luxury car field.[52]

To some extent, Hoffman may have been a captive of his own reputation. The image of the small but progressive automaker staying ahead of the competitor may well have led him to ignore the disadvantages, especially in advertising and distribution, that merger could have alleviated. The concept of America's Friendliest Factory may also have led him to minimize the problems of eroding work standards and persisting excess in labor costs. Below the surface, Studebaker did not quite live up to its favorable press.

On the other hand, Hoffman's achievements during his fifteen years at the helm should not be slighted. In competition with the Big Three and other independents, he did bring Studebaker back from bankruptcy to profitability. He launched two innovative and distinctive new models that won a growing share in the car market. During the war he operated with outstanding results as a defense contractor. Without resorting to speedup or other tough labor policies, he provided stockholders with satisfactory dividends. Measured by his so-called functional approach to managerial obligations, Hoffman's record at Studebaker was one of success—qualified by what happened after he left the company in 1948.

4 The Search for Stability and Growth, 1933-48

During the fifteen years that he led Studebaker, Paul Hoffman also emerged as an articulate voice for business within the public arena. Though not an original thinker, an intellectual, or even a well-educated person in a formal sense, he was intelligent and hardworking. He learned by reading a lot and by contact with a broadening circle of acquaintances and friends. Despite the fact that he found writing difficult, on the big issues of the day he expressed himself with clarity and cogency.

A low-keyed and amiable salesman, he knew how to sell himself and his ideas. With his naturalness, exuberance, and sincere conviction, he put people at ease and instilled confidence and trust. His personality and his performance at Studebaker gave him credibility both within the business community and to more general audiences. During World War II, he reached the level of business celebrity as chairman of a new business organization, the Committee for Economic Development.

Although some of his ideas changed during those fifteen years, Hoffman did not move far from a central core of values and assumptions. In an attempt to avoid conventional ideological labels, he usually called his views "responsible." Nevertheless, he clearly shared much with business progressives who had tried since the turn of the century to accommodate American capitalism to the conditions of a modern industrial society. Without necessarily agreeing among themselves about specific policies, business progressives had been seeking to prevent the harmful consequences of the business cycle, including heightened class conflict. They wanted economic growth with rational order and stability. By the 1920s, such businessmen as

E.A. Filene, Gerard Swope, and Owen D. Young had accepted the need for new bureaucratic techniques and for a larger government role. Bernard Baruch and Herbert Hoover figured prominently as political mediators for that effort to create for capitalism a satisfactory middle path between traditional laissez faire conservatism and statist or collectivist formulas.[1] Hoffman joined those efforts during the 1930s.

When Hoffman started to speak out on public issues during the Depression, business leaders faced widespread public criticism, labor unrest, and unwanted governmental intrusion. Large sections of the business community, including most leaders of the automotive industry, remained staunchly conservative, trying to defend their own interests against the New Deal. Hoffman, too, resented the New Deal and the antibusiness sentiments associated with it, but he also tried to combat wrong-headed, economically illiterate, reactionary businessmen. He wanted to educate them about the modern capitalistic system in order that they might help to preserve it and make it more prosperous.

Sharing the virtual mystique of mass production that had become part of the national self-image, Hoffman always defended American free enterprise as a system providing the average person with the world's highest standard of living. However, he recognized that in the modern industrial world Americans had to modify some of their most deeply ingrained values. Regard for individual integrity and self-reliance had hardened into a conservative philosophy of rugged individualism that rationalized injustice and undermined the democratic political system. For that reason, he welcomed some efforts toward providing common people with greater security. However, he warned against the dangers of conformity, including the kind encouraged by advertisers. People had to think independently and act cooperatively. Herbert Hoover called that combination "American Individualism."[2]

Like Hoover, Hoffman felt that the American free enterprise system faced greater threats from business reactionaries than from Communists. "If you are a capitalist who is seeking exorbitant profits," he told one business group, "you are sabotaging the free enterprise system."[3] Reactionary businessmen who opposed labor unions and collective bargaining also sabotaged the free enterprise system by heightening class conflicts and by refusing to provide an equitable distribution of society's benefits.

Hoffman urged businessmen and corporations, out of public favor during the Depression, to correct the abuses and injustices of the old order. Not from altruism or benevolence or paternalism—which he always distrusted—but from enlightened self-interest, they had to make sure that in an interdependent economy their policies were compatible with the public welfare. They had to treat labor unions with fairness, decency, and even friendliness. Business benefited in the long run from humane policies, including the highest possible pay for workers, for in the modern mass production economy the average person was the big customer.[4]

Because businessmen did not always act as they should, Hoffman praised the New Deal objectives for recovery with social justice. The New Deal properly sought to give workers and other low-income groups greater security, more generous shares of the material benefits of modern mass production, and protection against antisocial acts of exploitation by business. Although a Republican, he specifically endorsed laws promoting collective bargaining, minimum wages, unemployment insurance, pensions, public works projects to reduce the suffering of the unemployed, and some regulatory functions, especially those of the Federal Trade Commission (FTC). To the extent that they eliminated or reduced injustices, such government programs improved the public reputation of legitimate business and strengthened free enterprise. Therefore, he urged businessmen to accept the right of government to lay down rules of fair conduct. A case in point was the Wagner Labor Relations Act, which business vigorously opposed because it encouraged labor unions. But the government's attempt to solve the Depression was another matter.[5]

Recovery, according to Hoffman, depended mainly on businessmen's returning to American business traditions. Intensely competitive, even in his recreational bridge and golf, he believed that the risks and uncertainties of competition stimulated ingenuity and energy. As president of Studebaker and owner of other small companies, he knew how necessity could goad people into the creativity they otherwise avoided. Certainly, his description of businessmen in a competitive economy staying up nights worrying and trying to find new ways to make profits contained a large measure of autobiography. He hoped that with the spirit of adventure, courage, self-confidence, and resourcefulness, businessmen would innovate and speculate in the aggressive pursuit of profits. Then prices would be lowered, products improved, the economy expanded, and the American living standard raised even higher.

While Hoffman wanted the government to protect and strengthen that competitive system by enforcement of antitrust legislation, he recognized that some businessmen preferred security. Rather than face the risks and uncertainties of competition, a minority of reactionary and spiritually bankrupt businessmen sought political solutions to economic problems. Although they opposed efforts by farmers and workers to obtain government aid, those "political racketeers" subverted free enterprise by their own efforts to obtain special privileges from government. Silly and ethically outrageous, such behavior hurt the economy. Furthermore, he warned, "Legislation to help the businessman make a profit is dangerous because its natural concomitant is government control."[6]

On the national level, he regarded the NRA system of industry-wide codes controlling prices and production as the worst assault on competition and free enterprise. By expecting businessmen to rise to what they could not become—namely, public policy-makers—the National Recovery Administration undermined incentives and innovation. Expressing neither liberalism nor belief in progress but rather selfish pursuit by reactionaries of their own security, the NRA encouraged business complacency, monopoly, privilege, restricted output, and stagnation. Yet higher living standards and a more abundant life could never be achieved by producing less at higher prices; recovery depended upon expanded production and lower prices.[7]

Hoffman sharpened that criticism as the nation approached the presidential election of 1936. Privately, he lamented that President Roosevelt, "the absolute dictator" under the NRA, had turned for advice to "a strange group of young men" less interested in recovery than in moving toward a planned economy. Their bureaucratic harassment of competitive business actually retarded recovery and efforts to reduce unemployment. Nevertheless, the initiative, resourcefulness, and energy of the American people had brought about enough recovery, ironically, to make President Roosevelt virtually unbeatable.[8] And therefore, even though the NRA had been declared unconstitutional the previous year, its dangerous spirit lived on.

In new laws controlling prices and production, fair trade laws, retail license laws, and other governmental policies aimed at restricting competition, Hoffman saw a particularly ominous threat.

The nation after 1935 still moved toward a planned economy, with all the dangers of bureaucratic control, regimentation, and the ultimate destruction of both free enterprise and personal liberties. By just that path, which started with repression of individual economic freedom, some European democracies after World War I had become dictatorships under modern Caesars. From that perspective, he began to label the NRA, the Guffey-Vinson Act, the Miller-Tydings Act, farm price supports, and the whole effort at economic planning as state socialism or fascism or totalitarianism. Those modern forms of "feudalism" sacrificed economic dynamism and the welfare of the individual for stability and scarcity. Like Hoover, Hoffman warned that the New Deal outlook, even though not fascist by intent, assumed that the economy had reached maturity and therefore led to defeatist resignation and excessive reliance on government. According to Hoffman, free enterprise could still bring America greater prosperity than it had ever known. If unshackled, it would promote growth and provide new consumer products, such as air conditioning and television.[9]

As he readily admitted, this argument contained a large element of self-interest. Yet the connection between his ideas and his own business interests was neither clear-cut nor narrow. On one side, he felt that Studebaker suffered first because of rigid NRA codes and then later because of rigid limitations on overtime labor under the Wages and Hours Act. To compete against entrenched giants, it needed the flexibility to respond to sudden market shifts. Similarly, while most car dealers backed federal and state efforts to limit competition on the retail level, he wanted the market open so that Studebaker's superior service could bring expansion. On the other side, however, the NRA quotas actually benefited his own dealership in Los Angeles.[10]

Just as he opposed all efforts to restrict competition, Hoffman also opposed what he regarded as fiscal irresponsibility. Because of the Depression, he accepted the New Deal's monetary devaluation as beneficial for the nation, but like most businessmen he did not think the way to recovery could be found through deficit spending by government. We could no more spend our way out of the Depression, as New Deal Keynesians seemed to think, than we could spread work and loaf our way to recovery. Instead, he wanted budgets balanced by less spending and lower taxes.

By criticizing New Deal tax policies, Hoffman expressed sentiments common within the business community. Stunned by higher surtax rates, corporate rates, and an undistributed profits tax, business leaders charged that the New Deal was penalizing initiative and hindering investment, especially among small corporations; during the devastating recession of 1937–38, many members of Congress, not merely conservatives, agreed. In the Treasury Department, even Undersecretary Roswell Magill, a defender of the undistributed profits tax, argued for lower taxes, specifically mentioning the plight of companies like Studebaker. President Roosevelt reportedly scoffed at such arguments, however.[11]

Like many others of his class, Hoffman felt personally victimized by New Deal policies. By one set of regulations, the Securities Exchange Commission prevented him from selling a stock bonus held less than six months; by another set of regulations, the Treasury Department taxed him on the value of the stock when he received the bonus, not when he could sell. Thus, because stock prices dropped during the recession, before he was permitted to sell, he was taxed on bonus income he never received.[12]

Beyond that personal grievance, he regarded the existing laws as dangerously chaotic, excessive, punitive, and destructive. Not only did he suffer, but so did the Studebaker Corporation and the entire national economy. New Deal tax policies deprived innovative business of venture capital, which would be invested in risky and speculative business only when boldness was rewarded, not taxed away. Those tax policies excessively penalized profits without consideration of the risks of failure. Like the NRA and some other New Deal measures, tax policies were inhibiting economic expansion just when the nation most needed growth to create jobs.[13]

Much of what Hoffman said about the revision of tax policies stood well within the conventional wisdom of the business community. After a group of automotive industry leaders attended a White House conference in January 1938, he voiced optimism that relations between government and business would improve. He insisted, however, that constructive remedies for the recession had to include downward revision of taxes on top individual incomes, capital gains, and new or small businesses that earned high profits. In that way, those who invested and risked failure or who used their creativity to promote economic growth would see incentives for boldness. He agreed with business leaders who attended the *Fortune* Round Table, the symposium created by Henry Luce in 1939, that taxes for middle income groups should be raised, government budgets balanced, and debts gradually retired by reduction of government spending on needless services.[14] His brand of economics for the forgotten rich won at least a partial victory in June 1939 when Congress, against the wishes of President Roosevelt, repealed the undistributed profits tax.

For Hoffman, revision of the tax structure was only part of the bigger issue: the defense of free enterprise. With the recession of 1937–38, he felt that America had reached a crossroads: either the nation would continue its course toward complete bureaucratic control of business, or it would return to free enterprise. The recession generated public skepticism about government management of the economy, but it did not automatically make the public confident about the wisdom of businessmen. For businessmen to regain public favor, they had to show by their efficiency, innovativeness, and willingness to lower prices that the system worked well.[15]

Prolonged economic stagnation and massive unemployment demonstrated just the opposite: the system did not work well. With millions still unable to find jobs, in the late 1930s Hoffman started to speak out more frequently about the dangerous social consequences of unemployment as a threat to democracy. The recent histories of Italy and Germany convinced him that democracy could not long endure class conflicts exacerbated by large-scale and protracted unemployment. Even the United States was not immune to such dangers. When declining national income and rising unemployment made more people aware of the grossly unfair distribution of wealth and income, internal strife, class jealousies, and abusive epithets grew sharper. He worried that in an emergency such divisions carried the potential of degenerating into mass hysteria. Thus the survival of democracy depended on the reduction of poverty and unemployment. For the "haves," security could be achieved only by a social program that constantly decreased the number of "have-nots."[16]

The economic recovery and increased employment brought on by the advent of war in Europe in 1939 did not lessen Hoffman's concerns. Even more than the New Deal's economic planning, the war threatened to expand government bureaucratic control that could stifle free enterprise. When critics of business advocated that the government take over actual management of American industry to assure adequate military production, Hoffman claimed that so-called conscription of wealth or of industry could be achieved only through totalitarian methods. Furthermore, free enterprise based on management's ingenuity and resourcefulness could always produce more efficiently than could regimented business using slave labor.[17]

To protect free enterprise, Hoffman and other business opponents of the New Deal emphasized more than just economic benefits. They sought to convince the American people that all freedoms were connected and mutually dependent. Thus in 1940, the National Association of Manufacturers, never prominent in the civil liberties movement, launched its "Tripod of Freedom" campaign linking free enterprise, civil liberties, and representative democracy. Hoffman spoke out in defense of academic freedom, religious freedom, and freedom of the press; he urged other businessmen to do the same. The United States had to be more than the arsenal of democracy; it had to become the guardian of democratic ideals by protecting freedoms and democratic decision-making on all levels of society.[18]

Because the battle for public opinion eventually leads to the political arena and because he regarded government restrictions as the major threat to free enterprise, Hoffman himself became more active politically. Though not a Roosevelt-hater given to repeating the kinds of stories that circulated among the rich, he did very much resent the President's oratorical assaults on business leadership; more important, he worried that four more years of government fumbling and business timidity might seriously imperil private capitalism. Sound recovery depended on business confidence in government, something impossible with New Dealers in office.[19] As the election of 1940 approached, he thought that Republican chances were better than they had been in 1932 or 1936. In any case, the stakes were too high to let events pass without effort.

In August of 1939, through his work on behalf of traffic safety, Hoffman met the man he thought would be "a natural" as the Republican presidential candidate: Thomas E. Dewey. The ambitious young district attorney from New York was, he felt, the one man who could lead America back to democracy and away from the menace of fascist control of enterprise. In Dewey he saw a chance to move the nation back to a policy of economic expansion and to challenge the New Dealers' exclusive claim as custodians of all that was progressive. He especially liked the way Dewey had gone on the attack and put the New Dealers on the defensive for their defeatist attitudes regarding the Depression.[20]

Besides personally preferring Dewey, Hoffman also knew that circumstances required the Republicans to nominate a progressive candidate. Unlike Robert A. Taft, the conservative senator from Ohio, Dewey at least had "some chance" against President Roosevelt. Therefore, Hoffman worked for Dewey in Indiana and tried to arrange other contacts, such as with baseball executive Branch Rickey, a key Republican in Missouri and "a crusader of the first rank." However, he declined Dewey's suggestion that he devote all his activities to the campaign; he thought Dewey showed little political acumen if he believed that his candidacy would benefit from the fulltime support of one of those people New Dealers labeled an Economic Royalist or a Prince of Privilege.[21]

When the Republicans nominated neither Dewey nor Taft but Wendell Willkie, Hoffman became an easy convert. Earlier he had considered Willkie a "starry-eyed amateur" but was persuaded otherwise by his friend Russell Davenport of *Fortune*. Shortly after the nominating convention, Hoffman wrote to a friend that Willkie had the best chance of any Republican against Roosevelt, and—backed by the now popular Luce publications—the photogenic Willkie did indeed poll more votes than had any previous Republican opponent of F.D.R. His defeat naturally disappointed Hoffman, who worked for the ticket, but it did not dismay him. He hoped that Willkie's postelection call for a loyal opposition to challenge the New Deal would lead to a new and better day for America.[22] By then, however, he had other plans to try to save free enterprise in its time of peril.

During 1939 and 1940, Hoffman discussed with friends his concerns about such national problems as unemployment and economic stagnation. Too many Americans, in his view, seemed interested only in "getting all the swag while the getting is good." They needed to learn that properly enlightened self-interest required responsible concern for the welfare of the nation as a whole.[23] Only when Americans kept to that vision could the country enjoy stability and prosperous growth.

As a trustee of his alma mater, the University of Chicago, he proposed to its president Robert Maynard Hutchins and vicepresident William B. Benton that the university direct its experts to consider current economic problems. He thought that the gap between knowledge and practice could be closed by better communication between academics and leaders of important segments of the society, not only business but also labor. Benton, who had independently arrived at similar views, joined him in creating at the University of Chicago a new institute. Professor Harold Lasswell, who assisted them, suggested that it be called the American Policy Commission.[24]

In recruiting participants for this institute, Hoffman enlarged his already wide circle of personal contacts. In February 1941 he joined the Business Advisory Council, a group of business leaders organized by the Commerce Department during the early days of the New Deal. The BAC, which included some of the more pragmatic and moderate leaders of large national corporations, provided important connections for Hoffman and his project.

At the insistence of Benton, a Democrat, participation in the American Policy Commission was restricted to "literate" business leaders and academics; labor leaders were not invited. To finance the project, Hoffman said they needed about ten generous business leaders of "liberal" views.[25] Their initial group included Henry Luce; Marshall Field, department store owner and newspaper publisher; Ralph Flanders, machine tool manufacturer and banker; Beardsley Ruml, treasurer of R.H. Macy and former dean at the University of Chicago; Thomas B. McCabe of Scott Paper; R.R. Deupree of Procter and Gamble; and advertising man Ray Rubicam.

Even such practical and experienced men, Hoffman felt, should not debate current economic problems without adequate preparation. First, the experts must study the causes of the collapse of free societies elsewhere and conditions jeopardizing American freedom; then participants should read the experts' reports and meet with them in study groups. With different experiences and perspectives, they could educate one another. The result, he hoped, would be a better understanding of the principles of a free society and more thoughtful solutions to national problems.

Despite their hopes and efforts, Hoffman and Benton decided to put the American Policy Commission in mothballs when the United States entered the war, believing that businessmen would be too busy with war production problems to participate in the nascent organization. However, events soon proved that forecast wrong. With encouragement and support from Secretary of Commerce Jesse

Jones, a conservative Houston millionaire, in 1942 they broadened the scope of their project and launched the Committee for Economic Development.

Structurally, the CED consisted of two distinct components. Its small and rather elite research division sponsored study groups and issued reports on major questions regarding the economic policies of the government and the private sector. Its field division, organized in twelve regional sections corresponding with those of the Federal Reserve Banks, sought to use those reports to educate businessmen at the local level. This division, which by 1946 included about 75,000 members, provided the first audience for the CED's effort at molding public opinion.

Atop this structure was the CED's eighteen-member board, all selected by Jesse Jones. Benton described the trustees as "liberal, progressive businessmen."[26] Mostly the heads of very large national corporations, nearly all belonged as well to the Commerce Department's Business Advisory Council. This elite of big business came together in the new organization because of common concerns about how wartime government decisions would affect the postwar economy. To serve as the chairman, chief spokesman, and focal point of publicity for what was originally intended as only a wartime effort, the board chose trustee Paul Hoffman.

The chairmanship of the CED further elevated Hoffman's celebrity status. Journalists consistently praised him for personifying enlightened capitalism. In a cover story on the CED's first year, for example, *Time* noted that Hoffman, though "no world-shaking figure," had become a "recognized power" well beyond the size of Studebaker in the automotive industry.[27]

The favorable press served Hoffman well when he explained what the CED was all about. In a manner common among progressive elites since the turn of the century, he argued that a modern industrial society could not leave complex public decisions to outmoded traditions, ignorance, and emotional partisanship. According to him, the CED sponsored experts who studied important policy issues by gathering all relevant facts and then reaching objective and responsible interpretations. Such nonpartisan and scientific expertise, divorced from the ordinary politics of competing interest groups, was supposed to help Americans uproot prejudices and overcome narrow-mindedness. Thus, unlike other business organizations that lobbied or propagandized for special interests, the CED was "entirely non-political." Its chairman claimed that it focused on purely economic matters of business performance that contributed to prosperity.[28]

Hoffman's version of the CED did not tell the whole story however. Many scholars have pointed out that the CED resembled other elite-dominated organizations that sought to use claims of technical expertise and nonpartisanship to mold public opinion and influence government policy. In the area of foreign affairs, the Council on Foreign Relations provides the best example. And contrary to Hoffman's claims that the CED eschewed politics, it did advocate a point of view. Recent scholars have suggested that the CED promoted a vague and ambiguous ideology that they have categorized as a form of so-called corporatism.[29]

Although the corporatist label carries connotations not quite appropriate for Hoffman, he readily admitted that the CED's goal was the preservation of America's "free dynamic economy." Alternatives to the CED-charted middle path for capitalism simply did not make sense to him. Socialism he regarded as economically inept and politically threatening to all freedoms. He also denied that a modern economy could operate by rugged individualism, laissez faire, and the natural course of so-called immutable principles. Those who claimed that all economic problems could be solved by unshackling free enterprise indulged in what he called "loose, irresponsible talk." With a more sophisticated view, Hoffman argued that business cycles were man-made, not natural or inevitable. Therefore, proper planning and action by business and government could at least moderate them and provide greater stability and growth within capitalism.[30]

His endorsement of planning while chairman of the CED did not, however, represent a fundamental shift in his progressive orientation. Even when receiving the National Planning Association's Gold Medal in 1949, he advocated the kind of government planning that would foster capitalist freedom and competition—the basis, he said, for economic dynamism. The government had to resist all schemes by private interest groups to circumvent competition, to restrict output, and to penalize efficiency. "Action was needed," he told a Senate committee, "because capitalism without competition does not serve the people well."[31]

According to Hoffman, who insisted that the primary responsibility of business was to operate profitably, the war itself created conditions favorable for a capitalist revival. He urged businessmen to take advantage of the new opportunities, to shake off the slothful thinking of the 1930s with its talk of permanent stagnation, to become more daring by planning scientifically and by supporting constant research for new production methods, new products, new services, and new markets. With the application of modern technology, including robots, they could provide steady employment based on higher productivity, greater output, and low but reasonable profit margins. Within twenty or twenty-five years, real wages and the standard of living for the average worker could double. Americans could abolish poverty.[32]

Such unparalleled progress, in his view, depended on industrial peace and the right policies by government and business. To promote that kind of future, he and Benton decided—contrary to their original agreement—not to disband the CED when the war ended. Remaining as its chairman, Hoffman addressed more openly the postwar political debate about the economy. He told a disbelieving Senator Robert Taft that "maldistribution of income has been one of the serious deterrents to stability of our economy in the past." Too many Americans had too little in the way of material welfare and opportunity for individual development. Those conditions, which left many with inadequate purchasing power to sustain national prosperity, had to be changed.[33]

For the postwar era, the CED supported many of the government programs associated with the New Deal's effort to provide workers with greater security. To sustain their purchasing power and morale, it endorsed, for example, both minimum wage laws and unemployment compensation payments. Hoffman recommended that the government expand security for workers by protecting their pension rights. To cope with temporary and localized unemployment, the CED also endorsed public works.

Nevertheless, Hoffman continued to warn that too much reliance on public works would create complacency without generating enough useful, productive, and well-paying jobs. Only a healthy economy could do that. There was a sharp difference, he pointed out to Henry Luce, "between government intervention in the event of mass unemployment and government intervention to provide jobs for all."[34]

Thus, on behalf of the CED, Hoffman criticized liberal proposals in Congress to have the U.S. government guarantee full employment. He admitted that "the right to live is not meaningful unless included in the concept is the right to a job." But only a totalitarian society could provide full employment and perfect security. What America needed was a government policy that would give a "satisfactory level" of employment while preserving economic freedom and incentives for efficiency and productivity. Proposals for a thirty-hour work week to spread employment, he and Philip Murray of the CIO agreed, represented just a new form of featherbedding detrimental to the nation and its workers.[35]

Typically, Hoffman sought to depoliticize what he regarded as a technical economic problem of maintaining prosperity and high employment. He proposed, first in testimony before a Senate committee and then directly to President Truman, that the issue of employment be left for study by a presidential commission. That particular proposal was not implemented, but the CED did succeed in joining business efforts that transformed the Full Employment Bill into the less obtrusive Employment Act of 1946.[36]

By and large, the welfare and security of workers, Hoffman always insisted, depended on a prosperous economy and reasonableness within the collective bargaining process. When Senator Taft suggested at one congressional committee hearing that collective bargaining raised wage levels too high, Hoffman tactfully declined to respond. When Congress debated the Taft and Hartley bills, the CED proposed measures less likely to arouse hostility from unions. Hoffman declared that although most strikes were unnecessary, the government had to avoid restricting the right and freedom of unions to strike. In the hope of making the collective bargaining process operate effectively even under the Taft-Hartley Act, he agreed to serve as one of six management advisers to the newly created Federal Mediation and Conciliation Service. He regarded collective bargaining, like competition, as an essential part of the modern free enterprise system.[37]

Yet he also believed that that system, to function properly, needed moral restraints on excessive selfishness. Even while he proclaimed that the primary responsibility of business was to operate profitably, he preached the need for an enlightened and long-range view to restrain the narrow pursuit of profits and self-interest. Glossing over evidence to the contrary, Hoffman proclaimed that basically America measured up well to that standard. It demonstrated a "moral achievement" because it retained its sense of mission and principles "above selfishness and above self-interest."[38] Thus he and the other leaders of the CED claimed to speak not for their own interests but for the public welfare and the national interest.

For Hoffman, and probably for most business leaders who joined with him, the private sector held the key to national prosperity. But unlike the laissez faire conservatives, the leaders of the CED shared a more sophisticated view of the modern economy that assigned important functions of economic management to government. One such function involved the determination of fiscal policies.

The wartime fiscal policies of the Roosevelt administration worried Hoffman, a member of the Federal Reserve Board of Chicago beginning in 1942. He warned that the staggering deficits produced a phony and unhealthy prosperity that could not continue. Without inhibiting private investment, the federal government had to raise sufficient revenues to pay for the war and to reduce the debt so that deficits would not exceed those of the 1930s.[39]

After much discussion and division of opinion, in 1944 the CED worked out a comprehensive program for tax revision. As Hoffman explained, the CED recommended the abolition or at least the reduction of excise taxes because they limited purchasing power for the lowest income groups. The income tax was the best and fairest way for government to raise revenues. As a method of collection, the CED endorsed the withholding tax promoted by trustee Beardsley Ruml under the slogan "pay-as-you-go." While many more people paid taxes, the CED urged reduction of rates for all income brackets to stimulate demand and employment in the postwar era. With adjustments taking into account taxes paid by corporations, it also wanted capital gains taxed like other income, something Hoffman had earlier opposed.[40]

Beyond its specific recommendations, this program was significant because it revealed that the CED had adopted Keynesian concepts. As Hoffman said, federal fiscal and monetary policies had become the "balance wheels in a free enterprise system"; private business could do little to maintain "dynamic stability" with high levels of aggregate demand and employment.[41] Therefore, the government had the responsibility to adopt countercyclical measures to assure prosperity. To moderate the business cycle during recessions, it had to lower taxes, ease credit, increase spending for public works, and carry deficits. During inflationary periods when the private sector prospered, it had to raise taxes, tighten credit, cut spending, and avoid deficits.

Within the CED's own leadership, opinion differed over how much discretionary authority the government should wield. Beardsley Ruml argued for maximum flexibility in government management of fiscal policy. Hoffman, on the other hand, feared tax manipulation by politicians within a permissive system. With his typically progressive desire to depoliticize what he regarded as technical economic issues, he wanted experts to establish stable rates that would be automatically countercyclical. Such a system would provide businessmen with predictability for their own planning and would help maintain purchasing power sufficient for high employment, while minimizing the risk of politically induced inflation. On this issue he convinced other CED trustees to back a plan for stability and "automaticity" of tax rates.[42]

For fiscal policy, the CED advocated what it called a "stabilizing budget." It rejected both the conservatives' desire for rigidly balanced budgets and the liberals' desire for greater flexibility. During recessions the "stabilizing budget" would carry countercyclical deficits, but over a five-year period the public debt would have to be reduced and the budget balanced with a surplus.

During the postwar years, the CED sought to prevent runaway inflation by policies Hoffman called bold, positive, and sound. Alone among business organizations, in 1947 it supported the Truman administration's strategy of high taxes, tight credit control, and reduced federal spending. Such a credit policy, Hoffman confessed, ran counter to the wishes of most leaders within the automotive industry.[43]

Even with that apparent conversion to Keynesianism, Hoffman did not completely shake loose from his moorings. As he told a Senate committee in 1949, he still believed that balanced budgets were desirable and that "deficit spending of itself is very bad psychology." But he did prefer deficits to tax increases, specifically warning against the notion that tax increases could check inflation. A policy that increased government revenues actually ran the risk of promoting extravagant government spending and, therefore, more inflation.[44]

What he looked forward to was a time when inflation would cool so that the government could carefully reduce taxes. Small businesses and struggling corporations like Studebaker needed liberal depreciation allowances, income averaging, and carryover of losses. In other words, Hoffman never gave up his preference for government policies that provided incentives for business expansion, innovation, and "creative leadership" within the private market.[45]

Although he was mainly concerned about the domestic economy, from the late 1930s on Hoffman became increasingly aware of the importance of foreign affairs as well. For many years Studebaker had sold cars in Europe, Asia, and Latin America, but it was not business that turned his attention abroad; it was totalitarian aggression. When he heard Walter Lippmann's Walgreen Lectures at the University of Chicago in February of 1938, he found further evidence that geographic separation alone would not protect America from that foreign threat.[46]

Through friends such as Henry Luce and his sister Elisabeth Moore, the wife of Studebaker's legal counsel, and Professor Arthur Holcombe of Harvard, Hoffman became active in efforts to support beleaguered China. After working very hard as the chairman of the South Bend chapter of United China Relief, he became the national chairman early in 1942. His solicitation of contributions for China appealed to both humanitarianism and practicalism. China would become, he declared, a promising peacetime outlet for American goods, capital, and technological skills. He told the directors of Studebaker, which contributed several thousand dollars, that the automaker could gain valuable business there. But even when he emphasized economic self-interest, he did not believe that the U.S. needed international trade for its own prosperity.[47]

The fundamental argument of the CED rested on the assertion that the *domestic* economy could expand enough by taking advantage of unrealized opportunities. On its own, the United States could enjoy prosperity and high levels of employment; it did not have to suffer chronic underconsumption and underdevelopment. During 1944 and 1945, however, the CED did begin to suggest that the American standard of living would reach higher levels with international trade than without it. Therefore, the CED recommended that the U.S. adopt policies to expand trade.[48]

Hoffman agreed completely. He told a congressional committee that while prosperity depended mainly upon expansion of the domestic market, America had to abandon isolationism and nationalism by encouraging freer international trade. Endorsing Secretary of State Cordell Hull's efforts at reciprocal tariff reductions, he explained that Americans could not just expect to expand exports; international trade was a two-way street that required imports as well. With leaders of the National Association of Manufacturers, the U.S. Chamber of Commerce, and other business organizations, he joined a new committee on international economic policy headed by Winthrop Aldrich of the Chase National Bank.[49]

Even before the war ended, international economic issues were raising a political storm within the United States. Many bankers threatened to mobilize opposition against the new International Monetary Fund, and Senator Taft charged that support for that institution would be like "pouring money down a rat hole." At just that critical stage, in March of 1945, the CED released a public statement—mainly drafted by Beardsley Ruml—supporting the Bretton Woods Agreement and offering a plan to prevent the IMF from misusing its resources as bankers feared.[50]

Hoffman played a major role in shaping the CED's position on international affairs. Although he vehemently opposed trade subsidies, he actively supported both the IMF and the World Bank. Those institutions, he declared, could help the wartorn world rebuild and raise living standards, thus creating the prosperous, high-volume foreign markets America needed for its own prosperity. Furthermore, prosperity abroad would overcome the anarchy and hatred that caused political upheaval and war.[51] Thus Hoffman argued, as did a growing circle of business and government leaders, that an expanded role for the U.S. in international affairs was indispensable for peace and prosperity, which were really inseparable.

According to Hoffman, America had an opportunity for undisputed world leadership because of the power vacuum created by the war. To make the most of that opportunity, the country would need to display unusual generosity by extending loans and aid for relief in wartorn areas and perhaps by canceling foreign debts. He insisted, however, that the U.S. had no desire to use its economic power for political purposes; it did not wish to impose capitalism on others against their wishes. Minimizing the differences among political systems, he endorsed the right of all nations to their own political ideologies.[52]

Nevertheless, elements of the Cold War mentality began to emerge quite early in his postwar foreign policy prescriptions. At the August 1945 meeting of the International Chamber of Commerce in London, he voiced concern about how private enterprise and international trade could deal with state-controlled economies and cartels such as those of Russia. The following March, at a meeting of the Business Advisory Council, he heard Ambassador Averell Harriman deliver a speech strongly critical of the Soviet Union. Hoffman reportedly stood up to lead the applause and to urge Harriman to speak out across the country. He fully accepted the Truman administration's view that the Soviet Union was the major obstacle to true peace.[53]

In the spring of 1947, the Truman administration reached a fundamental shift in foreign policy to aid the economic reconstruction of Western Europe, Germany, and Japan. Secretary of State George C. Marshall delivered his famous call for a bold new aid program at the Harvard commencement in June. To mobilize significant groups and public support for the Marshall Plan, President Truman appointed a Committee on Foreign Aid under the chairmanship of Averell Harriman. Hoffman, whom President Truman had appointed the previous year to an advisory committee on international trade and reconstruction, was one of the nineteen members of the Harriman Committee; Truman selected him because he was a prominent Republican business leader who agreed completely with the administration's general outlook on foreign policy.

As a member of the Harriman Committee, Hoffman argued that the Marshall Plan was a great humanitarian gesture based on enlightened self-interest. If Europe did not revive economically, he told a congressional committee, the Soviets would pick up the pieces. By helping Europe to create a strong and productive economy and by expanding international trade, the Marshall Plan could preserve a free society and provide a powerful antidote for Communism. In short, Hoffman promoted the foreign aid program as an economic weapon in the ideological Cold War and a cheap way to prevent a hot war.[54]

What of economic benefits for the U.S.? Like other supporters of the Marshall Plan, Hoffman realized that in the long run the rehabilitation and modernization of the European economy would provide important markets and investment outlets for American business. But even though he advocated enlightened self-interest, Hoffman did not emphasize that long-term potential. Nor did he regard the Marshall Plan as a way to shore up American capitalism against an impending depression: as he had predicted, the American economy was enjoying a postwar boom, and its internal expansion was creating shortages and inflation that could only be worsened by a foreign aid program. Hoffman and others accepted the short-term consequences as one price of containing Communism.

In March of 1948, after completing his work on the Harriman Committee, Hoffman went off to the Far East on an economic mission arranged by Undersecretary of the Army William H. Draper, Jr. Working days and evenings, he had no chance to see Japan and Korea for himself. In a six- or seven-hour meeting with General Douglas MacArthur, he discovered attitudes and traits he could not abide; the report he coauthored with the mission's chairman, Percy Johnston of the Chemical Bank, fully endorsed Draper's criticism of MacArthur's effort to push for an early peace treaty to end the occupation. If Japan were again to operate the workshop of Asia, the Johnston-Hoffman report declared, it would need special assistance.[55] Thus for the Far East as well as for Europe, Hoffman supported American economic aid for the rehabilitation and restoration of industrial societies friendly to the United States.

On his way back from Japan, Hoffman stopped in Hawaii and there learned that President Truman wanted him to head the Marshall Plan. Later, Hoffman always insisted that he did not want the job and had told Truman that, but when Truman publicly announced the appointment, he felt that he could not repudiate the President and therefore agreed to serve.[56] A genuinely modest man without political ambitions, Hoffman probably was reluctant to take the position. He certainly did not actively seek it.

Nevertheless, his own behavior also made him the logical choice. As a member of the Harriman Committee, he knew what had to be done. He had told the Senate Foreign Relations Committee that because the administrator of the Marshall Plan would have to show toughness and operate in a businesslike manner, a businessman would be best qualified for the job. Furthermore, the administrator would have to possess stature and ability to recruit for the staff "our ablest citizens."[57] His record at Studebaker and the CED gave Hoffman just the credentials he had said the administrator would need.

Politically, too, he was the man Truman needed. The President knew that the Republican majority in Congress wanted a businessman, preferably a member of their own party. Hoffman was a loyal Republican who had backed the presidential candidacies of Wendell Willkie and Thomas E. Dewey. In 1946, Harold Stassen, former Republican governor of Minnesota, suggested that Truman name Hoffman to replace Henry A. Wallace as Secretary of Commerce. When

Truman considered the Marshall Plan appointment, Senator Arthur H. Vandenberg of Michigan, the powerful chairman of the Committee on Foreign Relations, told him that he wanted Hoffman, who, according to Vandenberg, represented "the common denominator of the thought of the nation."[58] What he meant, of course, was that Hoffman spoke for an elite of internationally minded leaders of big business.

Senate confirmation, as the New York Times observed, was a "foregone conclusion." Vandenberg quickly pushed the appointment through the Foreign Relations Committee, and less than an hour later, armed with the unanimous vote of his committee, Vandenberg asked the entire Senate to give its consent to the appointment of the man he called an unselfish and publicly responsible citizen. The voice vote in the Senate took only ten minutes. Paul G. Hoffman had become the administrator of the single biggest peacetime spending program ever.[59]

Henry Luce, a friend of nearly two decades, rejoiced: "I can think of no one," he wrote to Hoffman, "who has with greater modesty tried to avoid the attention of the gods. But Destiny so often unresponsive to its postulants has clearly marked you for its own." Luce's magazines went on to describe the new head of the Marshall Plan as a top-drawer, ebullient evangelist for enlightened capitalism, one of the new-style responsible businessmen who gravitated naturally to public service. If anyone could do the job, Life asserted, Hoffman could.[60]

Journalistic comments generally gave similar praise. Since many people in a time of great anxiety obviously wanted the Marshall Plan to begin well and to succeed, Hoffman became the repository of hope for America's foreign policy. In the spirit of bipartisanship, he was placed above politics or made to fit political biases across a wide spectrum that included both liberals and conservatives.

Yet despite the quick Senate confirmation and the well-orchestrated publicity, Hoffman's appointment drew immediate fire from enemies of the Marshall Plan. In the House of Representatives, which voted on all appropriations for the plan, the noisiest attack came from Ralph Waldo Gwinn. A "pre-Cambrian" Republican from Bronxville, New York, Congressman Gwinn denounced Hoffman as a "soft-shelled New Deal operator," "possibly the leading left-wing industrialist in America." "There is no greater influence to the left in our country today," he wailed, "than Paul G. Hoffman."[61]

Little wonder, therefore, that Hoffman began his stint in government service by bracing himself for personal attacks. After Gwinn's assault he expected a barrage of criticism that would leave his reputation tattered by the time he completed the job, but he told friends and relatives that he did not care, so long as the Marshall Plan succeeded.[62]

By accepting the appointment, Hoffman fulfilled the logic of his actions over the previous fifteen years. During that time he had emerged as a prominent member of the nation's business elite. Under the broadening influence of new contacts, especially as chairman of the CED, his own progressive inclinations matured and acquired greater sophistication. In order to preserve democracy and capitalism, he preached the need for businessmen to act with enlightened self-interest and to accept government policies that enhanced both stability and economic growth.

Although initially he emphasized domestic economic expansion, gradually he recognized the international implications as well. For Hoffman, for the CED, for a substantial part of postwar American leadership inside government and out, peace and prosperity seemed to require a more active U.S. role in world affairs. By 1948, Hoffman's commitment to responsible internationalism meant that he fully shared and supported the Truman administration's decision to aid the economic reconstruction of Western Europe and international trade.

Simple though it may seem, Hoffman's internationalism and support for economic foreign aid rested primarily on political considerations. He feared that in fighting Communism, an isolated America might become a garrison or corporatist state in which free enterprise and other freedoms could not survive. During the postwar boom he had correctly predicted, he believed that the United States could afford the enlightened self-interest of generosity to avoid isolationism and its harmful domestic consequences. Of course, he expected that with American guidance the European economy would revive so that both Europe and the United States would enjoy mutually beneficial trade. Whatever its limitations, however, this view did not stem from a corporatist or open-door expansionist ideology, as some scholars have recently suggested.[63] In his search for order and stability, Hoffman was guided much more by prevailing notions of the need to strengthen Europe in order to contain Communism.

5 The Marshall Plan, 1948-50

Scholars have usually portrayed the Marshall Plan as a policy of enlightened national self-interest. Within the framework of the containment of Communism, the United States pursued peace and prosperity by unprecedented generosity toward potential economic competitors. During a period of domestic shortages and inflation, it gave the countries of Western Europe billions of dollars so that they could reconstruct their economies and reestablish normal trading patterns.

Recently, some scholars have charged that the policies of the Economic Cooperation Administration differed significantly from its own rhetoric and the conventional view. According to one leading revisionist work, the ECA actually pursued a hidden agenda of shoring up American capitalism against a postwar depression. It defined successful economic recovery not by improvements in the living standard of the European masses but by the control of inflation and the narrowing of the dollar gap so that Americans could find markets for the surpluses they could not absorb domestically.[1]

Much can be learned by looking beneath the surface of events and of the rhetoric churned out by the government's publicity apparatus. However, the revisionist exposé compares the ECA with a standard to which the American policy-makers did not aspire. In a sense, revisionists have created a straw man of altruism and have then proved that reality fell short.

For two and a half years, ending 30 September 1950, Paul Hoffman occupied a key position and made major contributions within the complex process of government policy-making. He liked to say that no man did another a greater favor than President Truman did for him by drafting him to head the Marshall Plan. "It opened my eyes to many things of which I was totally unaware," he told one interviewer, "and it was the beginning of my real education."[2] His record at the ECA does not, of course, reveal the whole story about the Marshall Plan, but to understand that important part of American foreign policy, one must surely pay close attention to its first administrator.

Although the Marshall Plan started with a broad base of support, no one had drawn up a blueprint for putting the concept into operation. That task fell to Hoffman. He discovered quickly that being a government bureaucrat, however interesting, was also rugged. With the ECA often facing simultaneous crises at home and abroad, the amount and pressure of the work exceeded what Hoffman had known in private business.[3] Yet instead of the $96,000 a year he had earned at Studebaker, he was receiving a government salary of $20,000.

Widely acclaimed the capital's "busiest man," he led a particularly frenzied pace during the first couple of months. Living alone in a Washington hotel, he worked fifteen hours a day, with business conferences at nearly every meal. Even so, he felt that he could not keep on top of the situation. On the personal side, his life improved when he leased a modest house where he and Dorothy, who had initially stayed in Pasadena, could settle in with some measure of privacy. Thereafter, though conferences often intruded on meals, he usually worked only ten hours a day. "Definitely Main Street" by his own account, he and Dorothy rigidly avoided the capital's social whirl.[4]

Much of his time at first was spent recruiting personnel for both the headquarters in Washington and the ECA missions abroad. In that task he enjoyed complete freedom; neither President Truman, who earned his high regard, nor Congress imposed political patronage on the ECA. Some Democratic and Republican politicians tried to force party hacks onto the ECA's payroll but failed.[5]

According to Hoffman, the Marshall Plan itself attracted top-rate individuals who saw it as a way to preserve the free world. His own reputation among businessmen and labor union leaders also helped. To assist in sorting out applicants and finding well-qualified personnel, he turned to his own friends. Studebaker's legal counsel Tex Moore and its advertising consultant James Cleary proved especially valuable during those early weeks.

Within a short time the ECA had recruited a small team that Hoffman thought could play in the "big league."[6] Hard-working, dedicated to the cause, and closely knit, the Washington staff included people from other government agencies and from outside government. The first person hired was Richard M. Bissell, Jr., an economist who had served ably as executive secretary of the Harriman Committee. The mutual respect that grew between them allowed Hoffman to lean heavily on Bissell. Other key members of the staff included Wayne Taylor, former president of the Export-Import Bank; food expert Dennis A. Fitzgerald from the Department of Agriculture; and Baltimore businessman Howard Bruce, who served as deputy administrator.

Outside its Washington headquarters, the ECA's success most hinged on the U.S. Special Representative in Europe. As a member of the Harriman Committee, Hoffman had said that the position required an individual of special ability because "he may well become our first ambassador to a unified, modernized Europe." For that single most important position after his own, then, Hoffman chose Secretary of Commerce Averell Harriman. The two quickly developed and continued to maintain a relationship of extraordinary cooperation. Without reservations, Hoffman trusted and respected Harriman and his chief advisor, Milton Katz, who joined the ECA from Harvard's faculty.[7]

The Office of Special Representative in Paris served as theater command with authority over the ECA mission chiefs. Mostly leaders of big business connected with the CED or part of the foreign policy elite, the mission chiefs had responsibility for implementing policy in the various countries. Hoffman told them that their behavior would shape the attitudes of people in the countries where they served and therefore the success of the recovery program. He exhorted them to show sincerity, humility, and friendliness; to avoid arrogance, insensitivity, and personal pleasure-seeking.[8]

Contrary to its image as a free-wheeling, autonomous agency, the ECA maintained a fairly taut administration highly dependent upon other government departments. To get maximum creative effort, Hoffman was willing to accept some flexibility but not anything that might hurt the program. When no real scandal over money had surfaced after one year, he predicted that something was bound to happen and just hoped that it would not seriously damage relations with Congress. As it turned out, the ECA never did suffer such a scandal.[9]

Hoffman had good reason for his concern about relations with Congress. Anyone who thinks that the Marshall Plan was simply the instrument of the Truman administration makes a serious mistake. Congress had helped formulate the plan and continued to exert enormous influence on its implementation. Congress, not the administration, forced the ECA to use American vessels, when available "at market rates," for at least 50 percent of the tonnage it shipped. Congress forced the ECA to buy from American suppliers if the agricultural commodities it needed were declared in surplus. And members of Congress often tried to impose more rigorous "buy American" provisions to benefit their own constituents.

Even those members of Congress who did not seek to expand business for constituents at least wanted to prevent the ECA from harming the domestic economy. Several complained—rightly—that the ECA financed a foreign assault on American businesses and jobs. Some accused the ECA of pursuing the recovery of Europe without adequate regard for the plight of Americans who lost their jobs because of that competition. Such concerns posed serious problems for Hoffman when he appeared at committee hearings to present the ECA's budget appropriation requests.

President Truman privately referred to conservative opponents as "squirrelheads," but Hoffman usually avoided open conflicts. He told congressional critics that he was an administrator, not a debater. From his experience with the CED, he knew how to cultivate key individuals. That skill and strong backing from congressional supporters of the Marshall Plan made his encounters on Capitol Hill much less ferocious than journalists suggested; only once after a squabble with Congress did he threaten to resign. Nevertheless, he often did have to fight the budget cutters and the lobbyists. "It is amazing how many people there are in Washington," he commented to a friend, "who agree with you in principle but who would like to extract a few dimes for themselves or their clients."[10]

A big part of Hoffman's job required him to sell the ECA to Congress and to the American public. With a carefully planned publicity program (not, he said, a propaganda machine), the ECA continually tried to create favorable attitudes toward the Marshall Plan and foreign aid generally.[11] In one year, for example, Hoffman personally made about 150 speeches on those subjects. In addition, he often testified before congressional committees, sometimes two in the same day. For his ability to field difficult and varied questions about the ECA, Senator Richard Russell of Georgia called Hoffman a "mental acrobat."[12]

Hoffman said that within the U.S. he tried to keep discussion of foreign aid "at the very highest level" intellectually. Of course, he kept in mind that the Marshall Plan was the instrument of Congress and the American people and a means for promoting the national interest. But he also wanted to stir the hearts of Americans to make them see the reasons for foreign aid and its value.[13] He built his domestic campaign around the connection between Europe's economic recovery and winning the Cold War. He emphasized that the ECA was promoting economic recovery that would eventually lead to a better quality of life in the free world. It did so in part because all free people were joined together by a "fundamental morality." But the "real objective," he told a congressional committee, was "to stop the spread of communism."[14]

In the best rhetoric of the Cold War, he described the Soviet Union as a ruthless, barbaric dictatorship, probably the most powerful ever. Aggressive and insatiable for expansion, it operated by a "well-thought-out program of destroying all free institutions." This "Russian imperialism" threatened the survival of democracy and Western civilization. Europe was the key battleground and the vortex of the struggle, but the Cold War had become global in scope.[15]

To conservatives worried about the costs of foreign aid, he explained why the United States had to win the Cold War. "The *alternatives* are pretty grim," he declared shortly after he took charge of the ECA. America obviously could not afford to lose a hot war, but neither could it afford to win such a military encounter. The United States had already become a "semi-garrison state" and, if Western Europe succumbed to any form of totalitarianism, would have to become a complete garrison state. Just the expenditure of $15 to $20 billion a year on defense would create an enormous tax burden and would generate pressure for a regimented economy. To avoid those harmful consequences for the U.S., the ECA sought to promote the recovery of the European economy.[16]

The Marshall Plan and other foreign aid programs that encouraged economic recovery and development, according to Hoffman, were weapons for democracy in the Cold War: they bought time for the free world to recover from World War II and to prevent World War III. If the U.S. won the Cold War and if Europe's economy recovered, he predicted, then the Soviets would have to behave better and accept what later became known as peaceful coexistence. The Soviet bloc might even break down, perhaps after Stalin's death or during the 1950s.[17]

Hoffman used that broad view to resist congressional efforts to impose "buy American" restrictions on the ECA. He asked Congress to consider the Cold War and Russian propaganda before enacting restrictions merely for the benefit of domestic interests. He did not want the fact obscured that the Marshall Plan was the "most generous act of any people, anytime, anywhere, to another people." If Congress wanted to aid American farmers by giving away surpluses, he often said, it should find needy Americans at home.[18]

Rather than administering the Marshall Plan for the benefit of American exporters, Hoffman sought to ease Western Europe's shortage of dollars. The ECA declared that aid recipients should buy what they needed in Europe, where prices were lowest and where purchases did not deplete dollar reserves. It even favored the broadest possible nonmilitary trade between Western and Eastern Europe. Nevertheless, Hoffman did sometimes compromise his principles when Congress imposed trade restrictions or when American business interests limited his options.[19]

When Americans complained about European competition, he extolled its positive economic benefits. Just as he had while president of Studebaker, he argued that competition produced dynamism and efficiency by forcing managers to be alert and to lie awake figuring out new and better ways to operate. He did not sympathize much with people afraid of fair competition; such fears were "not the highest compliment that should be paid to American management."[20]

Perhaps Hoffman found it easy to defend the principle of competition because he assumed that the practice would not impose high costs for Americans. European competition did not concern him, partly because, as he told a Senate committee, American goods could provide consumers with much better value than did manufactured goods from other countries. In those rare cases when foreigners could compete, Americans needed to change their ways of doing business. Senator George "Molly" Malone of Nevada pointed to a simple explanation for Hoffman's view; according to the ultraconservative Republican protectionist and opponent of foreign aid, Hoffman favored free trade because he knew that the American automotive industry did not face foreign competition and would not for years.[21] To many in Congress, it seemed a question of whose ox was being gored.

Hoffman, recognizing that aspect of the debate, went directly to the textile workers' unions, for example, and assured them that he did not regard unemployment as merely a matter of statistics. But domestic unemployment could not be solved by reducing the modest volume of imports from Western Europe; in fact, cuts in imports would reduce the capacity of Europeans to buy American goods and thus actually increase unemployment. The United Textile Workers of America accepted that argument and in 1950 voted to support the reciprocal trade agreement program.[22]

According to Hoffman, the resourcefulness and imagination characteristic of a free economy could solve domestic unemployment: by greater efficiency, Americans could produce goods at prices people could afford; then domestic consumption and, consequently, domestic employment would increase. If European competition really did worsen American unemployment, the U.S. government should provide workers with special aid for retraining and relocating. To achieve its broad foreign policy objectives, the United States must avoid exporting unemployment to the poorer countries by excluding their products.[23]

In dealing with the Europeans, Hoffman followed the broad view suggested by the Harriman Committee. "Only the Europeans," he had written in the first sentence of the committee's report, "can save Europe," but as the aid donor, the U.S. did have the right to ensure that recipients used aid properly. Because of economic interdependence, it also had the right to demand that the Europeans cooperate for joint action. On the other hand, the U.S. would not try to buy up European property or to control the economies of aid recipients as the Soviet Union controlled Eastern Europe.[24]

Several times Hoffman went to Europe to observe developments firsthand and to deliver the ECA's message. Often he sounded very much like the progressive American business booster he was. He told the Europeans that they needed to recognize the tides of change and abandon their traditional desire for security and their fear of overproduction. He had concluded, from his observations during the 1920s, that Europeans suffered from both excessive labor costs and low wages. Greater mechanization and modernization could improve productivity and efficiency, making possible economic growth within larger competitive markets. Then workers could earn higher wages and all could enjoy higher standards of living.

The ECA started with the assumption that the Europeans had to put capital investment for long-term growth ahead of efforts to bring immediate improvements in the standard of living. But even before going to Europe, Hoffman realized that the ECA must modify its rigid separation of relief and reconstruction. Efforts to save money for capital investment by cutting the European diet would demoralize the people and impair recovery.[25] Because they suffered from chronic and debilitating undernourishment, Europeans needed more food; therefore, food relief was a necessary step toward greater productivity.

As early as his first official visit to Europe during the summer of 1948, Hoffman sensed that the Marshall Plan would succeed. With the arrival of American aid and promise of much more, the Europeans were regaining their self-confidence and hope for the future. They were psychologically prepared for recovery.[26] When he returned to Europe in October, he found still further reason for optimism. Each participating country showed some progress toward self-help. In France the Communist-led strikes had failed to sabotage the recovery effort, and the election defeats suffered by the Communists in both France and Italy suggested that the European Recovery Program was bringing desired results. Later he also admitted that the ECA's propaganda campaign in Western Europe against "the Commies" had achieved considerable success. "We found numerous ways to manipulate their [Europeans'] anxieties."[27]

When the European governments took action aimed directly at raising the standard of living for common people, Hoffman pledged that the ECA would not interfere. It would not oppose nationalization of industry or expansion of welfare programs, provided those policies did not hinder economic recovery. However, by warning the Europeans that Congress might cut appropriations, Hoffman did seriously restrict their policy choices. Despite his focus on technical economic issues, the European Recovery Program could not escape U.S. political interference.[28]

Of all the participating governments, the British caused Hoffman the most trouble. Without British cooperation the whole program might fail, but the British adopted a stance of noncooperation and even obstruction. The Labour government sought to protect from

American interference its domestic policies of nationalization of in-dustry and expansion of social welfare.[29] It also asserted a unique Anglo-American relationship and expected special consideration for the sterling bloc, countries that conducted trade through British cur-rency and thus provided Britain with easy markets for its manufac-tured goods.

When the ECA reached impasses with the British, Hoffman did find Chancellor of the Exchequer Stafford Cripps willing to listen to reason. He told Cripps, whose intellectual integrity and courage he respected, that the British Labourites were just too cautious. "If you were Americans," he reportedly said, "you probably would be Repub-licans . . . and right-wing Republicans at that!"[30] With Hoffman prodding him to accept the risks of a freer market, Cripps finally consented to reduce British trade barriers. The talks between Hoff-man and Cripps about ways to increase British productivity also eventually led to the creation of the Anglo-American Council on Productivity.

With the British Foreign Office, however, Hoffman had greater difficulty. The Foreign Office vigorously defended its policy of dis-mantling German factories so that equipment could be shipped as reparations. Many influential members of Congress, on the other hand, insisted that the dismantling cease; they did not want the United States to give aid for German industrial recovery while Brit-ain and France dismantled Germany's factories. Because Congress threatened to withhold the ECA's appropriations, Hoffman had to intervene.

Having seen firsthand the damage inflicted by the Nazis, he did not advocate a "get soft" policy toward Germany. "I think too many Germans today are sorry about only one thing," he told a House committee, "that is, that they lost the war." But he also agreed with other American policy-makers that European recovery needed the revitalization of Germany's industrial base. In response to congres-sional pressure, in August of 1948 he announced that a group of leading American industrialists—eventually headed by George Humphrey, president of the M.A. Hanna Company—would study the issue of factory dismantling and would advise him. The Hum-phrey Report, which called for Germany to retain key industrial fa-cilities, "profoundly disturbed" the British.[31]

Throughout the rest of 1948 and 1949, Hoffman complained

about the lack of British and, to a lesser extent, French cooperation on the issue of reparations. He tried to convince them that Congress and the American public opposed a policy that had the ECA financing a buildup of Germany's industrial base while Britain and France tore it down; their disregard for congressional opposition, he warned, produced an adverse reaction in the U.S. that could hurt support for the entire foreign aid program.[32]

Sometimes using what Secretary of State Dean Acheson regarded as an evangelical delivery, Hoffman preached to the Europeans his faith in salvation by exports. He emphasized that continuation of American aid depended upon proof that they were doing their best to earn dollars and to reduce trade barriers. The British, in particular, he exhorted to forgo easy markets in the sterling area, cut their production costs, and try harder to earn dollars by selling in the American market. Then they and the other Europeans could solve their balance-of-payments problems when the Marshall Plan ended in 1952.[33]

During the fall of 1949, Hoffman gave a new label to the themes of his sermon. At the time, the Organization of European Economic Cooperation was facing great difficulty and continued division following a wave of currency devaluations, and cooperation for joint action seemed endangered. Furthermore, Congress made clear its impatience and irritation with the Europeans. Therefore, Hoffman wanted to deliver to the Council of the OEEC a strong message. The American press called Hoffman's address an ultimatum to the Europeans. No other speech by him as administrator of the Marshall Plan had greater importance. None aroused as much comment by contemporaries or prompted as much analysis afterward. None showed as well how he added his personal view to the general consensus behind the U.S. policy in Western Europe.[34]

Entitled "An Expanding Economy through Economic Integration: The Major Task of Western Europe," his address in Paris, October 1949, declared that recovery depended upon "nothing less than an integration of the Western European economy." By economic integration he did not mean political unification or a federal United States of Europe; instead, he emphasized the creation of a single large market comparable to that of the American economy. Such a policy would set in motion rapid growth in Western Europe. With the genuine cost pressures of competition, the development of large-scale industries would accelerate; productivity and resource use would become more efficient; then Europeans could afford higher standards of living.[35]

Giving the impression that unless they made real progress, Congress might cut off aid, Hoffman requested that the Europeans take meaningful action within ninety days. Secretary of State Acheson, who usually did not interfere with the ECA, refused to support Hoffman's strong stand, but Congress did. The French did, too. They and other Europeans felt that he had earned credibility by resisting congressional pressures to use the ECA for American economic gains or selfish national goals.[36]

Progress toward integration proved disappointing, however. The British so annoyed him with a prohibition on petroleum imports that he threatened to reduce their aid allocation. Still, he did not want to coerce the Europeans; as he explained to a House committee, "At least in my business experience I have never gotten the same results from people who were coerced as I have from people who were persuaded."[37]

Hoffman continued his efforts to persuade the Europeans, including the British, that the benefits of integration outweighed the costs. Instead of the unrealistic goal of a United States of Europe, he encouraged the creation of a payments union with stable and convertible currencies. He pointed out that such integration was, after all, a European idea that dated from at least 1930. He particularly praised France for pointing the way toward integration.[38] In September of 1950, almost a year after his famous speech, the OEEC nations did formally agree to the creation of the European Payment Union, just as he had hoped. It is no exaggeration to say that Hoffman and the ECA gave Europe a major push toward the payment union and, beyond it, toward what became the Common Market.

In contrast with the well-thought-out European Recovery Program, the ECA's small missions in Asia were launched in a haphazard way that lacked clarity of purpose or much support. Marginal to its overall program, ECA involvement in Asia seemed badly flawed and out of touch with reality. Though Hoffman expressed sympathy for democracy and national independence, the ECA seemed mainly interested in checking the forces of revolutionary nationalism and Communism; though he talked about economic aid for development to raise the standard of living and to make Asian countries self-supporting, he opposed what he called uneconomic industrial development or other forms of economic nationalism. Leftist critics have seen in such a position a form of economic imperialism that would have left those regions as impoverished suppliers of raw materials, and markets for surpluses not absorbed by the richer countries.

The ECA's largest Asian mission was in China, where the Nationalist government was losing a civil war to the Communists. Although a friend of China since the early 1940s, Hoffman realized from the start that an aid program there was a desperate gamble that could not work any miracles. For the ECA the central question became what to do if a coalition government or the Communists replaced the Nationalists. Hoffman claimed that 95 percent of the Americans he spoke with in China during his trip in December of 1948 wanted aid to continue even if the Communists took over.[39]

As the Communists were sweeping to victory in 1949, Hoffman tried to persuade the Truman administration that it could still prevent China from becoming a Soviet satellite. First in a forty-five-minute presentation to the Cabinet and then in a top-secret meeting with State Department officials, he decried excessively emotional anti-Communism. Yugoslavia's break from the Soviets showed that ideology was not the exclusive issue. He urged the administration to keep the aid program in China and then sell that policy to Congress, which was "not too well informed on the whole problem." Because he realized that his was a "rather sophisticated point of view," he volunteered to help sell the policy to the American public.[40]

Contrary to Hoffman's hopes, however, the victorious Chinese Communists imposed terms that precluded continuation of the ECA's operations there: the Open Door finally closed. Abandoning the flexibility he had shown earlier, Hoffman went along with the Truman administration's policy of nonrecognition. In a letter that the American Ambassador blocked, he tried to tell Chiang Kai-shek to stay in exile because, despite his integrity and high purpose, the Chinese public had turned against him. To one of Chiang's backers, Hoffman expressed himself more candidly: by late 1948, Chiang's Nationalist regime was doomed because it had failed the Chinese people so completely.[41]

Hoffman felt that two lessons were to be learned. For the Chinese Communists, he predicted that regardless of their revolutionary ideology, they would have to turn toward the West in order to develop China economically. For the U.S., the Chinese experience showed the consequences of doing too little too late. To prevent Communist victories elsewhere in Asia, it would have to give more aid for economic development.[42]

Hoffman and the ECA applied that use of economic assistance as an instrument against Communism in South Korea and in Southeast Asia. When seeking congressional appropriations for the Republic of Korea, he indulged in the salesman's hyperbole, calling South Korea a "key outpost of democracy in the Far East" that could become a model for Japan and the rest of Asia. But because that democracy was fragile, it needed American economic aid to raise its standard of living and become self-supporting. Hoffman's enthusiasm for the regime of President Syngman Rhee was, however, more apparent than real. Because he and the ECA's mission chief feared corrupt officials, the ECA directly operated a relief and development program in South Korea, and when Rhee's government failed to curb inflation or to use aid properly, Hoffman bluntly threatened to cut economic assistance. Later, when the Korean War dragged on, he confessed privately that the U.S. had made a real mistake in accepting responsibility as midwife for South Korea.[43]

The ECA's involvement in Southeast Asia revealed additional difficult realities. For one thing, the ECA sought to aid the European colonial powers to use their possessions for their own economic recovery. Furthermore, the ECA wanted to prevent a European withdrawal in order to forestall a Communist victory. "Unless we step in," Hoffman declared in May of 1950, "we're going to lose Indo-China"; then India might be caught in the maelstrom of revolution. Very modest economic aid to supplement the French effort, he said, could save the area from the Communist—that is Soviet—menace.[44] By mid-1950, the ECA had launched small programs in Southeast Asia aimed at controlling Communist insurgency.

On 25 June 1950, Hoffman entered a Washington hospital under an assumed name to have his gallbladder removed, an operation decided upon several days earlier.[45] The same day that he entered the hospital, North Korea attacked South Korea. Suddenly, the Cold War had entered a new phase. The Truman administration shifted its position to place more emphasis on rearmament.

Before the Korean War, Hoffman had emphatically opposed the diversion of counterpart funds (American-controlled foreign currency accounts) from economic recovery to military expenditures; he said that such a diversion would hurt recovery and lend credence

to Communist propaganda attacking the Marshall Plan as preparation for war. Nevertheless, he did not oppose rearmament per se. As
he explained and Averell Harriman agreed, economic recovery had
to be separate from and on equal terms with increased rearmament.
Only the United States could afford to produce for both civilian and
military needs.[46]

Once the Korean War began, however, he modified his stance and
backed the administration. Something like Korea was needed, he
told a friend, "in order to make people appreciate the character of
the struggle in which we are now engaged." The war demonstrated
Communist intentions and willingness to resort to force. In response, he supported President Truman's request for an extra $4 bil-
lion for mutual defense assistance. In the cause of peace, the United
States and Western Europe must temporarily divert their industrial
capacities from production for improved living standards to military
production.[47]

Despite that apparent support for rearmament, when he returned
from convalescent leave in late August, Hoffman was already nego-
tiating for a new job outside of government. A month later the public
announcement of his resignation was coupled with news that he
would head the newly reorganized and fabulously rich Ford Foundation. His own denials notwithstanding, the question arises whether
he resigned because he opposed the Truman administration's decision to emphasize rearmament in the foreign aid program.

Within the broad consensus among policy-makers, Hoffman did
not want economic aid sacrificed before the new emphasis on military aid. Before departing on his farewell tour of the ECA's missions
in Europe, he raised searching questions about the impact of increased defense expenditures on European budget deficits. In Europe,
he pointed out that military strength, though necessary, could not
alone stop Communist aggression. The Europeans had to continue
efforts to modernize production, to avoid inefficient economic nationalism, and to pursue integration. With economic strength they
could afford guns *and* butter. In fact, he predicted that they could lift
their living standard within ten years to the level already enjoyed in
the United States.[48]

When Hoffman resigned, neither the administration nor Congress mentioned policy disagreements. President Truman and
congressional supporters of the Marshall Plan sent Hoffman their
thanks for a magnificent performance. Even many of the ECA's

congressional critics offered expressions of high regard for the job he had performed. Senator Kenneth Wherry of Nebraska, a budget cutter who had embarrassed and angered Hoffman, assured him that he had contributed to the nation's welfare; Senator Robert Taft, a more moderate critic, informed him that he always approved of the general theory of economic aid and of Hoffman's manner of administration.[49]

Hoffman could rightly receive such praise because by the time he resigned, the Marshall Plan had already succeeded. By pouring billions of dollars into Western Europe, the ECA paid for about a quarter of the region's total imports from 1947 to 1950. An addition of 5 to 10 percent of resources had enabled Europe to increase production more than 25 percent above prewar levels.[50]

The economic benefits in Western Europe were not, to be sure, shared equally. The ECA gave its money to those whom one journalist called the "unlovely and greedy men of Europe" who knew how to use it for investments that yielded economic growth. As Hoffman admitted in his book *Peace Can Be Won*, the standard of living had not risen significantly, and deep social, economic, and political problems in Europe had barely been touched. But with the increases in production, the desperation of 1948 had been replaced with hope and confidence for the future. Unlike leftist critics who have emphasized the failure of the living standard to improve, most people in Western Europe were willing to wait for the expected gains once they realized that the system provided the foundation for such improvements.[51]

According to Hoffman, the money spent in helping Western Europeans to rebuild their shattered economies, and thus achieve the foundation for prosperity, paid Americans real dividends. Again unlike leftist critics, he did not point to gains made by American exporters or the increases of American investments in Europe and in areas linked to it; instead, he emphasized the Marshall Plan's contribution to peace and security. When he claimed that it had prevented Western Europe from falling under Soviet domination, he meant that prosperity made Europeans less susceptible to Communist propaganda and better able to withstand external pressure from the Soviet Union. With the revival of Western Europe, the U.S. could shift some of the costs of rearmament to its allies and avoid becoming a "garrison state" forced to regiment business and to squander its resources on massive military expenditures.[52]

Hoffman and other policy-makers within the Truman administration built that argument on the premise that the Soviet Union possessed substantial power to back up its expansionist ambitions. If they did not expect a direct Soviet military assault on Western Europe, they certainly feared that Communist pressure could undermine postwar regimes vital to the U.S. From that perspective it made sense to conclude that the Marshall Plan had strengthened Western Europe within the anti-Communist alliance. On the other hand, it now appears that the architects of U.S. policy exaggerated both Soviet strength and inflexibility, and that the very success of the Marshall Plan promoted a sharper division of Europe between East and West and contributed to a prolonged arms race.

Although the ECA in Western Europe served its political premises well, in Asia the story was quite different. There the non-Communist regimes suffered from massive weaknesses and serious questions of legitimacy. For such poor and backward regions, President Truman proposed and Hoffman endorsed U.S. programs extending economic aid for development. When faced with concrete problems, however, the ECA seemed to focus less on economic development than on containing Communist revolution. For a short time, Hoffman did try to make the best of an undesirable situation in China, but his proposals lacked political support in an era when the administration had already embraced anti-Communism.

Hoffman himself did not, apparently, learn enough from the limitations of the ECA's efforts in Asia: he oversimplified what he realized was a complex situation. Using an expansive rhetoric, he declared, "We have learned in Europe what to do in Asia, for under the Marshall Plan we have developed the essential instruments of a successful policy in the arena of world politics."[53] With Western Europe on the road to prosperity, he wanted to promote economic development for the poor and underdeveloped regions elsewhere.

Hoffman regarded foreign aid as an instrument to preserve democracy and capitalism by providing stability and the foundation for economic growth. And just as his domestic policies had to be sold to an apathetic or hostile American public, so did foreign aid. To Congress and the public he tried to sell the concept of economic foreign aid as enlightened national self-interest. When he left government, he was still frustrated because the public continued to regard the ECA as just a big charity.[54] As president of the Ford Foundation, Hoffman hoped to persuade the public that foreign aid for economic development was a sound investment for the United States. There was nothing hidden about Hoffman's agenda.

6 The Ford Foundation, 1951-53

Given his performance as chairman of the CED and as administrator of the Marshall Plan, Hoffman seemed perfectly suited for the presidency of a major private foundation. By the time he assumed his new position, older foundations such as those created by Andrew Carnegie and the Rockefellers had already established rules for operating within the U.S. and abroad. Their wealthy founders and benefactors had turned over control to professional administrators, so-called philanthropoids who embraced the principles of nonpartisanship, scientific objectivity, and pluralism to retain tax-exempt status and to avoid political harassment. Hoffman brought to the Ford Foundation not only administrative experience but also the generally progressive outlook common among those who led the big foundations.

The place of large private foundations in American society has not been without its critics. Even some who recognize that the foundations have tried to better the lot of the world's poor have also charged that they function as class institutions. According to one scholar who recently examined their influence on American foreign policy, the foundations have supported the existing social order and a world view commensurate with the extension of economic, military, and political U.S. hegemony. Technocratic consciousness has permeated their programs because of their inherently undemocratic elitism.[1]

That kind of criticism has some merit, but like similar charges against the Marshall Plan, it makes too much of one aspect while ignoring other and more important truths. Of course the big foundations served the system that created them; they never claimed otherwise. During the early 1950s they functioned as forces for progressive reform within that system. As a result, they had to defend themselves against popular and reactionary accusations that they undermined the American system. Hoffman's own experiences suggest that exclusive focus on the foundations as institutions of the so-called ruling class is not so much wrong as it is lopsided.

Among American philanthropic organizations, the Ford Foundation was neither old nor significant before Hoffman became its president. Established in 1936 by the Ford family, it had concentrated relatively modest efforts within the Detroit metropolitan area, free from fanfare or public scrutiny. In the late 1940s, however, it suddenly emerged as the giant among all foundations because bequests by Henry Ford and his son Edsel gave it almost 90 percent of the stock equity of the Ford Motor Company. That arrangement, intended to preserve family control of the company, tied together at least temporarily the economic health of the foundation and the automaker. But regardless of the motives of its benefactors, the foundation was forced to expand its activities greatly because of provisions in the Federal Revenue Code.[2]

Sheer size as well as government requirements changed the character of the Ford Foundation and pushed it into the national limelight. After the death of Henry Ford in 1947, the foundation was run by his grandson Henry Ford II and a board of trustees. To determine how it would operate under the new circumstances, the trustees created a special committee. At the recommendation of trustee Karl Compton, president of MIT, the committee was placed under the direction of H. Rowan Gaither, Jr., Compton's wartime assistant director at MIT's Radiation Laboratory. Gaither had helped convert RAND, an Air Force research institute, into the Rand Corporation, an independent "think tank" for which he served as chairman.

In November of 1949, Gaither delivered to the trustees a meticulous and thorough report. On organizational matters, it recommended that the Ford Foundation not appear to be the instrument of the Ford family or any particular political interest. The family had to divorce itself from the control and operation of the foundation; authority should rest, instead, with an independent board of trustees. Furthermore, the administrators must avoid strong partisanship even on issues involving work they supported.[3]

On substantive matters, the report of the Gaither committee was expansive. It identified five general areas of activity to advance human welfare: the promotion of peace, the strengthening of democracy, the strengthening of the economy, the promotion of education, and the improvement of individual behavior and human relations. Given the assets of the Ford Foundation, the report left no doubt that it would surpass all existing foundations in the scope of its activities.

The trustees realized that even with so comprehensive a report, the foundation's success or failure could well hinge on the attitudes and performance of its president. Then thirty-two years old and obviously more interested in the automotive business, Henry Ford II announced his intention to resign the foundation presidency as soon as a successor could be found. The trustees therefore initiated a search for a new president, really the first for the expanded Ford Foundation. They wanted an individual with proven executive abilities and prestige of national or even international scope. Perhaps because they also wanted flexibility and adaptability, they did not look within existing foundations.

As the Ford Foundation trustees went through their evaluation process, rumors began to circulate that they wanted Hoffman. In December of 1949, Henry Ford II publicly admitted that the trustees were considering him, but Hoffman declared that, while flattered, he could not leave the ECA in the near future. Eight months later, Ford himself went to Washington and asked Hoffman to reconsider. By then, Hoffman had received indirect encouragement from foundation trustee Donald K. David, a former CED member who enlisted the help of their mutual friend William Benton. Responding to Benton's encouragement, Hoffman confided that he considered the competence of Ernest Breech, president of the Ford Motor Company, an important element in his own appraisal of the foundation's opportunities; after all, the value of Ford stock would determine the resources of the foundation. Thus at the time he first met Ford, in August of 1950, Hoffman admitted that if he could leave the ECA with a clear conscience, he would be interested in the presidency of the Ford Foundation. Ford left him a copy of the Gaither committee's report.[4]

When he met Ford again in September, Hoffman declared that the foundation would have to take very bold, imaginative, and even controversial action to provide the "venture capital of social progress."[5] Before accepting the position, he wanted assurance that the president would have a large degree of freedom in pursuing the foundation's general goals. Ford gave that assurance and left, convinced that

Hoffman was the man for the job. And as Ford hoped, at a third meeting a month later, Hoffman proved willing to make the commitment.

After lengthy negotiations with Henry Ford II, Hoffman conferred with the entire board of trustees on 6 November 1950. Before accepting the presidency of the Ford Foundation and a salary of $75,000, he made clear his preconditions. First, he insisted that the foundation's headquarters be located near his home in Pasadena. Second, he expected wide latitude, subject only to the trustees' general advice and ultimate authority over broad program decisions. Having just had to contend with misinformed members of Congress while he headed the ECA, he did not want petty interference from the trustees.[6] He rejected a routine ministerial role by which he would merely implement orders from the trustees. And he rejected the role of "just a banker" distributing funds. With personnel of his own choosing, he intended to operate boldly and to risk unpopularity by tackling controversial problems.

On those terms he started, full of hope. It seemed to him that the Ford Foundation had a greater potential than any private organization of its kind to contribute to the cause of freedom, human welfare, and peace. With relatively few dollars spent wisely, it could "change the course of history for the better." To his friend Robert Hutchins, he reportedly said that the foundation had "the biggest blank check in history."[7]

In electing Hoffman, Henry Ford II and the trustees presumably accepted his terms. Ford publicly praised his successor as the best man in the world for that job. Nevertheless, the trustees failed to define clearly the line between their prerogatives and executive direction. As it turned out, Ford and the trustees could not live with the kind of latitude Hoffman expected. And from the start, at least some of the trustees regarded the move to Pasadena as a mistake.

The unconventional home of the Ford Foundation became a subject of some controversy. Started in Hoffman's own residence, it eventually moved into a large mansion on a palm-lined estate with swimming pool at 2 Oak Knoll Terrace. There, the Tuerk House, dubbed "Itching Palms" by Robert Hutchins, was remodeled into offices and meeting rooms. Despite a reputation for lavishness, its expenses were not extraordinary. The comfortable atmosphere of Hoffman's modest office, for example, was more characteristic of a private home than of a place of business.[8]

To make the Pasadena programming office the foundation's intellectual center, Hoffman tried to gather together the best brains available. Given freedom to choose his own coworkers and assistants, he relied heavily on contacts made through the University of Chicago, the CED, and the ECA. He started by naming three associate directors of whom the first and always the most important was Robert Hutchins.

After two decades of controversy at the University of Chicago, Hutchins still possessed the inner fire of a nonclerical missionary of truth. Tall, slim, and strikingly handsome even at fifty-two, he intimidated many by his seemingly imperturbable and formidable dignity, combativeness, and—according to critics—arrogance. Hutchins never suffered fools gladly. The friendship and mutual respect that had developed between Hutchins and Hoffman during the 1930s lasted the remainder of their lives. Hoffman always found in Hutchins a brilliant mind ready with ideas on big issues that could excite men's imaginations. Many trustees, however, found him more than they bargained for or could bear.[9]

The other two associate directors, Chester Davis and Rowan Gaither, were quite different. Davis, an economist who specialized in resource development, had once headed the New Deal's Agricultural Adjustment Administration. When Hoffman, who knew him through the CED and the Harriman Committee, invited him to Pasadena, he was serving as president of the Federal Reserve Bank of St. Louis. While Davis apparently paid little attention to the foundation's internal politics, Gaither remained very much the trustees' man and did not join Hoffman's inner circle. As chairman of the Rand Corporation in Santa Monica, he could devote only half his time to the Ford Foundation.

Before he assumed the presidency, Hoffman did not have clearly defined ideas about how the Ford Foundation should be run, although even with his lack of experience, he did know that giving away money so that it helped society was a difficult job. For a time he seemed to think that the foundation would emphasize "responsible research" programs rather than more direct action. But the day after he assumed office, he received from Rowan Gaither a long memorandum reviewing the foundation's objectives and suggesting policies to be implemented, including a heavy emphasis on foreign programs.[10]

With the first planning sessions in Pasadena in January, the ambitious programs of the Ford Foundation began to take shape. During the lively exchange of ideas about big social issues, Hutchins forcefully insisted that the foundation had to emphasize projects that would actually do something, and none of the others disagreed with him that the foundation should not merely sponsor studies of problems. In emphasizing action rather than study, Hutchins expressed hostility toward the behavioral sciences, which Hoffman described as a "good field [in which] to waste millions and get nothing."[11] Gaither, whose committee's report in 1949 reflected current vogues in the social and behavioral sciences, did not immediately take up that veiled rebuke.

Although Hutchins emerged in the informal role of first minister to Hoffman, others within the organization also pushed for an ambitious program of action. Tex Moore, brought in as legal counsel and trustee, emphasized the need to start spending large sums of money quickly; otherwise, Moore warned, the foundation could expect trouble from the Internal Revenue Service and Congress. As a matter of fact, after the Revenue Act of 1950 the trustees had recognized that the foundation had to avoid unreasonable accumulation of capital in order to retain its tax-exempt status.[12]

Among others in the early stages who urged Hoffman to start spending, W. H. Ferry showed considerable boldness and imagination. Son of the chairman of the Packard Motor Company, "Ping" Ferry had moved from the Republican politics of his family to become a liberal Democrat and gadfly for causes. After working for newspapers in several states, in 1944 he served as the director of public relations for the CIO's political action committee and then became a partner in one of the county's largest public relations firms, Earl Newsom and Company, which handled the accounts of both the Ford Motor Company and the Ford Foundation. Often disagreeing with Newsom, Ferry backed Hutchins, particularly his proposals to defend civil liberties and dissent, then under heavy assault in America. Intelligent, hard-working, and blunt to the point of impatient abrasiveness and short temper, he became a friend to whom Hoffman turned for advice and administrative assistance. With Hoffman, he never hesitated to speak his mind.[13]

Within a few months, the organization Hoffman created had revealed its basic character. With a flurry of activity the foundation performed quite creditably, and much of the credit, according to the foundation's authorized history, rightly belonged to Hoffman himself. In Pasadena the small group he gathered around him developed an élan and a strong sense of purpose that produced a steady flow of ideas and programs.

The foundation's peculiar administrative structure also contributed to much confusion and turmoil. While the programming headquarters in Pasadena poured out ideas and proposals, the operations office in New York had responsibility for investigating those proposals and various grant applications. From the New York office, project proposals were supposed to pass to the trustees and, after their approval, to the fiscal office in Detroit for payment. Very quickly, the volume of paperwork between the offices in Pasadena and New York became elephantine. As foundation officials traveled across the country, delays and costs mounted. The staff recognized that it needed better control over grant applications and project proposals.

For the most part, Hoffman left administrative details to trusted subordinates and concentrated on broad policy matters. After all, he had taken the job to advance human progress and the cause of freedom, not to fill a bureaucratic niche. Although he described the Ford Foundation as a charming ivory tower,[14] he clearly did not intend to remove himself from the vital issues of the day. Two areas in particular interested him: foreign affairs and civil liberties. Both were risky because they impinged upon contemporary political controversy.

While president of the Ford Foundation, Hoffman played an active role in the new Committee on the Present Danger, which lobbied for military preparedness and negotiation from strength. In July of 1951, the day after William Foster appointed him a consultant for the ECA, he testified before the House Committee on Foreign Affairs, calling for consolidation of economic and military aid within a single independent agency with Cabinet status. But, as he explained to a State Department official, he was less firmly committed to the notion of a single agency, which the Truman administration opposed, than he was to the notion that economic aid should enjoy an equal voice with military aid.[15]

At the Ford Foundation, after receiving from Rowan Gaither a memorandum proposing a broad approach to current international problems, Hoffman advocated that the Ford Foundation develop programs that would enhance the American ability to wage peace and to prevail if war began. He considered it quite appropriate for the foundation to strengthen and supplement government efforts, especially where government activities were inappropriate, ineffective, or warped by political partisanship.[16]

From the start, Cold War issues loomed large. Thus, the foundation created the East European Fund and brought in George F. Kennan, then between assignments at the State Department, as a consultant with virtually a free hand. A serious student of U.S. foreign policy and an expert on the Soviet Union, Kennan was impressed by Hoffman's sincerity but doubted that the foundation could accomplish what its president hoped. Meanwhile, Hoffman got involved with the German question. Before providing a grant to a German group giving support to refugees who had fled Communism, he discreetly obtained approval from the State Department, the Central Intelligence Agency, and the U.S. High Commissioner. And when he, Henry Ford II, and other foundation officials toured Europe in June, they responded favorably to the High Commissioner's request that the foundation provide financial support for the Free University of Berlin.[17]

In spite of his contacts with U.S. government agencies, including the CIA, Hoffman did not allow the Ford Foundation to become an instrument for covert activities. When Edmund Palmieri, a former consultant to the Rockefeller Foundation and later a U.S. district judge, suggested that the foundation advance money for covert CIA propaganda, Hoffman rejected the idea; the Ford Foundation, he said, followed a policy of full disclosure.[18]

While Europe was the main theater for U.S.-Soviet rivalry, Hoffman also turned his attention on Asia. It seemed to him that too many Americans failed to understand Asians and presented themselves badly. They had to "stop talking about the Western tradition and the Christian tradition and start talking about the free world." The U.S. must convince Asians that it was leading a global struggle for freedom, not seeking to impose new forms of oppression and exploitation. American leadership had to be based on political wisdom, not the power of its military or the leverage of its foreign aid.[19]

In August of 1951, Hoffman went to Asia to see how the Ford Foundation might formulate programs to assist economic development. In India and Pakistan, where he maintained a hectic pace even in the oppressive summer heat, he received enthusiastic responses from government leaders and the press. Finding efforts for modernization and expressions of hope, he declared that, "Asia can still be saved from communism." But he realized that since Asians distrusted the U.S., identifying it with Western imperialism, Americans had to give positive proof of their willingness to help.[20]

Asia suffered from terrible poverty, disease, ignorance, and economic underdevelopment. For democracy to survive there, Hoffman observed, both rapid increases in agricultural and industrial production and a more equitable distribution of rewards were needed. In India and Pakistan people ought to overcome "weird" notions that physical labor was degrading and that those with education should avoid commerce; to that end, Hoffman went out of his way to give public praise to the concepts of equality and the dignity of honest labor.[21]

He returned from his travels without delusions of grandeur but with the firm conviction that the Ford Foundation could make significant contributions even in countries suspicious of the U.S. government. Within a few months the foundation launched a program for India. Hoffman, Chester Davis, and Douglas Ensminger, the economist who headed the program, all agreed that it would focus on aid for agricultural development at the village level. Leaders within India's central government and the new U.S. Ambassador, Chester Bowles, concurred with that approach. Although not entirely free from an ethnocentric vision of modernization, the Ford Foundation's program in India did manage to establish a firmer footing in local reality than did the earlier efforts of the Rockefeller Foundation in China.[22]

Meanwhile, back in Pasadena, Hoffman welcomed the foundation's fourth associate director, Milton Katz. Arriving in September, straight from the ECA, where he had served as one of the key members of the top command, Katz immediately joined Hoffman's inner circle. From their close personal relationship Hoffman regarded Katz as a brilliant source of ideas, and Katz regarded Hoffman as a very wonderful human being, always willing to bring together intellectually lively people to generate ideas.

Despite his admiration, however, Katz felt uneasy about the way Hoffman was running the foundation; the foundation's overseas program, he said, was based on naive and unrealistic premises. Unlike Hutchins (with whom he did not get along) and Hoffman, Katz did not believe that international conflicts and wars stemmed mainly from poverty, ignorance, and other misfortunes. Putting more emphasis on national and ideological rivalries, his anti-Communism fit more neatly into the Cold War mold. From that perspective, he held a narrower view of what the foundation could achieve, and worried that in his eagerness to aid world peace Hoffman was making the foundation into an ersatz State Department.[23]

Katz's warnings did not, however, change Hoffman's basic policies. Not only did he press on with programs touching international controversies; he also moved the foundation into the area of civil liberties in the United States. Ever since he had emerged during the 1930s as a champion of free enterprise, he had sought to defend all freedoms. To combat intolerance, he had worked actively within the National Conference of Christians and Jews and won its Brotherhood Citation for 1949. When he joined the Ford Foundation, he worked closely with his eldest son, Hallock, who had become a Quaker and executive secretary of the American Friends Service Committee, which attempted to reduce racial inequities.

During the early 1950s, Hoffman himself worried about the wave of intolerance, fear, and suspicion threatening American freedoms. His sense of decency was offended by the atmosphere in Washington supercharged with rumors and character assassination. Behind a veil of confidentiality, individuals were being accused as subversives or immoral persons. At the very least, Hoffman felt, the accused had the right to know the identity of the accusers and the nature of the allegations.[24]

For Hoffman, the issue of anti-Communism and civil liberties came to the fore during the struggle between his friend William Benton, then a Democratic senator from Connecticut, and Senator Joseph McCarthy, the reigning prince of anti-Communist demagoguery. Hoffman believed that McCarthy's methods actually resembled tactics of the Soviets and played into their hands. He advised Benton to make clear his own unswerving opposition to Communism in order to focus attention on American freedoms and respect for individual rights, rather than a negative anti-Communism.[25]

Hoffman forcefully stated his own beliefs in October of 1951, when he received the Freedom Award. His main theme was a defense of freedom of thought and criticism, without which society stagnates and dies. Criticism of injustice was essential, for an unjust society could not long endure, yet the current wave of hysterical fear of subversion threatened to stifle debate and criticism. "Of all forms of tyranny over the mind of man," he warned, "none is more terrible than fear." Already, fear of persecution by public opinion was leading to dangerous conformity. Too many decisions, even in high places, were being influenced by that fear. America needed courage and rationality, not suppression of irresponsible critics. It was perhaps as a result of those remarks that Hoffman appeared on McCarthy's public list of persons "soft" on Communism.[26]

Within the Ford Foundation, opinion was divided about involvement in the civil liberties controversy. From the start, Hutchins and Ferry pressured Hoffman to launch a new program to defend Americans' freedoms; they wanted him to get the trustees' approval to establish an independent fund for that purpose. Both felt that he dragged his feet and moved too slowly on so vital an issue.

If he did not move as quickly as Hutchins and Ferry would have liked, however, Hoffman did strongly back the idea of an independent fund for the defense of civil liberties. By late 1951 he had started to court Charles E. Wilson of General Electric to head such a fund; he felt that the fund would need a crusader, preferably one with good conservative credentials.

As a matter of fact, Hoffman and the Ford Foundation had already become targets of assaults by right-wingers. Their newspaper columns, magazines, and radio commentaries accused him of giving the foundation a "leftist slant." When such attacks linked the foundation's alleged radicalism with the Ford Motor Company, Henry Ford II began to receive letters of complaint from dealers, customers, and assorted cranks. Although he was not intimidated, Ford was concerned that his automotive business might suffer because of the way Hoffman ran the Ford Foundation.[27] As a result, his enthusiasm and confidence gradually diminished. By August of 1951, with rumors circulating of a pending congressional investigation of foundations, he had cooled toward the whole idea of a "Freedom Seminar." An October meeting with Hoffman and his associate directors at Ford's home in suburban Detroit revealed that the founding family felt uneasy about the foundation's top administrators, especially Hutchins.[28] Apart from the clash of personalities, the Fords and several trustees apparently thought that the foundation was pushing into too many controversies, subjecting them and the Ford Motor Company to needless abuse.

Some members of the foundation's executive staff also worried that conservatives in Congress would launch an investigation of foundations for possible "unAmerican activities." Ping Ferry alerted Hoffman to that threat and urged staff discussion of a proper response. Hoffman doubted that Congress would undertake such an investigation but did try to cultivate Representative Donald Jackson of the House Committee on Un-American Activities. He confessed to Jackson that the Ford and Rockefeller foundations had failed to make forthright statements about their unqualified support of the American way of life, including capitalism, but he assured the Republican from Los Angeles that that support could be clearly inferred from their actions.[29]

In spite of such efforts to calm troubled waters, the foundations could not avert investigation: in April of 1952, the House of Representatives created a special investigative committee chaired by Eugene Cox, a conservative Democrat from Georgia. Within a week Henry Ford II had prepared a confidential survey on congressional attitudes toward the foundation. According to that report, opposition stemmed from conservatives and opponents of racial integration and internationalism. Nevertheless, Ford and the other trustees went ahead with tentative approval for the creation of a fund to defend civil liberties.[30]

Hoffman still did not believe that the proposed congressional investigation would ever get under way, but in May he informed Ford that the foundation had to prepare for that possibility. If the Cox Committee actually started its probe, he wanted the Ford Foundation to testify first, and told Ford that he was eager to appear personally on behalf of the foundation.[31]

When Congress created the Cox Committee, Hoffman was just beginning a three-month political leave, which the foundation's trustees had reluctantly granted. His involvement in politics was no sudden development. During the early 1940s some Republicans had started to mention him as a possible presidential candidate; after the Republican defeat in 1948, he received further encouragement from friends, acquaintances, and ordinary citizens to seek the presidency in 1952. George Romney, then an executive with Nash-Kelvinator, declared that Hoffman was the only presidential candidate he could thoroughly believe in and go all out for. In the fall of 1951, a Gallup poll indicated strong public interest in a Hoffman candidacy, and *Look* suggested that he might be a GOP dark horse.[32]

Totally without political ambition, Hoffman never hedged in repudiating all such suggestions, but he did have firm convictions about what the Republican Party needed. Following the 1948 election, he commented that Republican leaders had yet to learn that the American people were "not interested in returning to the economies of the McKinley era." To avoid another disastrous defeat and possible oblivion, the party would have to modernize and attract independent voters. In his view, Senator Henry Cabot Lodge's program for "constructive conservatism" offered some hope for revitalizing the party.[33]

What he especially wanted for 1952 was to block the candidacy of Senator Robert A. Taft. As chairman of the CED and then administrator of the Marshall Plan, he had observed Taft in action and had come away completely disillusioned by the senator's "pedantic arrogance." It seemed to him that a contest between President Truman and Senator Taft would further divide the country and would likely mean one more Republican defeat. Yet if Taft somehow won, the results might be even worse, for the senator misunderstood the modern economy and the international situation. Calling him an "isolationist," Hoffman feared that Taft might neglect America's allies in Europe and might also imprudently lead the U.S. into a disastrous war with China.[34]

As early as April of 1951, Hoffman decided that instead of Taft the Republican Party and the nation needed General Dwight Eisenhower, then commander of the NATO forces. When he traveled to Europe for the Ford Foundation, Hoffman stopped several times in Paris to try to persuade Eisenhower to seek the presidential nomination, but the general, unwilling to admit his political ambitions, kept insisting that he wanted Hoffman to run instead: "I'd resign to work for him," he recorded in his diary after their meeting in June, and four months later he wrote Hoffman that "if *you* would only get into this particular ring, you can be sure of at least one man in the front row cheering you on—I would even carry the water bottle."[35]

To persuade Eisenhower, Hoffman used flattery, appeals to duty, and a sense of practical politics. As the Gallup polls revealed, some of the people but virtually no Republican politicians wanted Hoffman; meanwhile, more of the people and even many politicians did want Eisenhower. Hoffman concluded that Eisenhower could win, while he could not. In his last appeal to the general, he argued that only Eisenhower, beyond the control of "the boys in the smoke-filled rooms," could redeem the Republican Party. Only he could move the country away from an atmosphere of hatred and fear; only he could start the world toward peace.[36]

Hoffman alone did not persuade Eisenhower, but with others also urging him on, the general finally did admit that he was, at heart, fairly close to the "progressive branch" of the Republican Party. What he meant by that label had less to do with domestic than with foreign affairs. Like Hoffman and other internationalists within the party, Eisenhower regarded Taft as a threat to American policies aimed at promoting European recovery and security. Also like Hoffman, Eisenhower expressed doubts that the current political game always served the national interest. Both men agreed that pressure from private interest groups too often shaped the behavior of politicians.[37]

During the early part of 1952, Hoffman tried to confine his efforts on Eisenhower's behalf mostly to evenings and weekends, but some of those in the campaign pleaded with him to do more. According to Richard Bissell, the U.S. stood at the crossroads between peace with honor and the possible outbreak of World War III. The accession of Taft, he warned, would bring profound national disunity and other political catastrophes at a critical time in world affairs. Therefore, Hoffman must place Eisenhower's nomination ahead of duty and obligation to the Ford Foundation. Once Eisenhower had been nominated, Bissell added, "men like yourself can retire from the campaign secure in the knowledge that at least no catastrophy [sic] will happen."[38]

Swayed by such frantic pleading, and after conferring again with Eisenhower in Paris, Hoffman applied for and received a three-month leave from the Ford Foundation. On 10 April 1952 he became Chairman of the Advisory Committee of Citizens for Eisenhower, which was then a shambles. Hoffman's quick reorganization of the committee, his persuasiveness as a public speaker, his sense of the needs of journalists, and his knowledge of people who could help all greatly impressed Henry Cabot Lodge, the campaign manager.[39]

General Lucius Clay, Eisenhower's political advisor and liaison, expressed quite different views, however. "Paul Hoffman comes in like a hurricane," he reported to Eisenhower. "His values are great but he likes to be bridegroom at each wedding, the corpse at every funeral." According to Clay, Hoffman's good far outweighed the bad, but he did tend to move quickly in "dangerous areas." Clay, then president of Continental Can Company, lined up business support for Eisenhower among his "G.M. friends" and warned the general not to be oversold on Hoffman, who had a large public following but not the complete confidence of the business community.[40]

Until the Republican convention, which opened in Chicago on

July 7th, Hoffman worked sixteen hours a day for the Eisenhower campaign. To make the general look like a winner, he pushed attention beyond the nomination to the national election. Only Eisenhower, he claimed, could attract enough independent voters to win. In the heat of the contest, Hoffman's statements about Taft and his supporters took on a very sharp edge. He may not have actually used the phrase "Louisiana Purchase," but he certainly did accuse the Taftites of a desperate and unethical effort to steal southern delegates by trickery.[41]

Part of Hoffman's task was to use his own reputation to reassure liberals, moderates, and independents that Eisenhower was not becoming the captive of Republican conservatives. While the candidate remained silent, Hoffman gave assurances that he did indeed oppose McCarthyism. When campaign workers questioned Eisenhower's failure to defend civil rights, Hoffman declared that he felt very deeply about equal rights and opportunities for everyone. For those who worried that the general might overemphasize the military, Hoffman explained that Eisenhower, who supported foreign aid to help other free nations, could provide more security and economy than could the isolationist Taft.[42]

At the convention itself Hoffman played only a minor role. During the actual voting, he did join some of the inner circle and family members in Eisenhower's suite. He also participated in the final caucus that recommended Senator Richard Nixon as the vice-presidential candidate. After New York Governor Thomas E. Dewey called Nixon the only logical choice, Hoffman affirmed that everything in Nixon's background was an asset for Eisenhower and the party.[43]

When liberal Republicans later expressed shock over the selection of Nixon, Hoffman strongly supported the vice-presidential candidate's competence and character. Nixon was not a witch-hunter like McCarthy. On domestic issues, he was a forward-looking middle-of-the-roader. On foreign issues, he was a supporter of international cooperation in Europe and a legitimate critic of the Truman administration's policies in Asia. Because of Nixon's image problems, Hoffman urged him to respond to the smear campaign by showing his own support for civil liberties and minority rights.[44]

A week after the Republican convention began, Hoffman returned to the Ford Foundation and thereafter remained on the periphery of the political campaign. Only the scandal over Nixon's secret fund briefly brought him back into the center of the campaign: at the request of Eisenhower's chief of staff, Sherman Adams, Hoffman directed a speedy investigation of the fund. It was Hoffman who decided to retain the Los Angeles law firm of Gibson, Dunn and Crutcher to prepare an opinion on the fund's legality, and to have the firm of Price, Waterhouse audit Nixon's accounts. He then advised Nixon, who was preparing to defend himself in what became the famous "Checkers Speech," to use the reports of the lawyers and the accountants because they would carry great weight with the television audience, including Eisenhower's own advisors. To Hoffman, the whole episode showed that government officials should receive higher salaries so that they would not need supplementary income.[45]

Soon after Eisenhower's election, rumors circulated that Hoffman might become a member of the Cabinet, and before leaving for Korea, the President-elect did confer with Hoffman. Eisenhower's press secretary then released a statement that Hoffman "was not seeking and could not accept . . . any position at this time in the coming administration." Eisenhower deeply appreciated Hoffman's help during the election campaign and regretted that he would not serve in the new administration.[46]

Hoffman had nothing but praise for the way the new administration took shape. He expected that Eisenhower, who entered office without obligation to any special interest group, would become a great president. While critics condemned the appointment of so many corporate leaders to important government positions, Hoffman expressed confidence that they would get out of the "dog house" by their performance: businessmen in the new administration would of course have to prove that they could provide benefits for all people.[47]

Hoffman's main concern was that the Eisenhower administration get off on the right foot in foreign affairs. Worried that too much attention was focused on a military buildup, he recommended disarmament negotiations with the Soviets so that the U.S. would not become a "garrison state." He also urged Eisenhower to use his inaugural address to reach the "minds and hearts" of people throughout the world by reaffirming support for the struggling peoples of Asia and the Middle East. As for himself, Hoffman took pride and satisfaction in his relationship with Eisenhower, but he maintained that he could better serve the nation at the Ford Foundation than in government.[48]

Unfortunately, the trustees of the Ford Foundation, though mostly Eisenhower supporters, did not entirely share Hoffman's enthusiasms. They wanted a foundation president who would provide efficient administration without much controversy. Eager to preserve the foundation's tax-exempt status based on nonpartisanship, they greatly feared the threats of congressional investigation. Hoffman's political involvement and his many outside interests led the trustees to disillusionment and resentment. Increasingly, they questioned their decision in selecting him.

An important step in that process of disillusionment occurred while Hoffman was on leave. During those three months, Henry Ford II moved to Pasadena and temporarily assumed the foundation's presidency. Already disenchanted with the foundation's development, Ford discovered what seemed to him a lack of central direction and strong leadership. Hoffman had permitted associate directors too much freedom and too much overlap of responsibilities. Ford especially disliked the overly large role assumed by Hoffman's favorite, Robert Hutchins.

When Hoffman returned, he tried to mend his relationship with Ford and the other trustees. Praising the administrative changes Ford had initiated, he said that he wanted to continue if the trustees still had confidence in him. He not only promised to keep them better informed but also welcomed their greater participation in the foundation's management. Nevertheless, he still refused to serve merely as a banker passing out money according to the dictates of the trustees. He had no intention of avoiding public controversies just to protect himself and the foundation from embarrassment.[49]

Having already incurred the wrath of conservatives by his involvement in the Eisenhower campaign, Hoffman proceeded to make matters worse after he returned to the Ford Foundation. By dictating a deposition on behalf of Senator William Benton for his libel suit against Senator Joseph McCarthy, Hoffman became the target of a venomous assault by Westbrook Pegler in his nationally syndicated column. Less than a week later, Hoffman found himself verbally attacked when he appeared before the Los Angeles Board of Education to defend the use of materials distributed by the United Nations Educational, Scientific, and Cultural Organization (UNESCO). Badly shaken by that experience, he warned the board about the dangers of thought control in the schools. The board responded by rejecting the UNESCO materials and, later, a grant from the Ford Foundation.[50]

Hoffman's third involvement with controversy had much less to do with such high principles. In an exclusive article, the *Wall Street Journal* named him as the authoritative source for information that the foundation had considered the eventual sale of its stock in the Ford Motor Company. The fact of the matter was that in October of 1950 the trustees had decided to liquidate at the earliest date "consistent with maximum financial realization." But that decision remained a closely guarded secret. Hoffman's apparent indiscretion, which he denied, greatly infuriated Henry Ford II and Ernest Breech. From Rome, Ford sent an angry telegram rebuking Hoffman for the premature disclosure.[51]

Coincident with the growing rift between Hoffman and Henry Ford II, the Cox Committee called both of them to testify. Hoffman did most of the talking and adroitly defended the foundation as a source for the "venture capital of social progress" and a bulwark for a free society. The foundation operated, according to Hoffman, somewhere near "the middle of the road," avoiding the political ideology or bias of either the left or the right. It strengthened the American way of life by showing the world how the American brand of capitalism yielded real benefits for "the people."[52]

His appearance before the Cox Committee was a cakewalk for Hoffman. Chairman Eugene Cox told him that he had ably presented the Ford Foundation's case. "As a matter of fact," Cox added, "you have made a fine case for all the foundations." And after that congressional appearance, Hoffman followed the suggestion of public relations advisor Earl Newsom and expanded his public lecturing to show the contribution of foundations to the American way of life.[53]

Even while he attended to those responsibilities, he involved the Ford Foundation in preparations for the start of the Eisenhower administration and lent out Richard Bissell, on the foundation's payroll as a consultant, to the Mutual Security Agency. Yet he assured Henry Ford II that as he had stated to the Cox Committee, the foundation made full disclosure of its grants and did not engage in covert activities of any sort.[54]

None of Hoffman's explanations satisfied Ford and the foundation's other trustees. As historian Thomas Reeves has noted, Hoffman failed to be sufficiently self-effacing. He was constantly in the news, making speeches, accepting awards, winning applause, and generally linking his own personality with the Ford Foundation. But Henry Ford II, who may not have been prepared to let control of the foundation slip away so quickly, complained that Hoffman's loose administration often involved it in controversies and situations that made extraordinary and exasperating demands on him.[55]

At Eisenhower's inaugural, Ford removed the source of his irritation by telling Hoffman that his appointment would be terminated. Although Hoffman very strenuously fought his removal, at a meeting of the trustees nine days later they agreed to a deal: he would resign from the presidency of the Ford Foundation, and they would support him for the chairmanship of the Fund for the Republic, a newly incorporated independent organization to be financed by the foundation for the promotion of civil liberties.[56]

Six days later, after going to Washington and explaining the situation to President Eisenhower, Hoffman announced his resignation. According to the official explanation, he did not want to leave southern California when the trustees decided to consolidate all operations in New York; therefore, he had chosen to return to Studebaker as its chairman, using its Los Angeles assembly plant as his main base. Although that public version gave no hint that internal conflicts had forced him out, he later told friends that he left because he refused to play safe when Henry Ford II and trustee Donald K. David wanted less controversial and more traditional activities.[57]

If he felt bitterness about his removal from the Ford Foundation, he never let it show. When Dwight Macdonald was writing his history of the Ford Foundation, Hoffman decided not to grant an interview, and he refused to endorse Macdonald's book, which was unfavorable in its portrayal of his ouster.[58] His departure from the foundation, however well camouflaged for the public, meant personal defeat, really the first in his entire career. Nevertheless, Hoffman remained a man of the Establishment, and he still needed good relations with the foundation to launch the Fund for the Republic.

Despite the reasons for his firing, Hoffman did leave a personal stamp on the Ford Foundation. During the two years he served as president, the foundation began to move boldly into two controversial areas: civil liberties at home and economic development abroad. His successor, Rowan Gaither, differed greatly in his personality and his administration, but he did not alter the foundation's basic policies. Its ability to continue on the same track with different person-nel may confirm the judgment of critics that a common outlook permeated the foundation. On the other hand, the abuse directed at foundations by reactionaries should be a reminder that the so-called progressive Establishment did not always have its own way in these important matters. The Ford Foundation seemed ahead of popular opinion in the early 1950s.

7 Studebaker Strikes Out, 1952-56

In the fall of 1950, when Hoffman announced that he was resigning from the ECA to become president of the Ford Foundation, news commentator Eric Sevareid made an astute observation. He said that Hoffman—like Averell Harriman, James Forrestal, Robert Lovett, John McCloy, and others—had become too successful to remain satisfied with the rewards of business achievement. Men of that caliber craved the headier challenges of public affairs.[1] The Ford Foundation and the Eisenhower campaign had provided those challenges for Hoffman, but in 1953 he had to seek new endeavors.

Almost sixty-two years old and independently wealthy, Hoffman returned to Studebaker on March 1st. He still genuinely loved the automobile business and felt a strong loyalty to Studebaker. But in accepting the chairmanship, he did not expect to shoulder administrative responsibilities. For Studebaker he intended to serve as an ambassador of good will, with ample time for family, friends, and his wide-ranging interests in public affairs.

Unfortunately, he may have stretched himself too far when diverse tasks required greater concentration. In an automotive business quite unlike the one he had left in 1948, his tenure as chairman of Studebaker and its successor proved an unhappy experience. With McCarthyism a potent force, his tenure as the unpaid chairman of the Fund for the Republic generated new controversies. Hoffman obviously enjoyed being, as he put it, under the tyranny of the time clock, but he paid a heavy price. Even as a member of the national elite or Establishment, he saw his reputation nearly destroyed.[2]

Hoffman expected to give much of his time to the defense of civil liberties, and as chairman of the Fund for the Republic beginning in

February of 1953, he was not disappointed. Although incorporated on 9 December 1952, the Fund lacked financial resources because public criticism had intimidated the trustees of the Ford Foundation. Once Hoffman assumed the chairmanship, however, the foundation's trustees formally voted to provide the Fund, an independent organization, with $14.8 million. After being turned down by his first two choices, Hoffman then persuaded Clifford Case, a four-term Republican Congressman from New Jersey, to accept the presidency.[3]

Hoffman and Case proceeded cautiously. They knew that for the Fund to operate effectively, it had to avoid even the appearance of political or ideological deviation from its stated principles. From the start, Hoffman tried to ensure that the board of directors, which held ultimate authority over personnel and policies, was bipartisan. As a result, the board included both liberals and political conservatives presumably committed to the Bill of Rights.

Despite that initial caution, the Fund immediately attracted attention from politicians concerned about Communist subversion. First, Vice-President Nixon asked Hoffman, although not as an adversary, for information about the Fund. Then Senator McCarthy requested information. In the House of Representatives, Carroll Reece announced that he would resume the investigation of foundations. The Tennessee Republican, whom Hoffman privately called an "old gumshoe," delivered a blistering congressional speech in which he denounced Hoffman and identified the Fund for the Republic as a king-sized version of another organization the Attorney General had labeled subversive.[4]

Just when Congressman Reece launched his investigation, the Fund went through a major shake-up of executive personnel. Clifford Case decided to run for a Senate seat from his home state and therefore resigned from the presidency of the Fund. To replace the conciliatory Case, the Fund's directors chose a very different kind of person, Robert Hutchins. A friend of Hoffman since the 1930s, Hutchins had vigorously pushed him to start the Ford Foundation's civil liberties program and to create the Fund.

As chairman and president respectively, Hoffman and Hutchins agreed completely on the need for the Fund for the Republic to defend civil liberties. Hutchins promptly made Ping Ferry a vice-president in charge of the New York headquarters, and he appointed Hoffman's son Hallock his assistant in Pasadena. While they pursued a more active policy than had Clifford Case, the Fund's board left responsibility for public relations with Hoffman himself.

Although deeply enmeshed in Studebaker's affairs, in August of 1954, Hoffman responded to Congressman Reece's charges against the Fund for the Republic. According to his testimony, the Fund was studying not only individual rights in free institutions but also the "internal Communist menace." Elsewhere however, he minimized the domestic threat of Communism. Americans had to fight Communism abroad, where it existed, he declared, not by firing sixth grade teachers at home. He and the Fund sought to make the Bill of Rights once again a respectable document in defense of basic American traditions of liberty and freedom.[5]

Beyond traditional issues of civil liberties, Hoffman and the Fund for the Republic moved slowly into the area of civil rights and race relations. Hoffman said simply that he did not believe either creed, national origin, or color served as "reliable indices of character or competence." Although easy solutions did not exist, Americans must root out racial and religious discrimination. Just as the Ford Foundation had done while he served as its president, the Fund for the Republic gave grants to organizations working to reduce racial inequities. In 1954, Hoffman received the Gold Medal Award of the George Washington Carver Memorial Institute, with praise from Ralph Bunche.[6]

Later that year, Hoffman tried to persuade the Delta Tau Delta social fraternity, of which he had served as national president during the early 1940s, to abandon its policy of racial exclusion. He admitted that voluntary associations, essential for the American way of life, had the right to impose any conditions as qualifications for membership. But undemocratic and perhaps "Un-American" restrictions that denied social equality because of race, color, or creed weakened the country. He recommended a policy that would permit each chapter to determine its own membership. He did not, however, call for a national policy against discrimination.[7] Nor did he resign from all-white social clubs.

Of all his personal activities, none aroused right-wingers as much as his rather minor role in the campaign against Senator Joseph McCarthy. Hoffman believed that McCarthy had become not just a nuisance but a "deadly menace" to President Eisenhower, to the Republican Party, to the United States, and to world peace.[8] In 1954, when Senator Ralph Flanders, a seventy-three-year-old Republican from Vermont, attacked McCarthy and introduced a resolution calling for the Senate to investigate his behavior for possible censure, Hoffman sprang to the aid of Flanders, an old friend from the CED. He did limit his role in that effort. First, with C. D. Jackson, Eisenhower's long-time propaganda expert then back at Time Inc., he drafted a telegram sent to every senator urging support for the Flanders resolution. ("How any senator who has the slightest regard for morality and decency can possibly fail to vote for censuring," he observed privately, "is beyond me.") Then, to help build support for that result, he raised $12,000 for a special fund collected by the National Committee for an Effective Congress, which conducted a bipartisan effort on behalf of the Flanders resolution.[9]

But even so limited an involvement made Hoffman the target of more right-wing abuse. Of the several hundred letters he received on the subject, about 80 percent criticized him. To the minority of McCarthyites who identified themselves, he responded politely but firmly. "*I do not hate Senator McCarthy,*" he informed the political cartoonist for the *Chicago Tribune*. "My attitude toward him is entirely unemotional. I am concerned about him . . . because he is stirring up so much unreasoning hatred and hysteria."[10]

Besides his own actions, Hoffman had to defend Hutchins's leadership of the Fund. Two Hutchins statements proved especially troublesome. He proposed that the Fund sponsor a study of the American Legion's record on civil liberties. And on *Meet the Press*, a program carried by radio and television stations across the country, he refused to exclude Communists from possible employment by the Fund.

Hutchins's behavior simply gave critics of the Fund more ammunition. Commentator Fulton Lewis, Jr., kept up a steady assault; during one broadcast, he read excerpts from a letter Henry Ford II had written to an American Legion post criticizing some of the Fund's operations as "dubious in character." Ford, who had no legal authority over the Fund, had received criticism, often from responsible people, that he regarded as sincere and constructive. He told Hoffman that the Fund needed to review all its staff and its projects, past and intended.[11]

By the time the Fund's board convened on 6 January 1956, several directors wanted to remove both Hutchins and Ping Ferry, whom Ford privately accused of poor judgment. However, with Hoffman presiding at the day-long meeting, the badly split board reelected

Hutchins and gave him approval to begin reorganizing the Fund. Hoping to avoid further embarrassment, the directors reduced Ferry's executive responsibilities and tightened restrictions on the hiring of controversial personnel. When the Fund faced another possible congressional inquiry a few months later, the president of the Ford Foundation, Rowan Gaither, expressed "full confidence in the integrity and patriotism" of the directors of the Fund.[12]

Though still loyal to Hutchins and committed to the Fund's principles, Hoffman decided that he could no longer continue as chairman. At the board meeting in November, he asked the other directors to choose a replacement. The board complied by electing pollster Elmo Roper. Hoffman continued to serve as a director and periodically made important contributions to the Fund's management, but after he left the chairmanship, his connection became less visible to the public.

Hoffman's involvement in the Fund for the Republic and the struggle for civil liberties was a measure of his courage and his convictions. A man of pragmatic rationality, he always insisted that policy decisions, in public affairs as in business, had to be based on "the facts." Yet he shared with Robert Hutchins a common commitment to the values and principles of freedom apart from "the facts." That stand he placed above expediency.

Hoffman knew that he had to pay a personal price for taking unpopular positions; right-wingers regularly attacked him as a dangerous liberal who naively coddled Communists. What he did not fully anticipate was the extent to which his activities outside of business would hurt Studebaker. McCarthyites attacked the automaker's record and celebrated when it faced hard times.[13] As the ambassador of corporate good will, Hoffman could not operate as effectively as he had before all the public controversies sprang up.

Even if Hoffman had not been so heavily involved in controversial outside interests, Studebaker would have faced very serious difficulties. By 1953, when he rejoined the corporation, the automotive business was changing in ways that adversely affected Studebaker. Moreover, despite its still untarnished public image, the corporation suffered from internal problems that diminished its ability to deal effectively with the new situation. Later, Raymond Loewy claimed that "lethal complications" had emerged during the first year after Hoffman left to administer the Marshall Plan.[14]

A big part of the problem was Harold Vance, who ran the corporation as both chairman and president for five years in Hoffman's absence. Quiet, unpretentious, and hard-working, he had earned a reputation as a competent production manager. But although he believed in Hoffman's notion of the Friendly Factory, he lacked the personal traits to apply it with success. His leadership proved overly cautious, unimaginative, and lax. Disliking committees and subordinates with contrary views, he allowed Studebaker to drift while the rest of the industry changed. According to automotive historian Richard Langworth, Studebaker's board should have replaced Vance during the early 1950s because of his mismanagement.[15]

In January of 1953, however, Vance's deficiencies had not yet hurt his reputation. President Eisenhower even offered to appoint him director of the Office of Defense Mobilization. Vance rejected the directorship but did agree to serve as a consultant to that agency. He reportedly viewed Hoffman's return as a way for him to reduce his own responsibilities at Studebaker so that he could spend time in Washington.[16]

When Vance reviewed Studebaker's situation for Hoffman, he painted a rather rosy picture. During 1952 the dollar volume of sales had risen about 18 percent over the previous year and profits had moved up from $5.35 to $6.05 per share. Following the strategy of cautious expansion, Vance had bought a brand-new plant in New Brunswick, New Jersey, to place Studebaker closer to the populous eastern car market, and he was about to modernize the old plant in South Bend. Although operating capital declined about $10 million to pay for those improvements and retooling for new models, Studebaker's net worth increased.[17]

The new car models about to roll off the assembly lines seemed like real winners. Raymond Loewy's studio had designed a racy-looking coupe that would eventually win awards for excellence in styling. Studebaker engineers provided it with exceptional handling and roadability. Despite dull interiors and a lack of power, the coupes appealed to car buyers, and dealers already had a backlog of early orders.

Without indicating anything really serious, Vance did mention a few problems. On the technical side, Studebaker needed to improve the Champion's power by developing an eight-cylinder engine with high compression ratios to meet the competition. Although he did not provide details, Vance also informed Hoffman that tooling problems, comparable to those they had faced with the new 1947 models, had cropped up.

Personnel relations were causing trouble for Vance as well. In South Bend, some workers abused the Friendly Factory by holding back production, apparently hoping to extract higher wages. Production boss P.O. Peterson, already irritated by the prospect that Hoffman's return might thwart his own ambitions, had threatened to accept a highly lucrative job offer from Ford if Studebaker did not force a showdown with the union. Seeking to keep Peterson at Studebaker without a confrontation with the union, Vance had invited Emil Mazey of the UAW International to speak to local union leaders and members. After Mazey bluntly told them to cut out "monkey business" that hurt production, Vance met personally with union leaders to reiterate that slowdown tactics would not increase Studebaker wages, which were already the industry's highest. Both Vance and Peterson, who rejected Ford's job offer, felt that as a result of that effort, labor performance would improve.

Only after becoming chairman did Hoffman discover that Vance's rosy picture did not tell the true story. Extraordinary conditions during the Korean War had made Studebaker appear healthier than it really was: earnings depended too heavily on defense contracts that had now ended, and operating capital depended too much on provisions of the Defense Production Act. Without loans of $100 million, the largest under that law, Studebaker would have recorded a whopping loss in 1952. The company's share of the car market, over 4 percent between 1948 and 1951, had fallen below 3 percent.[18]

Nor did the 1953 models, which had seemed so promising, halt the decline in sales. Bad luck and managerial blunders had combined to waste a good opportunity. What Vance described as "tooling problems" had created a gigantic mess: lacking adequate capital to pay for new dies for both chassis and body, Vance and his top managers had tried to cut corners by modifying the old chassis to accommodate the new body. They set up the assembly line without sufficient experimentation and then discovered that the front-end sheet metal did not fit the chassis. Dealers ultimately refitted brand-new, factory-delivered cars in their own body shops.

Besides the production problems, which included a ten-week delay in obtaining transmissions because of a strike at Borg-Warner, its supplier, Studebaker suffered from other managerial miscalculations. For one thing, management decided to build the same proportion of sedans and coupes in 1953 as in the previous year, ignoring warnings from Raymond Loewy's staff that sedans with coupe styling looked ghastly. As a result, Studebaker could not build enough of the beautiful coupes while demand was strong, and dealers had to try to sell ugly sedans. As angry customers canceled many of the early orders, morale among dealers sank.

When he became chairman, Hoffman began to discover the nature of Studebaker's sales problems. In addition to customers' letters of complaint, he received firsthand reports from his son Lathrop, who owned a three-store dealership in southern California. Characteristically, he responded by recommending that Studebaker hire an outside polling organization to conduct a systematic survey of public opinion. Sound merchandizing, he reminded longtime vice-president Kenneth B. Elliott, required knowledge of the facts. Studebaker had to know more about its customers, its dealers, and the public.[19]

To restore the kind of relationship with dealers he had earlier nurtured, he toured the country with Vance and vice-president Chester K. Whittaker to listen to dealers' complaints and seek their advice about model designs and quality. Vance found that such meetings made him more aware of the dealers' problems and boosted their morale. Moreover, Studebaker's top managers promises to stop regarding dealers as merely captive selling outlets.[20]

A big part of Studebaker's problem was its uncompetitive retail prices, which were due to excessively high labor costs. While most Detroit automakers were introducing automation and thereby reducing the numbers of semiskilled workers—reportedly the most militant—Studebaker failed to keep pace technologically. While the once aggressive union steward system atrophied in the Detroit plants, and management asserted stricter discipline on the factory floors, Studebaker continued to rely on traditions of craftsmanship and worker loyalty—but according to both management and union leaders, new workers (especially university students in South Bend) were failing to perform their jobs properly. As a result of what competitors regarded as Studebaker's weak management, it was paying higher wages for lower productivity and poorer work.[21]

Hoffman and Vance realized that until they could upgrade technology, Studebaker had to take "drastic action" to make workers perform more efficiently. To raise the quality of the cars, they decided to establish a better system of inspection. To reduce costs, they decided to change the wage structure. What they proposed meant taking money and privileges away from workers accustomed to generous policies, but much as they hoped to avoid hostile confrontation, Hoffman and Vance were ready to risk that possibility.[22]

Studebaker's internal problems could not have surfaced at a worse time. By mid-1953 the nation's economy was slipping into a recession that turned the sellers' market into a buyers' market. For the small automakers, competitive pressures became particularly ferocious when the new car models appeared in the fall. Ford tried aggressive tactics to challenge the top market position of Chevrolet. Known as "the blitz," the fight between Ford and GM increased car output and forced new cars on dealers still trying to sell 1953 models.

Many dealers responded to those pressures by resorting to unethical sales schemes. Some lured customers with variations of "bait-and-switch" tactics, "packed" prices by adding on extra charges or by recalculating price or trade-in estimates, and used deceptive installment payment contracts for new buyers unfamiliar with car financing. Unwanted cars were bootlegged to nonfranchise dealers who could sell at cut-rate prices because they did not provide proper preparation or service. Such tactics angered customers and hurt honest dealers operating with low profit margins.

Hoffman responded on two levels to the changes in the business climate. In a burst of excessive optimism, he blamed the temporary downturn on talk about a national recession that could become self-fulfilling. If people had confidence, the country could avoid recession and serious unemployment. "There is absolutely nothing wrong with our economy," he declared in the booster's language, "that a higher volume of hard-hitting advertising and sales promotion by business, and good creative salesmen, could not cure."[23]

To help counteract dangerous pessimism, Hoffman expanded his role within the Advertising Council. In January of 1954, after becoming chairman of its public policy committee, he went to Washington to confer with President Eisenhower. Then he announced that public confidence had already improved. To carry the Advertising Council's optimistic platitudes to the rest of the nation, Hoffman also narrated a half-hour film entitled *The Future of America*, which all three television networks aired.[24]

On a different level, he urged the automotive industry to practice restraint. Although he had always preached the virtues of competition and high production, he urged automakers to limit production to volumes that vigorous, intelligent, and honest salesmanship could sell at profits for retailers. Hoffman, who possessed "more sales experience and savvy" than anyone in the business—according to George Romney, recently elevated to the top position at Nash—urged car dealers to operate by "just plain honest dealing." Razzle-dazzle tactics merely confused the public, demoralized the market, and wrecked dealerships. Salesmen had to learn to use good old-fashioned selling methods.[25]

Within a dealer network threatened by defections to other automakers, Hoffman reasserted the Friendly Factory theme. Top Studebaker management, he told dealers, took seriously their complaints and problems. He reminded them that his son Lathrop faced the same problems: despite cutting his operating costs, cleverly customizing new cars, and reentering the used car business, Lathrop's southern California dealership lost $85,000 in 1953. Nevertheless, the family put another $100,000 into the business so that he could acquire a store in Beverly Hills. That kind of investment showed the family's confidence that Studebaker would regain profitability.[26]

To address Studebaker's internal problems with labor management and quality control, Hoffman hired Anna M. Rosenberg Associates. Mrs. Rosenberg, whom he had known for years through William Benton and the Encyclopaedia Britannica board on which they served, specialized in the organization and efficient use of manpower. During the Korean War, she had served as an assistant secretary of defense under George C. Marshall. A liberal Democrat, she had a reputation for bluntness but also for friendliness toward labor.[27]

Mrs. Rosenberg gave Hoffman sound advice about how to restore the confidence of dealers and customers in the quality of Studebaker products. She recommended that Vance reaffirm the corporation's commitment to traditional quality by using a new production code and a seal that declared, "We Stand Behind the Quality of This Car"; that the president of Local 5, Louis Horvath, speak out about the workers' determination to live up to that standard; and that in his own speeches Hoffman emphasize the uniqueness of the company's craftsmanship in the machine age. She felt that Studebaker could gain respect by stressing that theme because "America has become a symbol of the biggest, the newest and, the shiniest—but not necessarily the best."[28]

Thus in speeches and in correspondence, Hoffman asserted that Studebaker had already achieved spectacular improvements in the quality of its vehicles. He frankly admitted recent defects caused by hasty expansion of the workforce from about 10,000 to more than double that number. He insisted, however, that Vance, Peterson, and their aides, in cooperation with the union, had found out how to instill the traditional spirit of craftsmanship. He assured Dewey Smith, Studebaker's sales representative in Asia, that "for the first time in years both supervisory personnel and the men in our factory are facing the facts of life."[29] They realized that good quality had to be built into cars, not inspected in.

About the 1954 Studebakers, he declared that no automakers offered better cars at *any* price. Designed and engineered for functional beauty, they were the only truly modern cars on the market. He personally enjoyed driving the sleek new Studebakers and rejected cricitism that they were underpowered, overpriced, and too European in appearance. Loewy's design was thoroughly American, resembling GM's dream cars—even far ahead of them according to Howard A. Darrin, former designer for Kaiser-Frazer. With its low center of gravity and light weight, the Champion provided greater safety, visibility, comfort, and fuel economy than did its larger competitors. Bowing to current tastes, Studebaker did "reluctantly" advertise the ratio of engine size to car weight; by that standard its 120-horsepower engine was not puny or lacking in reserve power.[30]

Hoffman wanted salesmen to emphasize those distinctive features for prospective car buyers. Recognizing the weaknesses of the 1953 sedans, he pushed the new coupe as a "sports car for the family." Salesmen had to show young couples, perhaps with two or three children, that the coupe would serve them better than a larger sedan. If they presented the facts properly, the Champion's higher price, always an obstacle in the market, would not seriously hurt sales. (By the late 1970s, one automotive publication had agreed with him, calling the 1953–54 Studebaker coupes, with their excellent and timeless styling, "beyond any question . . . the best buys today among all cars of the '50s.")[31]

Quite naturally, current talk about the plight of small automakers annoyed Hoffman. He claimed that Studebaker's management recognized its problems but was not overly concerned. After all, in the mid-1930s it had survived a worse crisis in spite of Wall Street predictions of failure. And just as small steel firms had competed well against giants in that industry, small automakers could achieve similar success. Hoffman still believed that small firms could hold their own against much larger by providing customers service and products as good as or better than the much larger companies were offering.[32]

Despite his enthusiasm and brave hopes, as Studebaker moved into 1954 its economic picture got bleaker. The "slugging contest" Ford initiated against GM disorganized the market with a flood of cars; while that "vicious dog fight" continued, the entire business suffered. With catastrophic declines in its sales and profits, Studebaker saw its capital reserve reduced almost by half.

Shaken by those circumstances, the board asked Hoffman to step in and help Vance run Studebaker. At the time, his wife Dorothy was very ill at their home in southern California, and he had no great desire to resume full administrative responsibilities. Certainly, the business was no longer fun. But out of a sense of obligation, he again subjected himself to a rigorous schedule and criticism from investors, dealers, and dissatisfied customers.

At the insistence of Chet Whittaker, Hoffman devoted himself to the effort of selling cars and had little time for anything else. He believed that the solution to one of Studebaker's problems was to match its superior products with superior merchandizing. The corporation needed more and better advertising, sales promotion, and training for salesmen. Like many businesses during the 1950s, it shifted advertising from magazines—which were then beginning to disappear—to other media, especially television.[33] It employed Hill & Knowlton, one of the largest public relations firms, to improve its image by concentrating on quality.

No amount of advertising, sales promotion, and public relations, however, could withstand the economic tide sweeping the automotive industry. As Studebaker's sales plunged below a 2 percent market share and losses mounted, bankers pushed management toward merger. Hoffman had always preached the benefits of the small and creative corporation; during the sellers' market of the 1940s, he had told Vance that Studebaker should consider merger only if it could buy Packard at a bargain price. But with new market conditions, in the fall of 1953 he started to pursue merger with Packard himself, even though Harold Vance predicted that Studebaker sales would rebound without it.

The first round of negotiations between Studebaker and Packard reached an impasse. James J. Nance, Packard's aggressive young president, recognized that merger could help overcome the serious disadvantages of his small company, but he had not decided whether to pursue Studebaker or Nash. As rumors circulated, Hoffman publicly admitted that an overture had been made and that merger, while not imminent, was yet possible.[34]

The second round of negotiations found both parties more eager. At Studebaker, the failure of Vance's predictions of a sales upturn had undercut his resistance to the plan. At Packard, James Nance decided he needed Studebaker when he realized that Nash was taking over Hudson to form American Motors. Thus on 22 June 1954, a meeting between the leaders of the two firms at the Waldorf-Astoria produced a public announcement of merger. Technically, Packard bought out Studebaker to create the new Studebaker-Packard Corporation. Hoffman became chairman of the board and Vance chairman of the executive committee, but operating power went to James Nance as president of the new company.

When the arrangement was made, Hoffman felt renewed confidence. In his view, Studebaker-Packard held "much promise," and he claimed that his biggest reason for seeking merger was to bring in Nance, whom he called "one of the most competent younger executives in the automobile business." Nance would head the world's fourth largest automaker, with a net worth over $175 million and the capacity to offer, as GM had long claimed, vehicles for every purse and every purpose. Publicly, Hoffman evaded suggestions that Studebaker-Packard could survive only by still another merger with American Motors, and George Romney, head of American Motors, certainly did not want it; he merely wished the new corporation well.[35]

Before Studebaker and Packard completed their arrangements on 1 October 1954, Hoffman and Vance had to negotiate a new labor contract. They fully realized that Studebaker's labor costs, despite previous efforts, remained quite out of line and contributed to noncompetitive prices, resulting in a loss of car sales and the company's last defense contract. The workforce had been cut to less than 11,000, and even those had had their hours reduced, but failure to improve labor efficiency further would jeopardize the merger with Packard and leave Studebaker in a desperate situation.

Unfortunately, Hoffman and Vance tried to cut wages at a time when Studebaker sales suddenly increased. What workers did not know and what management preferred to keep confidential was that in June, Studebaker had started giving bonuses to dealers to keep them afloat: the bonuses had enabled dealers to cut retail prices and thus to boost sales. But Studebaker could not continue that policy because it was losing money by selling below its costs.[36]

During July and August, while he had to contend with the Reece Committee and other McCarthyite assaults, Hoffman engaged almost every day in strenuous negotiations with leaders of Local 5. He opened Studebaker's books to them and explained why management needed significant wage concessions and greater prerogatives to tighten work standards. Accused by one union official of seeking "everything except the Union Hall," he insisted that Studebaker was trying to save the workers' jobs by preventing bankruptcy. Even the changes he proposed left the company at a "substantial disadvantage" that could be offset only by a spirit of teamwork and dedication to good work. In return for cooperation, he pledged to union president Louis Horvath that Studebaker would lower car prices in the hope of increasing sales and would seek to maximize workers' incomes by overtime before hiring additional workers.[37]

Once management and union leaders had agreed on the terms of the new contract, Hoffman published a newspaper ad to promote ratification among union members, explaining the terms of the contract and the merger with Packard. Union president Horvath, however, apparently because of the lengthy negotiations, had neglected to prepare his membership to accept a 14 percent wage reduction and new work rules. Meanwhile, Hovarth's longtime rival and former local president William Ogden was mobilizing opposition to the concessions. With only about 4,000 of the 10,700 eligible members participating, Local 5 stunned both union leaders and Studebaker's management by rejecting the contract by a three-to-two margin.

Studebaker responded the next day by announcing that it would terminate the existing contract in sixty days if the union did not reconsider. Then, as Hoffman predicted, the fireworks really started. For him, the tension day and night became terrible.[38] With the Packard merger at stake, management had no choice but to publicize Studebaker's plight in the hope of bringing the workers around.

In South Bend, rumors circulated that Studebaker would consolidate all work at Packard facilities around Detroit. From UAW headquarters, Walter Reuther and Emil Mazey urged union members in South Bend to accept the company's offer. Officials of Local 5, although they felt that they were committing political suicide within the union, displayed what Hoffman called responsible labor leadership. According to Louis Horvath, campaigning for ratification was "the hardest thing that we labor leaders ever had to do."[39] Finally, two weeks after the first vote, 6,000 members met at a high school football field and ratified the contract by a more than an eight-to-one margin.

By reversing its pattern of generosity and weakness, Studebaker had apparently achieved a great victory over high costs. The union's vote reaffirmed Hoffman's belief that collective bargaining contributed to business vitality, productivity, and democracy. He claimed that worker morale at Studebaker was excellent and that management had experienced less difficulty than it had anticipated in implementing its tighter work rules.[40] Yet the substantial savings achieved by the 1954 settlement still failed to make the company's labor costs competitive.

By the time Studebaker consummated its merger with Packard, Hoffman had spent an interesting but very demanding 150 days in South Bend. He came away from that concentrated effort feeling that the new corporation had a genuine chance to succeed and even to battle Chrysler for the industry's third position. Led by "complete realists" who understood the problems, it could improve its situation, he told a writer from *Fortune*, within six months.[41]

With the creation of Studebaker-Packard, Hoffman again said that he wanted to serve as a useful but not overly active chairman.[42] He hoped that under James Nance the corporation would not demand so much from him. Perhaps only on that account he was not disappointed by Nance's administration, for the Packard man had no intention of sharing executive authority with the leaders of Studebaker.

Very quickly, Nance discovered that Studebaker's plight was much worse than he had been led to believe. Pushed by labor costs nearly double the industry average, its break-even point was much higher than previous estimates, and the new president came to feel that Hoffman and Vance had deceived him and sold him damaged property. To rectify the situation, he decided to bring about sweeping changes.[43]

Like Hoffman and Vance he tried to reduce operating costs, especially for labor, but unlike them he was ready for a fight. Pointing out to union leaders that the Studebaker division lost money on

Paul G. Hoffman as Studebaker vice president, in the late
1920s. Discovery Hall Archival Collections

Hoffman, as president of the
Automobile Safety Founda-
tion, speaks on highway
safety at the Advertising
Club's Auto Show, 1937.
Discovery Hall Archival
Collections

Hoffman, Chief Justice Frederick M. Vinson, and President Truman at swearing-in ceremony, April 1948. United Press International, courtesy Harry S. Truman Library

Hoffman and Ambassador Averell Harriman confer with Rep. Charles Eaton before testifying on ECA's budget appropriation for 1949. International News Photo, courtesy National Archives

every car it produced, he sent time-study experts to South Bend and formulated new work rules to raise productivity. Local 5 responded in January by voting nine to one for a strike. Though management "won" the thirty-six day walkout, during 1955 unauthorized work stoppages plagued the factory.

Why did such problems persist in what was supposed to be the Friendly Factory? In March of 1955, manpower specialist Anna Rosenberg offered an explanation. Her report amplified her previous criticism that Studebaker lacked programs to train supervisors and to communicate with workers. Morale among supervisory personnel was low. Foremen, in particular, felt intimidated by the power of union stewards and the failure of their superiors to back them. As a result, the labor agreement was not being implemented, and factory discipline and efficiency remained poor. Although her report did not say so, she held Vance responsible for those conditions.[44]

James Nance had his own ideas about how to correct that mess. In January of 1956 he finally ended the incentive pay system and the incredibly disruptive "chain bumping" that had prevailed in the South Bend plant.[45] But after years of management leniency, his cost-cutting methods generated a backlash of antagonism that slowed production.

Nance repudiated not only Hoffman's labor policy but also his vision of car design. Hoffman had sought to give Studebaker attractive and distinctively styled cars, and to sell them by emphasizing safety and economy of operation. In 1953 he suggested that American automakers might again have to borrow innovations from European competitors, as they had earlier in the century. According to him, Americans needed a new, sensible, and advanced type of car. Raymond Loewy, whose $1 million contract was reportedly the biggest single industrial design account in the industry, thoroughly agreed that the independents should offer distinctive cars that would attract customers dissatisfied with the products of the Big Three. In his view, overdressed, square cars were on their way out, and Studebaker had the opportunity to pioneer in car design.[46]

Instead of taking the approach advocated by Hoffman and Loewy, however, Nance decided to meet the competition by imitating it. In August of 1954, even before he formally took charge, Studebaker announced that its new models would be flashier and more powerful. Early in 1955, Nance ended Studebaker's twenty-year relationship with Loewy—who had accepted less than he could have demanded

out of loyalty to Hoffman and to Studebaker. In the era when Virgil
Exner gave Chrysler its "Forward Look," Studebaker was "going Detroit." It gambled on an expensive new model called the Predictor—
only to discover that it could not afford to produce the car.[47]

Without executive authority over the operation of Studebaker-
Packard, Hoffman viewed Nance's administration with growing
alarm. Nance later claimed that in January of 1955, Hoffman phoned
him from Palm Springs in an effort to persuade him to soften his
labor policy and to prevent a strike.[48] Certainly, Hoffman did give
unsolicited advice about how the corporation should be run.

That advice emphasized the importance of good human relations
for a small automaker. He did not want Studebaker-Packard to imi-
tate GM and Ford by treating dealers as mere outlets and workers as
mere numbers. After the strike began in January, he warned that
workers already felt that the corporation regarded them merely as
"labor" to be dealt with as natural antagonists. Hoffman recommended that, instead, Nance should operate Studebaker-Packard as
a Friendly Factory, treating all parties as members of a team. Flatter-
ing Nance as a "warm and friendly person," he urged him to project
and communicate that personality through a systematic program,
perhaps developed in consultation with Hill & Knowlton or Anna
Rosenberg or himself.[49]

With respect to its distribution policies, Hoffman told Nance that
Studebaker-Packard needed a painful reevaluation. In view of the
continued growth of suburbs, about which Hoffman had been so enthusiastic, it had to reconsider the effectiveness of downtown dealerships in metropolitan areas. It had to discover how customers' attitudes toward the manufacturer and service affected their buying
habits. To answer such questions, he recommended the employment
of an outside expert on market research.

As president of the corporation, James Nance resented the advice
and the implied criticism of his administration. He followed his own
course and did not even reply to Hoffman's correspondence. However, he did see that the corporation might benefit from the experience of Hoffman and Vance; Hoffman especially had connections
that could help bring in business. For all his belief in competitive
free enterprise and eventual disarmament, Hoffman did not shun
using his connections to solicit government contracts. In August of
1953, he tried to promote sales, for example, in South Korea. Keeping his role confidential and in the background, he wanted Tyler

Wood—his former director of operations in the ECA and then economic coordinator of rehabilitation in Korea—to know that he had a personal interest in seeing that the United Nations Korean Rehabilitation Agency bought Studebaker trucks.[50]

After the merger, Hoffman eagerly sought to regain defense contracts, which he knew helped automakers spread their big overhead. Devoting himself exclusively to that part of the business, in the spring of 1955 he went to Washington and saw "nearly everyone." As a result, President Eisenhower asked Secretary of Defense Charles E. Wilson to discuss with Hoffman and Vance the possibility of government contracts for Studebaker-Packard. Before the end of 1955 the company had lined up contracts worth about $60 million but still needed $40 million more. Hoffman reported that Pratt & Whitney, the airplane engine manufacturer, was using "every trick and device" imaginable to prevent Studebaker-Packard from subcontracting jet engines, but after speaking about that matter with the Secretary of the Air Force, he felt that he had made some headway.[51]

Despite the contracts and Nance's retrenchment program, Studebaker-Packard found by early 1956 that it could not continue to operate without a $100 million loan. When bankers and insurance investors refused to extend that money, the corporation teetered on the brink of the biggest industrial collapse in American history. Nance scrambled for a way to shore it up through merger or sale.

For Hoffman the situation was particularly ugly. Deeply concerned, he felt frustrated and shackled by his lack of real authority. Like Vance, who joined the Atomic Energy Commission, and P.O. Peterson, who became president of Mack Truck, he might have left in 1955 had he not felt a sense of obligation because he helped to bring about the merger that had put Nance in charge. Thus he remained chairman, not even receiving compensation after February of 1956. Meanwhile, some stockholders abused him as an "international politician" and sought to block his reelection as chairman. Very pessimistic, he told President Eisenhower in April that he stayed on only to preserve the dealer organization and to raise capital.[52]

For some time, the President had involved himself because he believed that the survival of Studebaker-Packard was in the best interests of the economy as a whole. Doubtless reflecting what Hoffman had told him, he blamed the Big Three for blind hardheadedness in overproducing cars and thus weakening the market. He asked Secretary of Defense Wilson, who had previously been president of GM for eleven years, to discuss with the Big Three the possibility of shifting contracts to Studebaker-Packard, or buying some of its less efficient plants. However, no other automaker was interested in such arrangements.

Dealing with a difficult situation and difficult people, Studebaker-Packard found a solution: on 6 July 1956, after the Defense Department promised contracts worth $200 million, aircraft-engine producer Curtiss-Wright took over Studebaker-Packard (including its big tax write-off). It was both a sad and a happy day for Hoffman. Involved behind the scenes in the negotiations, he found the tough terms far from what he wanted. Though Studebaker was still much a part of him, he severed all association with it and sold most of his stock. A year later, after sustaining considerable losses, his son Lathrop closed the dealership in southern California.[53]

Much to his pleasure, however, Curtiss-Wright replaced Nance with Harold Churchill, who had been a valuable member of Studebaker's engineering department since the 1930s. Hoffman regarded Churchill as a man of integrity, courage, and unusual capacity for hard work. Reminding him of how they had pulled Studebaker through the receivership, Hoffman told Churchill that the formula successful then could succeed again. He hoped that Churchill would restore friendly relationships and would seek to build cars that could compete against those of the Big Three by their distinctiveness.[54]

Under Harold Churchill, Studebaker did make a brief recovery by scaling down its operations and by introducing an economical compact car, the Lark. It could not sustain itself, however, within the rapidly changing automotive industry. After further managerial shifts, it stopped automobile production in the early 1960s.

Studebaker's size alone contributed much to that failure. In the competitive market that followed the end of the Korean War, the Big Three enjoyed substantial price advantages over other automakers. With smaller volumes, the independents suffered from higher costs in advertising, transportation, and other elements of distribution. They could not survive errors of managerial judgment as Ford had survived the Edsel.

Many commentators have blamed Studebaker's management for tolerating excessively high labor costs. Even some of the former officials of Local 5, though regarding Hoffman and Vance as decent and humane, concluded that they neglected the balance sheets and thus failed both the stockholders and the employees. Hoffman had often said it was out of self-interest that the small company had to cultivate superior human relations by treating workers with decency and fairness. But when Studebaker enjoyed strong sales during the late 1940s and early 1950s, he and especially Vance had failed to get a fair return for those policies. By the time Hoffman returned in 1953, Studebaker suffered from work standards too loose for it to compete.[55]

During the nineteen months when he served as chairman of Studebaker, Hoffman did push Vance into corrective action. He tried to shore up the dealer network and to base policy more on systematic market research than on guesswork and tradition. But in the new economy after the Korean War, Hoffman's efforts were too little too late.

Like the leaders of other independents, Hoffman recognized that survival depended upon merger. He started with high hopes and confidence but, quickly discovering that he and James Nance were "miles apart" in their views about business, concluded that Nance's administration had been "utterly disastrous." Venting his own frustration, he told Chet Whittaker, "Never again will I permit myself to be put in a postion of responsibility without adequate authority."[56]

Hoffman's final assessment of Nance was correct but came too late. By turning Studebaker over to Nance, he had made a very serious error of judgment. Nance's hard line on labor policy replaced laxity with severity but failed to achieve the desired results. His decision for Studebaker-Packard to compete with the Big Three across a full price range abandoned Hoffman's more realistic goal of producing distinctive cars that could find a profitable niche in a competitive market. American Motors under George Romney adopted a small-car strategy and at least survived as an automaker.[57] Then foreign competitors entered the American market and proved how profitable that niche could become.

Out of the automotive industry after July of 1956, Hoffman found other pursuits to occupy himself. The family firm his father had started, the Hoffman Specialty Manufacturing Corporation, was still operating profitably. He remained a member of the board of the Encyclopaedia Britannica, which William Benton tried to make the GM of publishing. And he was still fighting battles for the Fund for the Republic. More important, by then he had decided to devote himself to what he called "trying to save the world."[58]

8 "Waging Peace" With Trade and Aid

For the first six years of Eisenhower's presidency, even while chairman of Studebaker and chairman of the Fund for the Republic, Hoffman stood close to the administration as a voice for liberal internationalism. A personal friend of the President and an acquaintance of many key members of the administration, he gently coaxed and prodded them to "wage peace" by enlightened policies. In particular, he sought to alert the administration, Congress, and the American public to the changes sweeping across Asia and Africa. He did not want the United States to stand on the side of reactionaries and imperialists obstructing the pursuit of progress and social justice.

Essentially a popularizer and conduit for expert opinions, Hoffman had nothing original or unique to say about America's global obligations. His views were shaped by his contacts through the CED, the Marshall Plan, and the Ford Foundation. During the 1950s, he leaned heavily on the new experts in economic development, particularly the collaborative work of MIT economists Max F. Millikan, who had served on the staff of the Harriman Committee, and W. W. Rostow, who had served with the Economic Commission for Europe. Sophisticated anti-Communists, they urged that the United States adopt liberal trade and economic aid policies to assist the evolution of stable, effective, and democratic societies abroad. America could not seek narrow-minded and short-term goals of winning friends or creating quick profits.[1]

Hoffman, too, advocated combining liberal trade policies with economic aid for the development of the poor countries. A business-oriented progressive, he believed that the policies of the United States should expand the world economy for the benefit of all countries. In that way, it could strengthen democracy and help to halt the spread of Communism. Unlike economic nationalists and protectionists, he did not fear that foreign competition would flood the American market with manufactured goods produced abroad; if foreign competition did displace some Americans, the domestic economy had the capacity to adapt. In any case, decency and morality called for the United States to take action to help alleviate human misery abroad.

Although conservatives often regarded Hoffman as a foolish gadfly for liberal causes, or worse, President Eisenhower appreciated his friend's views. During one controversy, he told a press conference, "I admire the man and his opinions; I listen to him."[2] Sometimes he used Hoffman as a sounding board or as an unofficial voice for policies the administration wanted to air. Hoffman certainly did not exercise the great influence on U.S. policies that right-wing critics attributed to him, but he did provide a significant counterweight against more conservative and nationalistic opinions that reached the President.

President Eisenhower did not need Hoffman to persuade him of the desirability of liberalizing world trade. He too hoped that a liberal trade policy and private investment abroad would strengthen the Western economy. And just as Hoffman argued, the President eventually recognized that the U.S. must also provide economic aid for the less-developed countries. His problem in attempting to do so, as he often told Hoffman, came from entrenched interest groups and protectionists, especially within the Republican Party, who stood vigilant against what they regarded as global giveaway programs.[3]

Because of Hoffman's well-known reputation as an advocate for aid to the new and economically underdeveloped countries, Eisenhower offered to appoint him Ambassador to India in the summer of 1954. Hoffman wanted to take on that assignment; he often said that the U.S. had to ensure India's success as the chief democratic alternative in Asia to the example set by Communist China. However, his commitments at home, particularly the merger of Studebaker with Packard, prevented his accepting the ambassadorship. Nor could he accept a special economic mission of the sort proposed by Secretary of State John Foster Dulles.[4]

When Curtiss-Wright took control of Studebaker-Packard in June of 1956, however, Hoffman ceased to occupy a demanding position in business. He then had to decide how to spend the rest of his life.

His wife Dorothy, in declining health, refused to leave southern California. He could have settled into a comfortable retirement with her in Pasadena and at their ranch in Palm Springs, but although he often talked about the joys of a leisurely life, he could not find satisfaction in daily rounds of golf and gin rummy with his many friends. He had come to expect a different kind of challenge and did not want to give up the habit of achievement.

Hoffman tried to explain his problem to White House chief of staff Sherman Adams. He said that a person who stopped growing started dying. Six months younger than the President and in excellent health, he was unwilling to start dying. He did not want to ask the President for a job; he just wanted to let him know that he was available to take on assignments that would tax his capabilities and his talents.[5] Even though public service provided less opportunity than business to make money and required long hours for those in top positions, such disadvantages were outweighed by the satisfaction of dealing with affairs of great importance. "There is no sacrifice involved in public service," he declared.[6] When he made that statement, he obviously hoped to find another challenge in public affairs.

Fortunately for him, just such an opportunity appeared. At the urging of Ambassador Henry Cabot Lodge, President Eisenhower nominated Hoffman to become a public delegate with the U.S. Mission to the United Nations General Assembly. At the time, Hoffman claimed that he had no advance knowledge of the nomination and that if he had, he probably would have declined the opportunity. When the nomination brought vicious new attacks from right-wingers, however, he decided to fight for the job.[7]

During the debate over his nomination, he told one of his sons that "some extremists on the right have been and are doing their best to make life rough for me." Senator McCarthy, no longer a political power but still a venomous character assassin, proclaimed that the U.N. appointment would elevate Hoffman from "a crackpot to a menace." His ally Styles Bridges of New Hampshire attacked Hoffman for past associations with people he called questionable characters.[8]

In the news media, right-wing commentators tried to generate a public tide against Hoffman. Fulton Lewis, Jr., kept up his usual barrage. John T. Flynn called Hoffman the perfect model of the individual who, ashamed of being a lowbrow moneymaker, posed as a political philosopher and ended up professing the "goofy philosophy" that served Communists and socialists. Subscribers to *National Review*, a new conservative magazine, launched a letter-writing campaign. "Please clean up the stink," one letter to Hoffman requested. "Ike has enough to carry without lugging you around, have the guts to lighten his load."[9]

The main issue was not Hoffman but Eisenhower's leadership. By nominating his friend, the President served notice that he would not permit the Old Guard to hold a veto over his appointments or to shape his foreign policy. In 1948, President Truman had mustered bipartisan support for the Marshall Plan, and the Senate had unanimously approved Hoffman's appointment. During the 1950s, however, the situation changed. Foreign policy had become not an issue of political debate but the target of political vendettas.

On 20 July 1956, the Senate voted on the appointment of Hoffman to the U.N. delegation. By writing in advance to Republican Senate leader William Knowland that he, too, opposed the admission of "Red China" to the U.N., Hoffman removed one potential obstacle, and the Senate approved the nomination by a bipartisan majority of 64 to 22. A hard core of sixteen McCarthyite Republicans and six Southern Democratic segregationists voted against him. One supporter noted with glee that the vote showed "the dwindling size of the atavistic group." Hoffman himself said that he "was proud of his support but would have settled for fewer enemies."[10] In any case, he would have the challenge of public service he so obviously wanted.

When Hoffman joined the U.S. Mission as a public delegate in the fall of 1956, the American attitude toward the United Nations showed less than unqualified enthusiasm. The U.N. was beset by chronic crises, bickering, hair-splitting formalities, and torrential rhetoric. The U.S. State Department and foreign service officers held it in low esteem. The appointment of public delegates to the U.S. Mission allowed the President to cultivate members of Congress and to give honorific patronage to political supporters without demanding much of substance from them.

Hoffman found matters quite different, however. During the Eleventh General Assembly the U.N. became not just a forum for discussion but a focal point for serious diplomatic negotiations to resolve conflicts around the world. Like the ECA during its first year, the

U.S. Mission seemed to face a crisis almost every hour. When the session ended in the spring of 1957, Hoffman looked back on a thoroughly interesting and exciting experience.[11]

Most of the General Assembly's attention had been riveted on the concurrent crises in the Middle East and Hungary, but other controversial issues also intruded on the agenda. Cyprus and Kashmir revealed the clashes of rival national claims, and Algeria demonstrated the continuing struggle of subject peoples against colonialism. Ambassador Henry Cabot Lodge initially assigned Hoffman the task of explaining the U.S. position on Algeria but then decided to take over that politically sensitive debate himself. He asked Hoffman to concentrate instead on the issue that most interested him: economic development for poor and underdeveloped nations.[12]

Hoffman seemed particularly well suited to deal with that issue. From his experiences with the ECA and the Ford Foundation and his subsequent travels, he enjoyed a wide network of contacts with leaders in Europe and Asia. Furthermore, he was known as a strong supporter of aid for economic development and of the U.N. technical assistance program. His personal closeness with Ambassador Lodge and, more important, with President Eisenhower seemed to make him someone who could speak with authority for the United States.

When Lodge assigned him to handle the issue of economic development assistance, Hoffman discovered that it had already become highly charged with emotions and politics. The underdeveloped countries were demanding the creation of a Special United Nations Fund for Economic Development (SUNFED). Proponents wanted countries to contribute about $250 million for capital investments, according to their means, but they did not want large contributors like the United States to control the agency the way they controlled the World Bank and the International Monetary Fund.

The U.S. Mission faced the difficult task of reconciling those demands with the position of the Eisenhower administration. Ambassador Lodge, sensitive to the political situation, proposed that the U.S. support a smaller U.N. program to assist the poor countries in building their so-called infrastructures—basic facilities that did not yield immediate revenues. He reportedly told members of his staff to work out details for a tame alternative to SUNFED. Like Lodge, Hoffman realized that an appealing alternative was needed for the popular but "dubious" SUNFED proposal. He joined Lodge in urging the President to go to the U.N. to announce a bold new development program, including modest American participation in a multilateral aid program.[13]

Convinced that the U.N. had to do more to assist economic development, he made the centerpiece of his own proposal an emphasis on resource surveys preceding capital investments. He urged the administration to support the creation of a special new agency, to be operated by the U.N. Secretariat, that would conduct preinvestment surveys in the underdeveloped countries. He even went so far as to arrange for the U.S. to hold a veto over the personnel and the operations of such an agency. And he assured Secretary of State Dulles that such an aid program, if "properly packaged," would find a "vast reservoir of latent support" in the United States.[14]

President Eisenhower and Secretary of State Dulles seemed to agree about the need for a constructive foreign aid program but felt frustrated. The shortsightedness and demagoguery of isolationists, according to the President, restricted his freedom to act. To win public approval, the administration had to make each of its proposals sound, sensible, simple, and easily understood. With Hoffman's aid proposal the President sought the opinion of Secretary of the Treasury George Humphrey. A bright, friendly, and plain-talking businessman whom Hoffman knew from their work on the Marshall Plan, Humphrey viewed with hostility any multilateral aid that did not return clear gains for the United States and for the private enterprise system.[15]

Hoffman agreed with Humphrey that private American investments would provide mutual benefits for all. But despite tax concessions and other government assistance, American businesses shunned investing in poor countries, except within oil and mining "extractive nations." Private investment lagged, he thought, in part because of the high risks and fear of the unknown. Therefore, he wanted an aid program that would concentrate on building infrastructures and providing resource surveys or "preinvestment inventories" to push back the statistical fog. That kind of program, which avoided the bottomless needs for consumer goods, would pave the way for private investment.[16]

For the U.S. the benefits from such a program would be twofold. In the long term, it would expand trade and help insulate the underdeveloped countries from Soviet subversion; as they grew stronger, the U.S. could reduce its military expenditures and could strengthen its own economy. In the short term, he claimed, the program would greatly enhance American prestige within the U.N. and might even "keep SUNFED from becoming a genuinely troublesome issue in the 12th General Assembly."[17]

Although he failed to persuade George Humphrey, Hoffman's efforts were not in vain. According to Ambassador Lodge, he had displayed an industry, skill, and fine judgment that made him a "veritable tower of strength" within the U.S. Mission. Lodge also advised the President to back his foreign aid proposals. With that urging from both Hoffman and Lodge, the President decided that the United States would have to deal more positively with poor and underdeveloped countries strongly moved by nationalism and rising expectations for a better life.[18]

Eisenhower turned the tide in favor of foreign aid, according to Hoffman, as an effective way of "waging peace." The State Department continued to oppose the creation of SUNFED but approved a plan for a U.N. Special Projects Fund that would include preinvestment operations, as Hoffman had suggested. In November of 1957, Representative Walter Judd, who replaced Hoffman on the U.S. delegation, formally presented the American proposal. The conservative Republican from Minnesota reportedly told Secretary of State Dulles that when the General Assembly adopted the U.S. resolution, it put SUNFED "in cold storage."[19]

For Hoffman, departure from the U.N. meant that he would again have to face the question of what to do with the rest of his life. To avoid loneliness and inactivity, he took a more active interest in the Hoffman Specialty Manufacturing Corporation, the Indianapolis-based business he had inherited from his father. He also served as finance chairman of the Encyclopaedia Britannica and remained involved with the affairs of the CED and the Fund for the Republic. Most important, he threw himself into work for the American Committee on United Europe and "stray jobs" for the U.N., "trying to save the world."[20]

When William J. Donovan, chairman of the American Committee on United Europe since 1949, became seriously ill, Hoffman as vice-chairman took over direction of its work. Early in 1957 he and William Benton spent several weeks in Europe evaluating the activities the committee financed, mainly democratic youth organizations and quiet promotion of the "European Movement." While assessing prospects for a common market, they discussed with

European leaders ways to win popular approval for economic cooperation and unity.[21]

Hoffman returned from Europe full of enthusiasm about the work of the American Committee on United Europe and about prospects for a common market. A Euromarket would extend the shift away from the disastrous policies of economic nationalism and toward economic integration. Western Europe would be able to compete with and keep ahead of the Soviet Union when it embarked, as he thought it would, on the production of consumer goods. Concurrent with NATO's defense effort, a common market would make a stronger Europe and a stronger free world. That combination of economic and military strength, he claimed, would induce the Soviets to negotiate in good faith for the prevention of war.[22]

He hoped that the superpowers could agree to reverse the arms race and to use the money saved from such an agreement to aid the poor and underdeveloped countries. By such policies they could reduce the dangerous instability within the Third World. Waging peace required bold action to address those complex problems.

President Eisenhower applauded Hoffman's readiness to think courageously about such issues but remained skeptical; the search for peace, he reminded Hoffman's eldest son, could not overlook man's ignoble qualities. More specifically, he felt that Communism could not be divorced from the readiness to use violence.[23] Though unable to trust fully in disarmament negotiations, however, the President did agree that the United States needed to wage peace by positive economic policies.

Aware that Hoffman regarded American tariff reductions and a European Common Market as complementary steps toward peace, Eisenhower asked him to run the campaign to build public support for extension of the Trade Agreements Act. In that role he testified before congressional committees and argued that extension of the trade agreement would help to keep Europe from retreating to regional autarky. Freer trade, he claimed, would boost European gross production and make Europe an even more wonderful customer for American products.[24] But neither Hoffman nor the President believed that American trade laws could help solve the problems and the needs of the poor, underdeveloped, and often nonaligned nations.

That issue Hoffman addressed in March of 1958 when he testified on behalf of Senator Mike Monroney's resolution calling for the U.S.

to support the creation of an International Development Association. Arriving in Washington after an overnight flight from California, he told the Senate subcommittee that the U.S. had a strong interest in friendly relations with the less-developed countries because they supplied critical raw materials, because they were the "largest potential consumer's market," and most of all because they had political and strategic importance. The proposed affiliation of the International Development Association with the World Bank would assure "sound, businesslike procedures" and a mechanism for speeding up international trade. Moreover, the multilateral IDA would provide a strong alternative to SUNFED, for which the Soviet Union had become the principal backer.[25]

Throughout the debates, Hoffman praised multilateral foreign aid over bilateral programs. The latter tended, he said, to combine economic and political goals, usually resulting in double failure. By concentrating on economic development without political goals, a multinational institution like the IDA would have a good chance of success. The Senate must have agreed, for it approved the Monroney resolution by a vote of 62 to 25. According to Monroney, Hoffman provided "splendid help" in mobilizing support for the creation of the IDA, which finally began operations in 1960.[26]

After he testified on behalf of the Monroney resolution, Hoffman resumed his work for the American Committee on United Europe. As its chairman, he undertook a written debate with French socialist André Philip and Italian Communist Palmiro Togliatti, whom he called "devilishly clever" with doubletalk. The debate, in which he defended the American economic system as a "genuine people's capitalism," attracted considerable attention in Europe. In the U.S., the American Committee on United Europe reprinted and circulated several thousand copies of the debate so that Americans could better understand the ideological issues behind international relations.[27]

During the summer of 1958, Hoffman undertook another demanding trip to Europe in an effort to ease international tensions. In Brussels he attended a meeting of the World Federation of U.N. Associations. Then he embarked on his first visit to the Soviet Union. In Moscow he met with delegates of the Soviet U.N. Association and with top staff members of the Institute for World Economy and International Relations. The fact that nearly all those he met at the institute could understand English impressed him. They did get "a bit fidgety," he told Senator Monroney, when he discussed the need for new capitalistic institutions.[28]

The Soviet Union impressed him; with its great crusading spirit still strong, it was definitely on the march and making real progress, although he thought that its ideological rigidity, elitism, and bureaucratic conformity would continue to limit its success. The visit did reinforce his belief that Khrushchev wanted peace but would not call off the Cold War on terms acceptable to the free world unless pressured to do so.[29]

In the Soviet Union he joined an old friend, Adlai E. Stevenson. The twice-defeated Democratic presidential candidate was concluding five weeks of exhausting travel in Eastern Europe and the Soviet Union. Calling himself "Ivan the Tired," the fifty-eight-year-old Stevenson could not help noticing that Hoffman, almost ten years his senior but full of energy, loved meetings and travel.[30]

From the Soviet Union they went on together in mid-August to a four-day conference of the World Brotherhood in Bern, Switzerland. Hoffman had arranged for a special group, known as the Working Party, to discuss ways to relax world tensions. Although the conference was difficult to appraise, he felt that it went beyond the anticipated results and had an impact that stretched from the West to behind the Iron Curtain. After conferring with Stevenson, he suggested to India's former Ambassador to the United States, G.L. Mehta, who had presided at the Working Party, that he organize a similar conference for the nonaligned nations.[31]

While engaged in those diverse activities, Hoffman tried to find still other challenges in the area of public affairs. Several times he had wanted to remind President Eisenhower that he was around and available for special assignments. But he decided against that course, he explained to Cabinet staff secretary Maxwell M. Rabb, because he did not want to give the impression that he expected the President, who had other burdens, to find some job for him. He did inform Rabb, a former administrative assistant to Henry Cabot Lodge, that he had a pervasive interest in only one field: progress toward peace.[32]

A week after Hoffman's letter to Rabb, Ambassador Lodge urged President Eisenhower to nominate Hoffman to serve again with the U.S. delegation to the U.N. General Assembly. Lodge claimed that because of his own busy schedule, he needed an individual who was "extraordinarily well-qualified." He felt that Hoffman, with his enormous popularity throughout the country, could gain confirmation in the Senate, where he had very few real enemies. He pointed out to the President that if he did not nominate Hoffman because of Senate opposition, the administration would be unable to use him for any task.[33]

Despite Lodge's best efforts, President Eisenhower reluctantly decided against the nomination, apparently heeding the warnings of the White House liaison with Congress that largely because of an article Hoffman had written for *Collier's* during the 1956 election campaign, the Senate would not confirm the nomination. Lodge held "a private suspicion that a little boldness and warm conviction might have brought confirmation." But he also knew that the administration would have faced a tough battle, which would have further bruised Republican leaders in Congress.[34]

Even without the nomination, conservative Republicans vented their wrath against Hoffman. Senator William Jenner, a McCarthyite from Indiana, called him "an Indiana idiot" who bankrupted Studebaker. Senator George "Molly" Malone declared that he was the only influential presidential advisor who had never succeeded at anything: "He has destroyed everything he has touched." Representative Clare Hoffman of Michigan cited the *Collier's* article as proof that he had insulted Republican members of Congress and that he wanted to become the party's dictator. Fulton Lewis, Jr., added his own gratuitous charge that Hoffman was leading "his ultra-liberal modernist Republicans" in an attempt to take over the party and "get Nixon."[35]

Although he did not rejoin the U.S. Mission, Hoffman did discover another and, in the long run, more important project at the U.N. In December of 1957 the General Assembly had approved a resolution sponsored by the U.S. to create a new U.N. Special Fund as an alternative to SUNFED. The Special Fund, much smaller in scope, would concentrate on helping poor and underdeveloped countries survey their resources and build their infrastructures. And unlike the proposals for SUNFED, it would not be controlled by aid recipients. In fact, Secretary-General Dag Hammarskjold assured Ambassador Lodge that the managing director would be an American acceptable to the U.S. government, which would contribute 40 percent of the funding. As one of the early proponents of such a fund, Hoffman was a logical choice for the top position.

The State Department, however, initially instructed the U.S. del-

egation to support the candidacy of John Davies, an American dip-
lomat not widely known at the U.N. But the Danish delegate lobbied
hard for Hoffman, whose name attracted broad support, and Ambassador Lodge then phoned the State Department and persuaded officials there to make Hoffman the U.S. candidate.[36] That decision de-
lighted Dag Hammarskjold, an old friend of Hoffman's from the
Marshall Plan era.

Hoffman himself was apparently unsure that he wanted a fulltime and demanding job in New York. In late September he tenta-
tively agreed to undertake some work for the project, perhaps only
as a consultant, but in mid-October, Hammarskjold told him that
he already had enough consultants and offered him the position of
managing director. Hoffman delayed accepting the offer and found
that he had to fend off job-seekers, who appeared almost as quickly
as the rumors of his appointment.[37]

Without settling the matter of the Special Fund, he went off with
publisher John Cowles to meetings in India and Hong Kong. His
main goal was to persuade Prime Minister Nehru to play a larger role
in the peace process. He pointed out to Nehru that unless the spread
of nuclear weapons were halted, the whole world might find itself,
to use the title of a then popular novel, "on the Beach."[38]

After returning from Asia, he wrote to Hammarskjold in December of 1958, accepting the position as managing director of the Special Fund. He said that he looked forward to the opportunity to work
with the Secretary-General, World Bank president Eugene Black, and
U.N. officials Philippe de Seynes and David Owen. He saw no possible conflict stemming from his position as a director of the Fund
for the Republic, because that organization confined itself to the
civil liberties field within the United States.[39]

Once Hoffman had accepted the job offer, events at the U.N.
moved quickly. The countries of the Soviet bloc briefly objected to
the appointment, but Hoffman had many friends at the U.N. from
European and Asian delegations, and Hammarskjold insisted upon
his right to have chief aides of his own choosing. Without great turmoil, the General Assembly then confirmed the appointment. Upon
hearing that news, Adlai Stevenson declared that no one he knew
was better equipped to marshal the thought and the moral influence
of leading intellectuals on world problems. "I am sure," Stevenson
predicted, "this influential area of transcendent importance will
stretch wholesomely and lengthily beyond the assignment itself."

Hoffman expressed more modest expectations. He realized that the task of advancing world peace required much more than he could provide. He just hoped that by assisting the underdeveloped countries, the Special Fund could help reduce world tensions.[40]

When he became a top-ranking official of the U.N. Secretariat, Hoffman's relationship with President Eisenhower altered. During the six previous years, he had been the President's liberal conscience on foreign affairs. Because they were friends who basically agreed about the general course of the international situation, he had been able to educate and to encourage the President, especially about the needs of the emerging nations. After he became the managing director of the Special Fund, he continued to offer the President friendly advice, but clearly he made the U.N., not the Eisenhower administration, the focal point of his energies.

Although he had to deal with the hard realities of domestic and foreign politics, President Eisenhower fully appreciated Hoffman's efforts. A week before delivering his famous farewell address, he sent Hoffman a personal expression of gratitude for his friendship and help, both official and unofficial. According to Eisenhower, Hoffman's record of public service commanded the respect of any thinking American.[41] Such praise between highly placed friends can often be regarded as merely *pro forma*, but in this case it does indicate that Hoffman retained the confidence of President Eisenhower throughout his administration.

9 The U.N.'s Development Programs, 1959-71

In January of 1959, Hoffman began his new career as a top-ranking official of the U.N. Secretariat. Though nearly sixty-eight years old, he looked and felt younger and still wanted the challenge of worthwhile work. His post at the U.N., constantly changing and sometimes frustrating, kept him active and alive by forcing him to grow intellectually. He remained at what he called his "most fascinating job" for thirteen years, finally retiring in December 1971 at nearly eighty-one years of age.[1]

When Hoffman retired, *Fortune* observed, "More than any single individual Paul G. Hoffman deserves to be regarded as the father of foreign aid."[2] As the head of the U.N. development program, he had carried on the work he had begun as administrator of the Marshall Plan and furthered as president of the Ford Foundation and confidant of President Eisenhower. Besides administering programs that spent billions of dollars and touched the lives of tens—perhaps hundreds—of millions of people, he had made himself the foremost American advocate of policies to help the poor and backward countries. *Fortune* might well have called him the leader of the Development Establishment, or at least its personification.

On the subject of economic development, Hoffman never pretended to be an original or profound thinker. As a busy administrator, he lacked time for critical analysis; as a popularizer of the views of experts, he realized that complex issues required simplification for consumption by politicians and the public. Nevertheless, Hoffman should not be dismissed as a shallow salesman or mere functionary. He addressed serious questions about U.S. relations with poor countries and about the meaning of development. Surely, the story of his career is central to an understanding of the Development Establishment and American policy toward poor and underdeveloped countries.

Not surprisingly, as a U.N. official Hoffman shared a common ideological framework with American policy-makers who emphasized the global responsibilities of the U.S. Like most other so-called internationalists, he rejected violent revolution as a solution for economic grievances. Having long preached the benefits of business competition, he never questioned the efficacy of private enterprise and the capitalistic international market. Thus he and other prominent spokesmen for the Development Establishment sought to promote peaceful economic development as an alternative to revolution and other threats to the system that benefitted the United States.

Despite that ideological agreement, Hoffman sometimes found his relationship with the U.S. government rather strained. While he advocated multilateral economic aid administered by the U.N. for the development of poor countries, American leaders expressed serious reservations. For one thing, American policy-makers increasingly regarded the U.N. as a political annoyance. Then, too, they regarded the poor countries outside of Europe as less important than Western Europe had been when it received Marshall Plan aid. And finally, the goal of economic development seemed much vaguer and more elusive than did the Marshall Plan's statistically measurable goal of recovery.

Hoffman's relations with aid recipients also proved more troublesome than had been the case when he administered the Marshall Plan. From his experience as a member of the U.S. Mission during the Eleventh General Assembly, he knew that the poor and underdeveloped countries did not really want the rather small and restricted program he administered. From time to time, they demanded a large-scale capital investment program and a fundamental change in trade between poor commodity producers and rich industrial nations. With a strong undercurrent of resentment, some sought development not just as improvement but as the narrowing of the gap between the rich countries and the poor ones.

The conflicting goals of the U.S. and the underdeveloped countries found expression within the complex bureaucratic and political structure of the U.N. Hoffman's previous experience provided only a small sample of what he faced as an international civil servant. Shortly before he retired, he told an interviewer, "There's a real danger of bureaucracy in business, doubled in national organizations and quadrupled in international organizations."[3] Although the bureaucratic and political side of his job did not overwhelm the pursuit of economic development, Hoffman could not escape the institutional limitations. At times the internal squabbles at the U.N. did assume too large a role.

From the start, Hoffman enjoyed a special position of power within the U.N. Secretary-General Dag Hammarskjold made him a member of his informal Cabinet and looked to the Special Fund to assist his efforts to strengthen the central Secretariat. Hammarskjold's successor, U Thant, also relied heavily on him and often publicly praised his efforts. In December of 1962, the General Assembly approved without objection Hoffman's reappointmment as managing director of the Special Fund.

To a great extent his U.N. position rested on his ability to cultivate support from the U.S., the Special Fund's largest contributor. As a personal friend of Eisenhower, and with strong backing from Ambassador Henry Cabot Lodge, he persistently urged the President to assist the poor countries through the U.N. and to suggest to other countries' leaders, including Nikita Khrushchev of the Soviet Union, that they do the same. The President responded favorably to that advice but complained that some members of Congress remained obstructionists who menaced the best interests of the country.[4]

Hoffman knew quite well that many conservatives in Congress opposed the Special Fund and particularly disliked him. Representative H.R. Gross of Iowa, a Republican traditionalist who long served as Congress's burglar alarm, led the attack, calling Hoffman a New Deal internationalist medicine man who promoted a "multi-billion dollar giveaway carnival." He especially resented the fact that Hoffman, "an unsuccessful auto manufacturer," received from the U.N. a tax-exempt salary of $23,000, more than his own salary. Congressman Omar Burleson, a Texas Democrat, alleged that the Special Fund, though receiving 40 percent of its money from the United States, would be run by foreigners, socialists, and radicals and would cost too much.[5] Nevertheless, Hoffman's personal lobbying in Washington managed to obtain substantial bipartisan support for the Special Fund.

After Eisenhower left the White House, Hoffmann tried to make sure that the next administration would also support economic foreign aid. Though he had opposed John F. Kennedy's election, he urged the new President to use his inaugural address to rally the American people behind foreign aid for development. The U.S. should emphasize that it welcomed the worldwide demand for progress and regarded the less-developed countries as the "great new frontier"; Kennedy should make clear that he would not use foreign aid as an instrument of economic warfare against any country.[6]

President Kennedy and the liberal Democrats who gathered around him gave the impression of eagerness to adopt flexible policies toward the aspirations and the political neutralism of the less-developed countries. In practice, however, the Kennedy administration did not initiate a sharp break from the policies of the 1950s, in part because of congressional power. At the U.N., Ambassador Adlai Stevenson told the poor countries to rely more on private capital, and an administrator of the Agency for International Development declared that the Kennedy administration used foreign aid to pursue long-range political goals and to open up opportunities for private initiative and private enterprise. It did not promote development for the sake of sheer development.[7]

President Kennedy put a slightly different face on the matter when he addressed the General Assembly in September of 1961. On that occasion he strongly endorsed the principle of national self-determination and denounced colonialism, which he linked with Communism. On the positive side, he urged the U.N. to make the 1960s the Decade of Development, with expanded efforts for promoting economic development within the poor countries.[8] In December the General Assembly approved an American resolution calling for greater effort during the period it designated the Decade of Development. Thus, even though Hoffman was not personally close to President Kennedy, the Special Fund seemed to enjoy the support of his administration.

With other contributors, too, Hoffman achieved success. As a fund raiser, he prepared carefully by studying his briefing memoranda and then made personal appeals to national leaders, traveling about 150,000 miles a year. According to one associate, he gave new meaning to the old saying, "robbing Peter to pay Paul."[9] European leaders who appreciated what the Marshall Plan had done for their countries usually had difficulty refusing his requests. By 1962, contributions reached nearly $75 million, almost three times as much as the Special Fund had started with in 1959.

Because of his ability to solicit voluntary contributions, Hoffman functioned as a kind of de facto finance minister for the U.N.'s entire economic and social program. That leverage quickly allowed the Special Fund to dominate the older but smaller Extended Program for Technical Assistance headed by Sir David Owen, a British bureaucrat with long experience at the U.N. That leverage also allowed the Special Fund to stand up to the specialized agencies—such as the International Labour Organization, the World Health Organization, the Food and Agriculture Organization, and UNESCO—that actually carried out development projects under contracts paid by the Fund. That leverage further allowed the Special Fund to impose rigorous standards on the poor countries clamoring for its aid.

In dealing with requests for aid, Hoffman relied heavily on the ideas of his first deputy director, W. Arthur Lewis. A pragmatic Jamaican economist and future Nobel laureate, Lewis provided a hardheaded theoretical model based on the notion that the poor countries had to concentrate on earning income through exports within the world market. Hoffman followed that line of argument by applying a policy of "unfair shares." The Special Fund financed development projects where results seemed most promising by the criteria of the market, not where need was greatest or where governments sought direct improvements in living standards. By evaluating projects according to such economic criteria, the Special Fund attempted to avoid impractical schemes and to concentrate on building the infrastructures for long-term gains among the poor countries.[10]

Hoffman called his view of aid for economic development "a new practical humanism on a world scale." "The goal," he declared, "is to meet human needs, to give each individual among the hundreds of millions of the poor a chance to build a life that is really worth living." Although he regarded morality as the best reason for the rich industrial countries to contribute, he knew that moral outrage alone would not bring the needed effort. Therefore, he offered solid political and economic reasons for the rich countries to make that commitment.[11]

His political case for economic assistance rested, for the most part, on the advantages of peace. Poverty clearly bred and exacerbated world tensions that threatened all countries and led to excessive military spending. The progress of poor countries, he warned in 1960, was "dangerously slow and would not put an end to the unrest throughout the world." Two-thirds of the world's population still lived with poverty, illiteracy, and chronic ill-health. For the average person in the poor countries, progress did not mean much. And the gap in living standards between rich countries and poor had actually grown larger. Without better results, the revolution of rising expectations would spread violence, war, and chaos.[12]

For the rich countries, the political reward for assisting the development of the poor countries would be peace, not gratitude. The early stages of development might actually increase turmoil while progress lagged behind rising expectations, but without progress violence would surely grow worse. In the long run, progress toward a better life for people in the poor countries would help to solidify the national security of the rich countries and enable them to reduce their defense spending.[13]

For the U.S. and other rich democracies, Hoffman made more pointed political arguments. Economic assistance, he often stated, should be divorced from international politics. Nevertheless, as managing director of the Special Fund, he linked the development program to the free world's struggle against Communist revolution. He told President Eisenhower, for instance, that the U.S. had to assure that poor countries could achieve their own "great leap forward" to prove that free institutions could achieve what Communist China attempted by authoritarianism. On other occasions he asked Americans, "How many Cubas do you need before you realize what poverty can do?" He claimed that economic development could prevent more Cubas or Congos and could create examples of what he regarded as democratic success, such as Puerto Rico, Mexico, and India.[14]

Even when he avoided blatant anti-Communist statements, Hoffman made quite clear his belief that "progress should come through evolution and not through violence." Apart from their frightful destruction, revolutions often failed to deliver the benefits their supporters claimed. They did not necessarily solve social inequities, and they did not advance economic growth. In fact, they frequently led to practices that retarded growth and left the masses of common people poorer.[15] Thus Hoffman argued that aid for economic development provided an evolutionary alternative to revolution for the benefit of poor countries and rich ones, too.

Besides those political benefits, he contended that the rich industrial countries would also receive economic benefits from economic development. The underlying cause of poverty, he said, was not lack of resources but their underutilization. By assisting the poor countries to overcome that deficiency, the industrial countries would make a sound business investment. The expansion of a "globally integrated economy," he insisted, was as critically needed by industrial countries as by the underdeveloped ones. Development of those countries offered a "great new economic frontier" of the world's largest potential market. Access to such a market would enable industrial countries to operate at their full productive capacities and to avoid the huge social and financial costs of idle men and idle machines.[16]

The kind of prosperity he envisioned required cooperation between the industrial countries and the underdeveloped countries. He thoroughly rejected the notion that the underdeveloped countries belonged to a Third World whose needs and aspirations totally differed from those of the industrial countries. The poor countries had to realize that they were hurt by reverses among their trading partners. The industrial countries did not have to apologize for the fact that they were getting richer; nor did they have to feel that their wealth resulted from unfair exploitation. In an integrated world economy, "an improvement in the living conditions of people anywhere," he declared, "is a matter of rejoicing for all."[17]

Although aid from rich countries could act as a catalyst for development, Hoffman emphasized that the main burden fell on the poor countries themselves. They could not rely exclusively or primarily on external help. For those with so little, the task might seem cruel; nevertheless, they had to make real sacrifices and assume proportionate responsibilities, with maximum self-help.[18]

Hoffman tried to administer the Special Fund by that attitude: aid recipients had to contribute to their own development projects, but they also shared in decision-making. "Paternalism in international relations, like paternalism in industry, generates and results in half-hearted effort," he observed from experience. "For there is a direct link between the degree of participation and the depth of motivation."[19] Yet as the dispenser of aid, he could not avoid giving advice about how to achieve development. The poor countries should modernize food production and increase output for their rapidly expanding populations. Rather than programs that substituted domestic goods, often inefficient to produce, for imports that required foreign currency, they ought to expand exports to earn their way in the world market. To achieve that kind of development and growth, they would often have to break the chains of custom and their traditional attitudes. They also needed extensive social reforms to distribute wealth and opportunities more widely and thus provide incentives for increasing productivity. One big obstacle, he realized, was that reforms depended upon action by governments that were controlled by elites, who often callously sought to preserve their own privileges.[20]

Despite all the complexities and difficulties, Hoffman insisted that for the first time mankind had the power to wipe out hunger, disease, destitution, and despair. By the year 2000 it could enjoy "a world without want." Unlike Secretary-General U Thant, he did not expect the poor and backward countries ever to catch up with the rich countries, but he believed they could reach a stage where their people lived with dignity and hope of a better life.[21]

For the most part, Hoffman succeeded in implementing his strategy while staying clear of national political maneuvering. As an international civil servant, he did not hesitate to serve the interests of the U.N. regardless of the wishes of the United States, but he did make clear that he would resign his post if forced to carry out any disservice to U.S. national interests.[22]

To avoid political controversies, he adroitly guided the Special Fund by an unspoken rule. Members of the Governing Council could engage in official posturing against particular projects they opposed without forcing separate votes that could wreck the entire program. Accordingly, the Soviets spoke against but did not block projects for Taiwan, South Korea, and South Vietnam; the Arabs spoke against but did not block projects for Israel; and the U.S. spoke against but did not block projects for Poland. In that way the Special Fund won acceptance by judging development projects on their technical merits without political interference.[23]

Hoffman maintained that position until Cuba requested help for an agricultural development project. U.S. sentiment against the Castro regime was very strong; nevertheless, Hoffman felt that he had to present the project proposal to the Governing Council after the Special Fund's staff had evaluated the technical merits. The American representative on the Governing Council was Philip Klutznick, an old friend from the CED. Klutznick voiced technical objections to the project but did not force a vote on that specific issue because he knew that the United States would lose. The Governing Council then approved the entire program, including the Cuban project.[24]

Although he considered the American objections more emotional than rational, Hoffman delayed action in the hope that tensions would ease. However, in January 1963, after the Special Fund's staff had reevaluated and again approved the project, he urged the Governing Council to support implementation. As a concession to the United States, he said that after six months of partial operation the staff would review the project again, and no American money would be used in Cuba for that preliminary work. With those restrictions, on 13 February 1963 the Governing Council announced publicly that the Cuban project would proceed.

That announcement brought sharp American criticism of Hoffman and the Special Fund. Critics complained that his statement about not using American money in Cuba was ridiculous or at least not wholly candid, for there was only one fund. A subcommittee of the Senate Foreign Relations Committee quickly launched an investigation. It discovered, ironically, that the Special Fund had operated much more to the advantage of non-Communist than Communist countries, and that if the Soviets started to block projects *they* found objectionable, the United States would face even more requests for bilateral aid.[25]

As it turned out, the Cuban project went ahead without noticeable damage to the United States, the Special Fund, or Hoffman. His dedication to efforts to help the poor countries won special praise from internationalists within the United States and abroad. The United Nations Association in Canada declared, "Surely no one in our time better deserves the Nobel Peace Prize than Paul Hoffman." And President Lyndon Johnson named him one of sixteen distinguished consultants on foreign affairs. Johnson seldom sought advice from him, but Hoffman did use that relationship to urge the President to spend more for aid to promote economic development.[26]

Meanwhile, Hoffman's personal life had taken on a new dimension. While serving with the U.N., he lived alone in a New York apartment for nearly two and a half years. His wife, Dorothy, restricted since 1952 by an apparent heart condition, stayed on at their Smoke Tree Ranch in Palm Springs. It was Hoffman's habit to work long hours five days a week and then spend weekends relaxing in Palm Springs with his family and a large contingent of old friends.

Each Sunday he would drive about a hundred miles to Los Angeles to board a night flight, sleeping en route so that he could return to work on Monday morning.

That routine came to an end when Dorothy died in May of 1961. After more than forty-five years of marriage, Hoffman told his children that he had no desire to remarry. But without the weekend visits to his wife, his loneliness in New York grew worse. Disliking the obligatory social engagements at the U.N., he sought out the company of old friends with whom he could relax.[27]

One such person was Mrs. Anna Rosenberg, whom he had known since the early 1940s. In many ways they were quite dissimilar. Born in Budapest, she had come to the United States with her parents when she was ten. In 1919, at the age of seventeen, she had ended her formal education and married Julius Rosenberg; in 1956, after thirty-seven years of marriage, she legally separated from her husband, a New York businessman. Called by critics excessively brash, blunt, and opportunistic, she nevertheless impressed most who knew her by lively intelligence, energy, charm, and driving ambition. A liberal Democrat, she had achieved—in both government service and business—successes rare for a woman of her generation.[28]

In August of 1961, three months after Dorothy Hoffman's death, Mrs. Rosenberg and Hoffman began a new relationship. It started when she and their mutual friend William Benton attended a conference on world tensions in Oxford, England. Hoffman, in England soliciting the British contribution to the Special Fund, joined them at the conference. Once back in New York, he started seeing her socially on a rather regular basis.

With Anna Rosenberg, he felt entirely comfortable and relaxed. She made clear that she did not want to marry for a second time, and he said the same thing about himself—but in a totally unexpected turn of events, he discovered that he was "very much in love with her." He explained to his children that "being without her did not make good sense."[29] In June of 1962 he overcame her reluctance and convinced her to marry him.

After she obtained a quick divorce in Mexico, Anna Rosenberg and Paul Hoffman were married on 19 July 1962 in a Unitarian Church in New York City. It was her sixtieth birthday, and he was seventy-one. Despite obvious differences in temperament, theirs was a very good marriage. They enjoyed each other and a wide circle of common friends, whom they entertained at the small townhouse they bought on Sutton Square. Anna, who had been a director of Lathrop Hoffman's Studebaker dealership in Los Angeles during the troubled 1950s, now became a director of the Hoffman Specialty Manufacturing Corporation, the family firm in Indianapolis. She also became a combative defender of her husband when he faced difficulties at the U.N.

During the mid-1960s, Hoffman's position at the U.N. grew even stronger. In January of 1966 he became the first administrator of the United Nations Development Program (UNDP). This new agency, formed by the merger of the Special Fund and the older but smaller Extended Program for Technical Assistance, seemed to some observers the result of a natural evolution. The United States, the largest contributor to U.N. programs, wanted the merger in order to make the Decade of Development more effective. Secretary-General U Thant, who continued Dag Hammarskjold's effort to centralize the U.N.'s administration, helped to lead the campaign for merger. Although decentralists tried to resist, in November of 1965 the General Assembly approved the plan without a single negative vote. U Thant called that decision "a seemingly undramatic but certainly significant milestone."[30]

For Hoffman, then in his mid-seventies, the merger meant a new level of importance but not major change. Except for the larger scale, he continued to operate pretty much as he had, concentrating on the solicitation of contributions and on top-level negotiations. The management of operations, including evaluations of all projects and project proposals, he left to his chief assistants, American Myer Cohen and Frenchman Paul-Marc Henry. Deputy Administrator Sir David Owen, formerly chairman of the Technical Assistance Board, tried to cooperate but never won Hoffman's full trust.

Because the UNDP had to work closely with the specialized agencies, Hoffman also served as chairman of the newly created Inter-Agency Consultative Board. Bringing together the Secretary-General and the executive heads of the specialized agencies, the IACB tried to foster cooperation but lacked coercive power and could not overcome the rivalry and independence of the specialized agencies. Organizational friction continued to plague the U.N.'s development efforts.

Nevertheless, things seemed to go smoothly for Hoffman, whose reappointment the General Assembly approved in December of

1968. At the World Bank, Robert McNamara became president and launched a much-acclaimed "poverty orientation" to assist development. Within the U.N. structure, increased reliance on voluntary contributions rather than on assessments gave Hoffman and the UNDP more influence. By the end of the 1960s the agency's annual budget reached $225 million, about 65 percent of all voluntary contributions or about 50 percent of the U.N.'s entire budget for economic and social programs. With those resources it not only contracted for work by the specialized agencies but also began to operate as its own "executing" agency.[31]

One new field the UNDP entered was population control. In view of Hoffman's previous positions, that new policy reflected some shift in attitude. During the 1950s, he had argued that economic progress would encourage voluntary family planning without government involvement. As the head of the Special Fund, he had told an American television audience that government promotion of birth control would not provide an answer for the problems of the less-developed countries; in fact, he denied that those countries suffered from serious overpopulation.[32]

To a considerable extent, he sought to avoid the subject because of his political sensitivity. President Eisenhower had firmly declared that promotion of birth control was not a proper government activity, function, or responsibility. Like the President, Hoffman had recognized that Congress might use the birth control issue to destroy the entire economic foreign aid program. He had also recognized strong resistance to birth control in the less-developed countries, where large families were regarded as providing security.[33]

By the late 1960s, however, the Development Establishment had convinced many political leaders in the West and in the poor countries that birth control programs were needed to raise living standards. In 1967 the U.N. created a small Population Trust Fund, which the UNDP supervised. Hoffman told the Governing Council that the UNDP had to encourage people in the poor countries to change their attitudes about the status of women, about family size, and about child rearing. To avoid the threat of widespread famine, governments must take the lead in promoting population control.[34] Accordingly, he appointed Rafael Salas, a former government official from the Philippines, to direct the U.N.'s program for assisting governments to limit population growth.

The UNDP, like the Special Fund before it, did not satisfy the demands of the low-income countries, however. Their goal was faster development and more freedom from economic domination by the rich industrial nations. The poor countries that depended upon commodity exporting especially resented trade imbalances. They demanded new international trade agreements and a large-scale capital investment fund—similar to the SUNFED proposal—which they, not the big contributors, could control. Although they succeeded in establishing the U.N. Conference on Trade and Development, the U.N. Capital Development Fund, and the U.N. Industrial Development Organization, the poor countries received no substantial benefits from their political victories. The rich countries simply refused to support the new organizations. Therefore, Hoffman's UNDP remained the key agency for multilateral development aid.

Hoffman himself acknowledged that the first Decade of Development had not achieved enough. "This is an age of hope and unprecedented prosperity for the fortunate minority," he declared in 1967, "but for a majority of mankind hope is limited and progress inadequate." Difficulties unanticipated at the start had tragically led to a widening gap between rich and poor countries. Too often, aid programs had financed big, wasteful projects that failed to bring rapid development and improvement for the masses.[35]

So that humankind everywhere could realize its full potential, Hoffman called for a "global war on poverty," an extension of the Great Society on the broadest scale. The United States and other industrial countries must double the amount of their aid, and make trade agreements that would allow the poor countries to earn greater income within the international market.[36]

He realized, however, that the biggest contributors to development aid programs had raised their own complaints. Former President Eisenhower, for example, expressed a common American view that the influence of growing numbers of new small countries would make the U.N. a less effective organization.[37] Certainly, the Kennedy and Johnson administrations showed little confidence in the U.N. when the United States could not control events in the General Assembly. American officials even expressed misgivings about the procedures of the UNDP under Hoffman's management. They wanted closer monitoring of projects to avoid waste, and they questioned whether the UNDP, already too slow in implementing its projects, could efficiently handle heavier loads.

In preparation for the second Decade of Development, Hoffman attempted to meet such criticism by shoring up his organization. He delivered to the Inter-Agency Consultative Board a confidential critique and a call for reform. "Frankly, the UNDP has financed too many projects of doubtful priority," he confessed, "and too much of the UNDP's and the agencies' time has been wasted in preparing low-priority project requests." While both requests for help and cash reserves had increased, the speed of operation had decreased. Hoffman urged the U.N. to evaluate and to improve its entire development effort.[38]

Within the UNDP's Governing Council, the United States and other big contributors pushed for a thorough appraisal of the future needs of poor countries and the part the agency should play. Therefore, the Governing Council decided to finance a comprehensive and independent capacity study. It requested that Hoffman submit an unexpurgated report and a commentary from the Inter-Agency Consultative Board.

Although he had admitted to the Governing Council his own disappointment with the pace of development among poor countries, Hoffman also felt that the UNDP had made much progress.[39] He wanted the capacity study to endorse his views by emphasizing the need for both reform and expansion. He apparently expected a report that was politically useful but essentially unmemorable, like most of the documents produced in the U.N.'s paper blizzard.

In July of 1968 he hired an Australian, Sir Robert G.A. Jackson, to serve as commissioner of the capacity study. Their acquaintance had begun in the 1950s, during the Marshall Plan era, when Hoffman exchanged ideas with Jackson and his wife, economist Barbara Ward, who were both involved with efforts to promote economic development in the poor countries. During the early 1960s, Hoffman had made Jackson a senior consultant for the Special Fund. Thus, the Australian seemed well qualified for the new job, and Hoffman had no reason to suspect that the capacity study would cause much trouble for him or for the UNDP.

Long familiar with the ways of the U.N., Jackson did not regard his assignment as routine or *pro forma*. He took seriously the encouragement of some members of the Inter-Agency Consultative Board and the Governing Council to "pull no punches," to be bold and imaginative, and above all to be independent. Some suggested that the report should be "hard hitting" and written in "non-UN

President Truman, Secretary of State George C. Marshall, Hoffman, and Special Representative Harriman confer, November 1948. National Park Services—Abbie Rowe, courtesy Harry S. Truman Library

Senator James Duff, Senator Henry Cabot Lodge, and presidential candidate Dwight Eisenhower listen to Hoffman at a Washington conference in June 1952. International News Photo, courtesy Dwight D. Eisenhower Library

Harold S. Vance and Hoffman receive gold watches twenty-five years after joining forces as vice presidents of Studebaker. Discovery Hall Archival Collections

President Eisenhower presents father-of-the-year medal to Hoffman, June 1954. National Park Services—Abbie Rowe, courtesy Dwight D. Eisenhower Library

language." Jackson himself sought to evaluate the administrative effectiveness of the U.N. system in relation to the needs of the low-income countries for development assistance.[40]

At the end of September of 1969, Jackson submitted to Hoffman a 600-page, two-volume report entitled *A Study of the Capacity of the United Nations Development System*. In an organization renowned for circumlocution and impersonality, the Jackson Report was remarkable. Written in first person singular, it used what one observer called "startlingly forthright language." Especially in the short first volume, Jackson's criticisms were brutally frank and pungently phrased. According to an outspoken admirer, it was "possibly the most thoughtful document ever to come out of the United Nations."[41]

Though beginning benignly enough with positive impressions, Jackson concentrated on the negative side. He charged that the U.N. development machine suffered from inertia that no one could change. The world's most complicated organization seemed "incapable of intelligently controlling itself." At the headquarters level, no central coordinating organization existed to exercise effective control. As a result, the development effort was "becoming slower and more unwieldly, like some prehistoric monster."[42]

"For many years, I have looked for the 'brain' which guides the policies and operations of the UN development system," he declared. "The search has been in vain. . . . There is no group (or 'Brain Trust') which is constantly monitoring the present operations. . . . The UN development system has tried to wage a war on want for many years with very little organized 'brain' to guide it. Its absence may well be the greatest constraint of all on capacity."[43]

Jackson placed most of the blame on the top-heavy and misdirected administration. The entire operation suffered from a "donor bias" and too much of a headquarters orientation. While the situation called for unorthodox and heretical proposals for new action, the U.N. had become disproportionately old and bureaucratic. Though he admitted that "some of the oldest are youngest in spirit," Jackson found a clear relationship between excessive age within the organization and an attitude of negativism. The U.N. had "more than its share of 'experts' in the art of describing how things cannot be done."[44]

Jackson considered his report favorable to the UNDP, but he realized that others did not view it that way and admitted that some senior U.N. officials resisted his recommendations. The fact was that Hoffman and his top aides quickly read enough of the report to feel deeply hurt. Jackson had called into question much of what Hoffman's administration had done during the previous decade.

Moreover, the discussion of excessive age seemed a cruel jibe at Hoffman, who was nearly eighty. For a long time he had impressed observers with the appearance and the vigor of a younger man. Although he continued to work long hours in the office and traveled extensively each year, he knew how to conserve his energies, (often taking short naps) and how to use them effectively. But in the late 1960s age had suddenly started to catch up with him. He became repetitive and forgetful. He tired easily and sometimes fell asleep at meetings. After particularly demanding work, he seemed exhausted, sick, and unable to concentrate. Friends and associates began to wonder about his ability to carry on, and some delegations tried to mount a campaign to get him to step down in favor of fresh leadership.

Perhaps understandably, therefore, Hoffman responded to the Jackson Report more emotionally than rationally. He regarded it as unfair, inaccurate, and harmful. He became furious and refused to listen when a senior consultant suggested that the UNDP might improve operations by using parts of the report. Anna Hoffman, who knew how much the job meant to him and who wanted him to stay on, was especially embittered. She accused Jackson of betraying her husband and of taking actions that would shorten his life.[45]

Publicly, however, Hoffman couched his response to the capacity study in polite and diplomatic language. He praised Jackson's overall effort and declared that the UNDP would act on some of the recommendations, but he did emphatically deny that the UNDP had reached its capacity and could not handle greater efforts with efficiency. The needs of the poor countries, he asserted, cried out for an expanded program of assistance. To help less-developed nations reverse the widening gap between the living standard of the rich countries and their own, he joined others in calling for massive increases in aid and more democratic sharing of international power.[46]

In the summer of 1970, attempting to minimize the bad feelings and bad publicity that followed the Jackson Report, the UNDP's Governing Council reached a so-called consensus agreement to use the report to improve the development system without fully embracing Jackson's language. By reorganizing the UNDP's structure, the

Governing Council clearly interfered with the operations much more than Hoffman had previously tolerated. Nevertheless, his personal reputation, still unsullied, was valuable for soliciting contributions, and despite privately expressed criticism the U.N. was not prepared to replace him. During the UNDP's Pledging Conference in 1970, delegates publicly reported that they expected Secretary-General U Thant to ask Hoffman to stay at least one more year after his term expired.[47]

A wave of favorable publicity had restored the aura of success. Then in February of 1971, the U.N. Secretariat finally announced big changes in its top positions. At year's end, both Secretary-General U Thant and Hoffman would retire. According to the *New York Times*, the U.N. would not easily find a suitable replacement for Hoffman. His administrative ability, vision, generous gift of persuasion, and impartial honesty had made him a "sort of Rock of Gibraltar."[48]

During the fall, Hoffman prepared to leave the job he so dearly loved. His farewell address to the U.N. General Assembly's Committee II, which was responsible for economics and finance, characteristically balanced realism and optimism. He warned that because of the enormously expensive and lethal arms race, "our planet is in many ways a more dangerous and less humanly satisfying homesite for the entire race of man." Nevertheless, he added, "conditions *are* demonstrably better in several respects than they were ten years ago."[49]

Compared with any similar period, he said, the 1960s had witnessed the greatest progress toward fuller use of the world's natural and human resources. In the poor countries, governments were showing a "rising tide of common sense" and realism by relying less on the public sector. Those willing to sacrifice for modernization showed "spectacular progress," and nearly everywhere the daily lives of ordinary people showed real improvements: they ate more, used more manufactured products, received better services, and found better-paying jobs. Meanwhile, development experts and administrators were showing a good deal of humility about their own capacities to transform the world. With that record, he felt justified in lobbying Congress on behalf of President Nixon's appropriation request of $100 million for the UNDP.[50]

When Hoffman finally stepped down from his $73,000 post, he did so amid a chorus of tributes from both Republicans and Democrats. Senator Charles Percy of Illinois, a liberal Republican friend since the 1950s, said that Hoffman—"one of the most gifted and dedicated Americans who has ever served an international organization"—had proved that economic assistance could lead to dramatic progress among the poor countries. At the U.N., Secretary-General U Thant called him "a model of a great world citizen and pioneer for peace," and even the Soviet delegation expressed admiration for him.[51]

One cannot help asking, Hoffman's aide Myer Cohen confessed, "Did we accomplish anything worthwhile?" With a certain amount of what he called faith, Cohen concluded that the U.N. development programs provided a "very great net plus." By helping to build the infrastructures, they paved the way for the World Bank, for bilateral aid programs, and for efforts by the less-developed countries themselves. Hoffman said he was under no illusions about utopia being around the corner, but he believed that by dispensing $3.4 billion in so-called seed money for development, those programs he administered did help create incremental improvements within the poor countries.[52]

This is not to say, however, that the enterprise he administered lacked serious critics. First of all, the emphasis Hoffman placed on support from rich countries based on enlightened self-interest did not generate the level of assistance poor countries needed. Voters in Western democracies, according to Swedish expert Gunnar Myrdal, simply did not believe that foreign aid and liberal trade policies were in their self-interest. Even when trade did expand, it often brought dislocations that required difficult and costly adjustments. Myrdal called for promoters of development assistance to emphasize moral arguments. In the end, he said, the issue came down to a matter of humanity, not economic and political gain.[53]

Hoffman, too, believed that morality should have led the rich countries to help the poor ones, but he felt that morality alone would not bring action. Therefore, he contrived practical arguments to persuade the rich countries to help. Of course, he genuinely believed in the benefits of modernization and economic integration. By calling poor countries the new economic frontier, he sought to mobilize Americans' desire both for gain and for a sense of mission. Unfortunately, the cause of economic development involved too many political complications and lacked the dramatic flare of the new frontier of space exploration. Thus he could not make the development program as big as the poor countries needed.

Those who worked hard within the Development Establishment often felt frustrated. World Bank president Robert McNamara, for example, observed that global poverty remained deeply rooted "in the institutional framework, particularly in the distribution of economic and political power within the system."[54] His "poverty orientation" tried to ensure that development projects actually benefited people below the poverty line. However, what he and Hoffman and other leaders of the Development Establishment achieved did not alter that framework in a fundamental way.

After observing that situation, economist Robert Heilbroner questioned whether the liberal formulas of Hoffman and other leaders of the Development Establishment could really benefit the poor countries. He acknowledged that Hoffman had persistently and admirably strived, despite endless discouragements, to bring about real development. But according to Heilbroner, political necessity led Hoffman to ignore the basic fact that economic development depends on political and social revolution, not mere reforms. Without such revolution, the liberal formulas for economic aid would not likely bring about the kind of progress Heilbroner called the "global Great Ascent."[55]

During the late 1960s and early 1970s, that kind of criticism became more common. One of the most thorough philosophical critiques of the liberal formulas of the Development Establishment appeared in the work of Denis Goulet, a founder of the Center for the Study of Development and Social Change, based in Cambridge, Massachusetts. In several works, culminating with his book *The Cruel Choice*, Goulet tried to demystify prestigious blueprints for development. From a common New Left perspective, he charged that the United States and other donor countries failed to make the needs of the poor countries the normative standard for development aid. By seeking to domesticate the development of the Third World so that their own strategic, ideological, and economic interests would not be threatened, they adopted policies that distorted the economies of the poor countries. The world market benefited and the elites in the poor countries benefited; the masses in the poor countries, however, continued to suffer from underdevelopment.[56]

To replace such injustice, Goulet advocated "authentic development" under noncapitalist models that would enable the masses in the Third World to enjoy a better quality of life. Within a worldwide system of cooperation, nonelitist planning could consider the ethical implications of technological and ecological transformations that the promoters of capitalist models of development largely ignored. Such a change, according to Goulet, might well require political upheaval and even violent revolution. Holding up as desirable examples the experiences of China, Cuba, and Tanzania, he declared that underdevelopment itself was a chronic state of violence. For him, the choice was not between violence and nonviolence but between the different kinds and degrees of violence needed to bring about change.[57]

From Hoffman, that criticism elicited a sensitive response. He even wrote a draft of a foreword for Goulet's book, which he called a major philosophical work that filled a critical gap in thinking about development. According to him, Goulet had made a sound point in saying that development was too important to be left solely in the hands of so-called experts. As a matter of fact, the "developers" had improperly tried to impose the Western model by emphasizing gross national product as the most important measure. Progress was better measured by the standard of living index.[58]

Nevertheless, Hoffman did not endorse Goulet's critique of modernization; on the contrary, he argued that the poor countries probably would have pursued a similar line even without Western-oriented aid programs. "Realistically, I do not see how it [improvement in the standard of living index] can be accomplished at all without a good deal of 'Westernization'—if by Westernizing one means the importation of modern technology, production and distribution methods, and mass training."[59]

Obviously, Hoffman did not want to abandon the main thrust of the development effort. To be sure, he recognized that the development process was far from purely technical or even economic and that it required the restructuring of whole societies—"not only in the developing world but to some extent in the wealthy industrialized world as well." But the extent of the restructuring he had in mind did not resemble leftist prescriptions. "I do *not* see the need for radically new approaches either in strategy or in tactics," he told the State Department's Foreign Service Institute in 1969. "I *do* see the need for a greatly expanded, much more intensified, and somewhat better planned application of our principles and techniques."[60]

Countries seeking economic growth and development, he believed, benefited most from responsible, progressive capitalism. "It is only dynamic capitalism," he reaffirmed for Henry Luce, "that can support a welfare state."[61] That economic model depended upon incentives, especially for educated people and the middle class. He hoped that aid programs would not merely help the rich in developing countries get richer, but as the price of development, those countries had to allow the rich and talented to receive the biggest shares. Ironically, by the late 1970s Communist China, which Hoffman had often criticized, may have accepted the same conclusion. Without abandoning Communism, it started to seek technological help and better commercial relations with the West, just as he had predicted thirty years earlier. On the other hand, Hoffman's examples of successful democratic development—Puerto Rico, Mexico, and India—may not have achieved the successes he hoped for.

Despite his basic belief in capitalism, Hoffman revealed a good deal of ambivalence about the private, multinational corporation. Publicly, he claimed that such businesses, even when they repatriated profits, benefited the poor countries by investing capital and skills in modernization; privately, he condemned their plunder of the poor countries. He tried to use the U.N.'s preinvestment resource surveys to provide the less-developed countries with the information they needed to deal with large corporations.[62]

At the U.N., Hoffman's legacy survived his retirement, but with serious difficulties. By an informal agreement, the United States had the right to name the administrator of the UNDP. The Nixon administration chose Rudolph A. Peterson, the Swedish-born former president of the Bank of America and a firm supporter of multilateral aid. Despite Peterson's efforts to carry on as Hoffman had, in 1974 the UNDP faced a serious financial crisis. While the United States failed to expand its contributions, the UNDP had tried to use contributions from the Soviet bloc as if they were liquid currencies. After overextending commitments, Peterson suddenly had to impose drastic retrenchment: the UNDP fired many of its experts and backed out of commitments. Those incidents shook the Development Establishment but did not change its course. The UNDP remains the world's largest source of technical cooperation grants for development.

For Hoffman, too, his retirement was followed by reverses. In May of 1972, only five months after leaving the U.N., he suffered a debilitating heart attack followed by a stroke. Paralyzed on the left side, suffering pain and impaired speech, he was incapacitated for the rest of his life. Often confined to a wheelchair or bed, he could not concentrate enough even to play cards or to watch sports on television for long. Though his memory was unreliable, he fully understood and was frustrated by what had happened to him, yet he did not become an irascible old man; he retained his good humor and was always pleasant with his wife Anna and with his children when they visited. He died on 8 October 1974 at the age eighty-three. The year before, President Nixon had awarded him the Medal of Freedom.[63]

Conclusion

A man of the Establishment and a progressive—that is how Paul G. Hoffman should be remembered. In business and in public affairs he headed important institutions and stood close to those with greater power, sharing many of their values, attitudes, and limitations. Yet even while he sought to preserve the American system, he also helped to change it. Within his multifaceted career he demonstrated a capacity for recognizing modern trends and new ways of coping with them. By his deeds and his talents as a promoter and publicist, he gave progressive attitudes wider currency, especially within the Establishment.

In the first place, Hoffman made himself one of the automotive industry's brightest stars. Neither a production man nor a financial man, he rose through marketing when that aspect of business was increasingly important for mass production industries. Doubtless, he benefited from his winning personality and his attentiveness to others, but he also combined the daring of the entrepreneur with the organizational skills of the modern corporate executive. He relied on systematic and scientific analysis of the market and on bureaucratic teamwork to sell cars and to train others to sell cars.

When he moved up from his dealership in Los Angeles to become a top executive of Studebaker during the mid-1920s, Hoffman proved himself adept at the broader aspects of business leadership. He picked up the progressive human relations approach to management and, with the slogan "America's Friendliest Factory," tried to cultivate good relations with Studebaker's employees and with its dealers. For him, the human relations approach was a way to motivate members of the corporation to give their best efforts. Corporate decency simply made good business sense.

After he took over the management of the bankrupt Studebaker Corporation in 1933, he had the opportunity to apply his progressive notions more fully. Making the best of the situation, he developed a distinctive vision of the small corporation competing successfully against giants by emphasizing superior human relations and innovative adaptability within the market. Thus, during the turbulent 1930s, Studebaker alone in the American automotive industry did not resist unionization. Hoffman tried to make the union feel secure in the hope that it would behave responsibly. Eventually, the rest of the industry abandoned its anti-union stance and accepted collective bargaining.

The superiority of the small corporation with alert management, according to Hoffman, could be seen in its product line. Studebaker's new models for 1939–41 and for 1947–48 seemed to prove his point. Uninhibited by the complex committee system at General Motors, for example, Studebaker produced distinctive and innovative cars that won approval from buyers and experts. Hoffman's strategy enabled it to find a profitable niche with a growing share of the market. When he left the company in 1948, Studebaker appeared to have found the road to continued success. Moreover, his extraordinary promotional skills had given it a reputation as a progressive and innovative force much beyond its size.

When he returned in 1953 as chairman, he discovered that appearances were deceptive. A combination of misadventures during the five years of his absence had brought Studebaker to the verge of collapse. Although he did not want to assume administrative responsibilities, he threw himself into the management in an effort to rescue the company. Quickly recognizing that in the new conditions Studebaker was too small, he engineered a merger with Packard. Even then, he argued that the new but still small Studebaker-Packard Corporation could succeed by following his old strategy of superior human relations and a distinctive product line.

As chairman after the 1954 merger, Hoffman suffered frustration and disappointment. The new chief operating officer in whom he had placed great confidence repudiated his strategy: in both its product line and its labor policies Studebaker-Packard attempted to follow the practices of the Big Three. The results, as Hoffman feared, brought further decline. He remained the neglected chairman only until another merger in 1956 finally ended his long tenure with the automaker.

Many observers, then and afterward, blamed Hoffman for Studebaker's decline and eventual disappearance from the automotive industry. They accused him of coddling labor while the company suffered from costly inefficiencies and low-quality work performance. They accused him of failing to recognize soon enough, in contrast with George Mason of Nash, that survival depended upon merger. And when he did act, he pursued the wrong partner and chose the wrong successor.

Although the critics have raised several valid points, one should not conclude that Studebaker's fate proved the failure of Hoffman's management and his strategy. Had he not left in 1948, the company might well have adapted better to the changing national economy. Even during the affluent 1950s, his market strategy of distinctive and economical cars could have found a profitable niche; the sale of small foreign cars by the late 1950s proved that many American car-buyers did not want just what the Big Three offered. As for labor policies, of course Studebaker could not survive with costly and inefficient practices. But eventually, other automakers also recognized that cooperation between labor and management, not an adversarial relationship, produced the best results.

Besides his management of Studebaker, Hoffman earned his reputation as a progressive business leader by making himself the automotive industry's "Apostle of Safety." He first became involved when public concern about traffic congestion and accidents threatened to hurt car sales and to bring undesirable government regulation. Characteristically, he responded by urging that government action be based on the recommendations of technical experts, not on public emotionalism. The experts agreed, he said, that government on all levels had to address the problem by spending more on street and highway construction and on law enforcement aimed at unsafe drivers.

Like the rest of the automotive industry, he strenuously resisted proposals that government impose restrictions on car design or other aspects of manufacturing. According to him, the industry was acting responsibly and producing safe vehicles without government interference. At Studebaker he operated on the assumption that safety features helped to sell cars. That kind of enlightened self-interest and willingness to cooperate with government, he claimed, provided the best solution to the traffic safety problem.

Hoffman's characteristically progressive response to the safety issue too easily reconciled corporate pursuit of profits and protection of the public interest. As critics charged, the industry's handling of the problem was often more cosmetic than substantive. By the 1960s, Ralph Nader and other consumer advocates were arguing that the automakers had abused the public, and Congress responded by enacting legislation that empowered government to mandate safety in car designs. What Hoffman, then no longer connected with the industry, thought about this repudiation of his preference for management initiatives is not clear.

Whatever his lasting contribution to automotive safety, Hoffman's involvement in that cause did start to move him toward greater participation in public affairs. Not until after he took over control of Studebaker in its crisis, however, did he emerge as a politically conscious businessman who addressed the broad social and economic issues of the country. Then, beginning in 1934, he took upon himself the task of speaking out to preserve capitalism and democracy.

That system, of course, had rewarded him handsomely. Even though he was not driven by burning ambition for great wealth, he had become a millionaire by the age of thirty-four. As a successful businessman he lived very well. And even if he could not admit it, he obviously enjoyed the limelight and association with public affairs that came with his business success. Thus, self-interest played a big part in Hoffman's move onto the national stage of public debate during the 1930s.

Like many other progressive Republican businessmen, he feared political extremism during the Depression as a threat to the American system, whereas rugged individualism and laissez faire doctrines clearly did not fit the needs of modern capitalism, and they provoked dangerous class antagonism. He also condemned statism and collectivism because they led to economic inefficiency and stagnation and because they threatened to destroy democratic freedoms.

Instead of those extremes, he advocated a middle path. In a modern society, he argued, the common people were entitled to a large measure of security and an equitable share of the nation's vast wealth. Because the private sector alone could not provide those advantages, government had to do so. For this reason he gave his approval to many of the New Deal reforms and programs to protect the common people. Nevertheless, he complained bitterly about the economic policies of the Roosevelt administration. He resented, of course, antibusiness rhetoric and appeals to class antagonisms, but the main thrust of his criticism focused on substantive matters: not only did the New Deal fail to bring economic recovery, but its policies actually retarded the economy.

Most of all, he attacked government efforts to address the Depression with policies of planned scarcity and price-fixing. Like cartels, the NRA and other New Deal programs that limited production and subverted the competitive market protected inefficiency at the public expense. According to him, only profit incentive and consumer sovereignty within free enterprise would promote efficiency, innovation, progress, and abundance. For economic recovery and prosperity, America needed antitrust enforcement and other government policies to encourage competition and expansion.

To businessmen, Hoffman preached a brand of managerialism that tempered self-interest and the pursuit of profits with enlightened views about long-term implications. But he did not want business to adopt paternalism or to substitute for the pursuit of profits some vague notion of social responsibility. Instead, he urged business leaders, especially in the mass production industries, to adopt policies of large volumes and low profit margins. For their own well-being and that of the free enterprise system, they needed policies that benefited their customers, their employees, and the public. That kind of enlightened self-interest, which reconciled seemingly conflicting forces, would ensure prosperity.

As he spoke out on those issues, Hoffman began to discover other corporate leaders who shared some of his concerns and attitudes. For him they became a reinforcing peer reference group and allies in the effort to influence public opinion and government policies. Thus, during the early 1940s, he joined with similarly minded businessmen to create a new organization, the Committee for Economic Development. With Hoffman as its chairman, the CED advocated a brand of business progressivism that encouraged government and private sector cooperation in the sharing of technical expertise. Among business organizations, it was probably the first to endorse

Keynesian economic theories that called upon government fiscal
and monetary management to stabilize the business cycle in order
to prevent protracted slumps and massive unemployment.

Hoffman himself absorbed Keynesian concepts within a basically
conventional framework. He continued to express concern about the
excesses of bureaucratic power weakening free enterprise. Too much
taxation on business carried the risk of reducing the incentives that
made capitalism efficient and productive. Too much government
spending raised the prospect of inflation. He believed that the stabilizing force of government had to be limited to preserve the dynamic
force of the private sector.

Impressed by how such views differed from traditional business
conservatism, some scholars have linked the CED with a type of
American "corporatism." Of course, as a theoretical model, "corporatism" calls to mind the fascist system that substituted for the instability of competitive markets the stability of cartels and func-
tional-occupational groups operating in concert with government.
Presumably to avoid that pejorative association as well as to take
American peculiarities into account, scholars have referred to "neo-
corporatism" or "liberal corporatism" or "technocorporatism" in
the U.S.

The question arises, then, does the corporatist label—however
modified—fit Hoffman, the founder and first chairman of the CED?
The answer may depend on how one defines "corporatism." If the
word refers to the economics of scarcity and avoidance of competitive markets, it clearly does not apply. But if it refers to the blurring
of the public and private sectors to promote the common good, perhaps Hoffman might seem a corporatist to some observers. He did,
after all, promote government reliance on experts and appointive
commissions; he did advocate greater harmony and cooperation between business and government, just as he sought to reduce the adversarial stance in labor-management relations. However, one
should not forget that for him such attitudes grew out of a pragmatic
American progressivism and continued to reflect a deep suspicion of
the statism associated with European "corporatism."

As a progressive, Hoffman feared excessive government power
not only because of economic inefficiency and stagnation but also
because of political risks. Free enterprise and other democratic freedoms rested on the same foundations; therefore, government power

that stifled any of those freedoms endangered the others. During the 1930s, the growing power of statist corporatism or fascism in Europe proved that point for him, and he became convinced that the United States faced a grave threat from foreign totalitarianism.

What particularly alarmed him was the prospect that the United States might resist that threat by adopting similar methods, and he began to warn against becoming a "garrison state" that would shackle business and labor and restrict other freedoms. Later, President Eisenhower, to whom he was both friend and counselor, expressed similar concerns and in his farewell address sounded the alarm over the dangers of the military-industrial complex. What such attitudes suggest is that those who categorize Hoffman and Eisenhower as corporatists may be stretching the definition of the word too far.[1]

Hoffman certainly did not raise the specter of excessive government power merely as a ploy to protect business from regulation. He openly linked the defense of free enterprise and the survival of democratic freedoms because he genuinely believed that they were mutually dependent and that they faced threats from the same sources. Thus as a trustee of the University of Chicago, he vigorously supported academic freedom and freedom of expression generally. Thoroughly repelled by bigotry, he became an active member of the National Conference of Christians and Jews.

To the cause of civil liberties and minority rights, he made his most important contributions during the 1950s. With encouragement from friends like Robert Hutchins and William Benton, he lent institutional support—through the Ford Foundation and its offshoot, the Fund for the Republic—as well as his personal prestige. In his view, the greatest domestic threat to American freedoms came from the hysteria and recklessness of the crusade against Communists and their sympathizers. He simply did not believe that the country really suffered from an internal Communist menace. He did believe that the tactics of Senator Joseph McCarthy and all his ilk divided and weakened the country unnecessarily.

While he sought to defend the American system from what he regarded as internal abuses, Hoffman also became concerned about threats from abroad. During the late 1930s he came to feel that American democracy and free enterprise could not survive surrounded by hostile and aggressive forces. Furthermore, he sympathized with the victims of totalitarian aggression. Unlike some of his friends, he rejected isolationism and insisted that the United States needed to take a more active part in international affairs.

During World War II those concerns led him to address the whole question of how the United States should fit into the postwar international scene. He and the CED urged the adoption of generous trade and economic aid policies to assist economic recovery abroad. To overcome isolationist and nationalist objections, they argued that the United States would benefit from the recovery of its trading partners. In an interdependent world economy, it would gain markets for its products and thus boost its own prosperity.

Although Hoffman genuinely believed in the mutual benefits of international trade, he never regarded economic gains as the main reason for internationalism. By 1946, certainly, much more important in his mind was the need to prevent the spread of Soviet power without excessive reliance on military methods. By assisting the economic recovery of the non-Communist industrial countries, the U.S. could invest in its own security. Within the Cold War framework, his internationalism merged peace and prosperity in a formula common among national leaders after World War II.

Hoffman's outlook made him an ideal choice to head the Marshall Plan. He firmly believed that by assisting the economic recovery of Europe, the United States was alleviating the conditions that Communists exploited. The notion held by critics that the United States aided Europe in order to solve its own economic problems he called a "delusion"; as he correctly pointed out, the booming postwar American economy suffered more from scarcities than from surpluses. Some American interest groups did try to convert the Marshall Plan into a program for their own benefit, but Hoffman resisted those efforts with considerable success.

He administered the Marshall Plan with straightforward economic objectives. The rebuilding of infrastructures and commercial networks took precedence over European desires for higher living standards and social reforms. He stressed that cooperation among the Europeans for economic integration had to replace nationalistic and inefficient trade barriers. In the long run, the Europeans would benefit most by following the progressive economic practices of the United States. Higher productivity, freer trade, and competitive markets would eventually raise living standards. Reflecting the policies he and other leaders of the CED promoted within the U.S., this doctrine of salvation by production had, of course, a clear capitalist orientation.[2]

So thoroughly did he believe in the beneficial results of economic development by that model that he thought the lessons of the Marshall Plan could apply outside Europe. He realized, of course, that conditions elsewhere differed enormously, but observing the terrible suffering and misery of the poor and underdeveloped countries, he felt that American aid and expertise could make a crucial difference. The question was, would Americans respond to the need in such areas?

During the 1950s, Hoffman tried to persuade Americans that an affirmative answer to that question had to be part of the national mission. As president of the Ford Foundation, he launched development projects in poor countries and urged American political leaders to support foreign aid for that purpose. After he lost his position at the Ford Foundation, he continued to crusade for American trade and aid policies that would benefit poor and backward nations.

Although he saw morality and humanitarianism as the best reasons for such action, he felt that Americans needed other reasons as well. In order to "sell" his program for development, therefore, he tried to "package" it with the kinds of arguments that would persuade Americans. Thus he talked about "waging peace" with "practical humanitarianism." Economic development among the poor countries, he claimed, would make them less vulnerable to Communism; as a result, the U.S. and other Western countries would be able to spend less on a military defense against Communism. Economic development among the poor countries would also make them better trading partners. An economically integrated market on a global scale would benefit all nations.

Hoffman's packaging seems naive not because he lacked sophistication but because he believed that to sell his cause he had to keep it simple. He knew that aid would not buy allies for the United States. He knew that it would not easily or necessarily create stable, effective, and democratic societies. Like the needs, the obstacles to development were enormous. But without an American commitment and a sense that the task could be achieved, development would have been even more difficult.

On these matters Hoffman did not stand alone. By the late 1950s, a pervasive intellectual climate had developed among American experts on economic development and "nation-building." Viewing the

Third World as the new battleground of the Cold War, they claimed to know how the United States could win the struggle and stop the spread of Communism. During the administrations of both President Eisenhower and President Kennedy, the United States proclaimed itself the friend of economic development for the Third World as well as the defender of its own national interests. Like Hoffman, American policy-makers could not admit that those goals might not be compatible.[3]

That unwillingness to face up openly to hard choices cast over American policies in the Third World the cloak of hypocrisy. On the one hand, the United States held out its money and technical expertise to promote development, while American rhetoric embraced the principle of national self-determination for poor countries often newly freed from foreign rule. On the other hand, the United States frequently intervened in those countries for its own interests. Even if not guilty of a form of imperialism, as its critics charged, the United States displayed cultural arrogance and a refusal to accept revolutionary changes.

No less than those who shaped American policy, Hoffman suffered from that failing. As head of the U.N.'s economic development program for thirteen years, he operated by an essentially Western and capitalistic model. On the international level as on the domestic level, open-ended economic growth seemed a plausible and painless goal to benefit all. He did encourage poor countries to adopt needed social reforms, but he concentrated on economic development, not reform. He was convinced that underdeveloped nations must modernize and make their economies more efficient and more productive; only then could they earn their way to an integrated global market and provide a decent and rising standard of living for their large populations.

In important ways, the international effort to aid economic development among the poor countries resembled the contemporaneous War on Poverty within the United States. In both cases, liberal experts and dominant groups identified and tried to correct serious problems without changing the fundamentals of the existing systems. But the problems proved more resistant to solution than the experts had assumed. Moreover, political constraints limited the nature and extent of the efforts to reduce poverty. The best examples of success may have been among those who did not really need help and who might have succeeded without it. For the very poorest who remained locked in poverty, however, heightened but unfulfilled expectations led to frustrations and anger.[4]

As with the War on Poverty, the programs of the Development Establishment became the target of leftist criticism. Some Third World spokesmen charged that the system through which development aid programs operated actually exploited the poor countries and failed to benefit the great masses. Despair over the persistence of backwardness and poverty converged with militant demands for radical change. Those critics assumed that the rich industrial countries depended on the primary commodities of the poor nonindustrial countries; therefore, they thought that the producers of primary commodities could force a redistribution of rewards from trade. Only the oil-producing nations, however, managed even temporarily to force that kind of change. Rather than yield to demands for redistribution, industrial countries have seemed more likely to seek technological solutions to reduce their dependence.[5]

For the United States and Western Europe, the demands of the poorest countries have been less threatening than the growing competition from newly developed and industrializing countries, especially in eastern Asia. With older technology and higher labor costs, Western countries have suffered from serious unemployment since the early 1970s. People displaced by competition from developing countries with lower labor costs have taken little comfort from the argument of internationalists like Hoffman that their economies could benefit by upgrading technology and taking advantage of expanded markets. Instead, pressures have mounted for protectionism.

Thus for many reasons, the prospects that Hoffman saw during the Decade of Development now appear less bright. A mood of pessimism, accompanied by forecasts of catastrophic famines and environmental disasters, has replaced the optimism he helped to generate. The arms race reaches new levels; military spending far exceeds economic aid for development. Perhaps the rich industrial countries are only suffering a temporary failure of nerve, an unwillingness to risk the global development and competition that Hoffman claimed would benefit all. But perhaps unpleasant realities have made his vision of a better world beyond attainment.

Notes

Preface

1 Paul G. Hoffman to Eugene Whitmore, 6 March 1951, Hoffman Papers, box 4, Harry S. Truman Library.
2 Hoffman to Paul F. Douglass, 16 Sept. 1953, ibid., box 51.
3 Theodore H. White, *In Search of History* (New York, 1978), 282–85, 528.
4 Quoted in Crane Haussamen, *The Story of Paul G. Hoffman* (Santa Barbara, Calif., 1966), 59.

1. Making a Million Selling Cars

1 Hoffman to Stuart Abel, 2 March 1962, Hoffman Papers, box 52, Harry S. Truman Library; "Genealogy of the Grays of Grayland," n.d., ibid.; Hoffman, Interview by Bela Kornitzer, 15 Oct. 1951, ibid., box 123.
2 Hoffman to Stuart Abel, 9 Dec. 1963, ibid., box 52.
3 Hoffman, Oral History, Columbia University, 27 July 1963, p. 1.
4 Interview by Bela Kornitzer.
5 Ibid.; Hoffman, Oral History, 1–2, 32–33.
6 Hoffman, "No Short Cut to Learning," in D. Louise Sharp, ed., *Why Teach?* (New York, 1957), 100–103.
7 Hoffman, Oral History, 12–14.
8 Ibid., 18–22.
9 Paul Barrett, *The Automobile and Urban Transit: The Formation of Public Policy in Chicago, 1900–1930* (Philadelphia, 1983), 73–74, 80. See Thomas S. Hines, *Burnham of Chicago* (New York, 1974), 401, n. 8, for an explanation of the difficulty in documenting Burnham's credo.
10 Hoffman to Jack Pollack, 23 June 1953, Hoffman Papers, box 92; Hoffman, Oral History, 24.
11 Kevin Starr, *Americans and the California Dream 1850–1915* (New York, 1973), 200–201, 304, 441.
12 Interview by Bela Kornitzer; Hoffman, Oral History, 3–5. In 1942, Hoffman

Specialty moved to Indianapolis; before the family sold its remaining interest to ITT in 1970, the company had acquired plants in California and Pennsylvania.

13 Hoffman, Oral History, 15–17.

14 "Hoofman," *Sales Management* 52 (15 Jan. 1938): 40; Noel Busch, "Paul Hoffman," *Life* 26 (4 Apr. 1949): 124–26.

15 Lathrop G. Hoffman, interview, Detroit, 6 Aug. 1981.

16 Hoffman to Jack Pollack, 23 June 1953; Hoffman, Oral History, 50–53.

17 Lathrop G. Hoffman interview.

18 Hoffman to Albert Russel Erskine, 23 Mar. 1925, Hoffman Papers, box 150; Hoffman and James H. Greene, *Marketing Used Cars* (New York, 1929).

19 Bill Davidson, "Paul Hoffman: Salesman for Democracy," *Coronet* 24 (July, 1948): 99–106; Lathrop G. Hoffman interview.

20 Hoffman, Oral History, 95–96; "KNX-CBS Radio—Continuity, Growth and Creativity," 16 Aug. 1961, p. 3 (copy supplied by the station).

21 Hoffman, "The Traffic Commission of Los Angeles," *Annals of the American Academy of Political and Social Science* 116 (Nov., 1924): 246–50.

22 Mark S. Foster, "The Model T, the Hard Sell, and Los Angeles's Urban Growth: The Decentralization of Los Angeles during the 1920s," *Pacific Historical Review* 44 (Nov. 1975): 459–84, argued that decentralized development resulted from the coincidental spread of cars, the real estate boom, and local planners consciously promoting horizontal growth.

23 *Los Angeles Times*, 4 April 1925.

24 Hoffman, Oral History, 95–96.

25 *Los Angeles Times*, 4 April 1925.

26 Hoffman, Oral History, 56, 61.

2. An Apprenticeship, 1925–33

1 On Dorothy Brown Hoffman the best sources are Obituary, *Pasadena Star-News*, 18 May 1961; Hoffman, Oral History, Columbia University, 27 July 1963, pp. 32–36; Theodore H. White, *In Search of History* (New York, 1978), 282.

2 Richard W. Fox, "Epitaph for Middletown: Robert S. Lynd and the Analysis of Consumer Culture," in Richard W. Fox and T.J. Jackson Lears, eds., *The Culture of Consumption* (New York, 1983), 118–19.

3 Albert Russel Erskine, *History of the Studebaker Corporation* (South Bend, Ind., 1924); Kathleen Smallzried and Dorothy Roberts, *More Than You Promise* (New York, 1942); and Stephen Longstreet, *A Century on Wheels* (New York, 1952), all presented what amounted to authorized histories and company publicity.

4 Harold Katz, *The Decline of Competition in the Automobile Industry, 1920–1940* (New York, 1977), 183.

5 *South Bend Tribune*, 26 July 1919; "Studebaker Comes Back," *Fortune* 11 (Feb. 1935): 89–94, 154–59; *Made in South Bend/Mishawaka* (South Bend, Ind., 1980), 8–10.

6 E.D. Kennedy, *The Automobile Industry* (New York, 1941), 81–84; James J. Flink, *The Car Culture* (Cambridge, Mass., 1975), 168–70.

7 Robert P. Thomas, "Style Change and the Automobile Industry during the

Roaring Twenties," in Louis P. Cain and Paul J. Uselding, eds., *Business Enterprise and Economic Change* (Kent, Ohio, 1973), 118–38; Kennedy, *The Automobile Industry*, 181.
8 *Chicago Tribune*, 2 July 1933; *South Bend News-Times*, 2 July 1933.
9 *South Bend Tribune*, 5 Jan. 1927.
10 Hoffman, Oral History, 57, 69.
11 *Automobile Topics* 96 (4 Jan. 1930): 809; Hoffman to Albert Russel Erskine, 30 Oct. 1929, Studebaker Papers, box 5, Discovery Hall Museum, South Bend.
12 *Automobile Topics* 78 (14 July 1925): 739; Hoffman, "Studebaker's Latest Plan for Qualifying Salesmen," *Sales Management* 18 (27 Apr. 1929): 177, 216–17. "Automobiles II—the Dealer," *Fortune* 4 (March 1931): 38–43, 134ff. Hoffman, Oral History, 64–65.
13 *Automobile Topics* 88 (4 Feb. 1928): 1257; Hoffman and James H. Greene, *Marketing Used Cars* (New York, 1929), 179; *Automobile Topics* 96 (1 Feb. 1930): 1242–44; Hoffman, foreword in David R. Osborne, *Salesmanship for Today for Sales Managers of Tomorrow* (New York, 1939); "Automobiles II—the Dealer," *Fortune*.
14 Hoffman, "America's Highways—New Frontiers," *Roads and Streets* 83 (Jan. 1940): 35–36; Hoffman and Greene, *Marketing Used Cars*, 179.
15 *Los Angeles Times*, 4 Apr. 1925; Hoffman to Albert Russel Erskine, 23 March 1925, Hoffman Papers, box 150, Harry S. Truman Library.
16 Hoffman to Albert Russel Erskine, 4 Feb. 1925 and 30 March 1926, ibid.
17 Claude Hopkins, *My Life in Advertising* (New York, 1927), 120; John Gunther, *Taken at the Flood: The Story of Albert D. Lasker* (New York, 1960), 85–86, 159, 167; Hoffman, Introduction to Charles H. Sandage, ed., *The Promise of Advertising* (Homewood, Ill., 1961); Hoffman, "Will the *Talkies* Talk Their Way into Mass Selling?" *Magazine of Bankers* 56 (Aug. 1929): 149–50, 194; *Automobile Topics* 96 (1 Feb. 1930): 1242–44.
18 Robert Atwan, Donald McQuade, and John W. Wright, *Edsels, Luckies, & Frigidaires: Advertising the American Way* (New York, 1979), 153–54.
19 "Less Speed and More Safety," *Literary Digest* 114 (20 Aug. 1932): 27; Hoffman to Louis I. Dublin, Oct. 1929, Hoffman Papers, box 150.
20 Charles A. Lippincott, "Promoting Employee Team Work and Welfare without Paternalism," *Industrial Management* 71 (March 1926): 146–50; Glenn Griswold, "Humanized Employee Relations: Studebaker an Example," *Public Opinion Quarterly* 4 (Sept. 1940): 487–96.
21 Hoffman to President and Fellows of Harvard University, 16 June 1926, and Hoffman to A. Lawrence Lowell, 25 April 1928, Abbott L. Lowell Papers, folder 508, Harvard University Archives; *Automobile Topics* 95 (28 Sept. 1929): 648.
22 "The Unseen Half of South Bend," *Fortune* 1 (March 1930): 52–57, 102–11; "Automobiles II—the Dealer," *Fortune*; "Studebaker Acquisition of White Consolidates Truck Position," *Business Week*, 28 Sept. 1932, p. 9.
23 Minutes of the Board of Directors of Studebaker, 1 April 1930, Studebaker Papers, box 5.
24 "Studebaker Comes Back," *Fortune*.
25 Minutes of the Board of Directors of Studebaker, 7 Jan. 1930 and 1 April 1930, Studebaker Papers, box 5; Albert Russel Erskine to Frederick S. Fish, 1 July 1930, ibid.

26 John E. Harris to Albert Russel Erskine, 16 Feb. 1931 and 4 March 1931, ibid.; Gunther, *Taken at the Flood*, 189–90.

27 "Studebaker Comes Back," *Fortune*; Kennedy, *The Automobile Industry*, 190, 195. Harold Fleming, *Gasoline Prices and Competition* (New York, 1966), 88–89, used data showing that retail prices including taxes increased; however, when adjusted by the Consumer Price Index, retail prices actually declined during the 1920s.

28 Minutes of the Board of Directors of Studebaker, 26 June 1928, Studebaker Papers, box 5; Federal Trade Commission, *Report on the Motor Vehicle Industry* (Washington, 1939), 795–823.

29 Minutes of the Board of Directors of Studebaker, 27 Jan. 1931, Studebaker Papers, box 5.

30 *Chicago Tribune*, 2 July 1933.

31 *South Bend News-Times*, 2 July 1933.

32 Hoffman, Oral History, 59.

33 *Automobile Topics* 109 (25 March 1933): 340; "Studebaker," *Business Week*, 19 March 1933, p. 13.

34 Thomas, "Style Change and the Automobile Industry during the Roaring Twenties."

3. Bringing Studebaker Back, 1933–48

1 *South Bend News-Times*, 19 March 1933; *South Bend Tribune*, 21 March 1933; "Studebaker Comes Back," *Fortune* 11 (Feb. 1935): 89–94, 154–59; Hoffman, Oral History, Columbia University, 27 July 1963, pp. 73–75.

2 Harold Katz, *The Decline of Competition in the Automobile Industry, 1920–1940* (New York, 1977), 186.

3 Eustace Seligman, Oral History, Columbia University, 22 Oct. 1974, pp. 110–14.

4 Sanderson & Porter Report, 1 June 1934, excerpted in Minutes of the Board of Directors of Studebaker, 14 May 1938, III:316–18, Studebaker Papers, Discovery Hall Museum, South Bend.

5 Salary and Option Agreements, 8 March 1935, Studebaker Papers, box 19.

6 Hoffman, "Spreading Responsibility for Expense Control," [Metropolitan Life Insurance Co.] *Executive Service Bulletin*, 16 (Dec. 1938): 1–2, 6; Hoffman, "How We Sliced Our Overhead 58 Per Cent," *American Business* 6 (Aug. 1936): 9–11, 42–43.

7 *Time* 26 (4 Nov. 1935): 72; *Automobile Topics* 117 (16 Mar. 1935): 250; Kathleen Smallzried and Dorothy Roberts, *More Than You Promise* (New York, 1942), 299–301.

8 Smallzried and Roberts, *More Than You Promise*, 308; Hoffman, speech to Press Prevue, 15 Aug. 1939, Hoffman Papers, box 102, Harry S. Truman Library.

9 Hoffman, Oral History, 88; Glenn Griswold, "Humanized Employee Relations: Studebaker an Example," *Public Opinion Quarterly* 4 (Sept. 1940): 487–96; Frederick H. Harbison and Robert Dubin, *Patterns of Union-Management Relations* (Chicago, 1947), 105–22.

10 Alton A. Green to William Green, 5 March 1935, US MSS 117A, AFL Papers,

Series 7, Strikes and Agreements File, 1898–1953, Box 4, Local 18310, State Historical Society of Wisconsin; Hoffman to Studebaker Supervisors and Department Heads, 28 June 1935, Hoffman Papers, box 150; Hoffman and Vance to Studebaker employees, 24 March 1936, ibid.

11 *Automobile Topics* 131 (19 Sept. 1938): 239; Hoffman, speech to Buffalo Dealer Driveaway, 5 April 1937, Hoffman Papers, box 100.

12 Morrell Heald, *The Social Responsibilities of Business* (Cleveland, 1970), 197–98.

13 Hoffman, speech to Studebaker sales representatives and dealers, 9 Sept. 1937, Hoffman Papers, box 100; "Studebaker in Low-Price Field," *Business Week*, 25 March 1939, pp. 3–4; "Studebaker's Light Car," *Fortune* 19 (Apr. 1939): 86–89, 144ff.

14 Minutes of the Board of Directors of Studebaker, 26 April 1938, Studebaker Papers; Sanderson & Porter Report, III:311–16, ibid.; Minutes of the Board of Directors of Studebaker, 16 May 1938, III:318.

15 Alan R. Raucher, "Paul G. Hoffman, Studebaker, and the Car Culture," *Indiana Magazine of History*, 79 (Sept. 1983): 209–230.

16 Minutes of the Board of Directors of Studebaker, 27 Jan. 1939, III:352–53, Studebaker Papers; *South Bend Tribune*, 5 March 1939; A. St. John, "Meet Mr. Hoffman," *Barron's* 20 (8 July 1940): 9.

17 "Studebaker's Light Car," *Fortune* 19 (April 1939): 86–89, 144ff.; "The Studebaker Champion," *Consumers Union Reports* 4 (Aug. 1939): 3; Dewey H. Palmer, "Automobiles of 1940," *New Republic* 100 (29 Nov. 1939): 160–62; Palmer, "Automobiles of 1941," ibid., 103 (3 Dec. 1940): 891–93.

18 Minutes of the Board of Directors of Studebaker, 25 April 1939, III:374; 19 Dec. 1940, IV:464, Studebaker Papers.

19 E. D. Kennedy, *The Automobile Industry* (New York, 1941), 310.

20 Minutes of the Board of Directors of Studebaker, 28 Feb. 1941, IV:478, Studebaker Papers; *New York Times*, 23 Jan. 1940; A. St. John, "Meet Mr. Hoffman."

21 U.S., Congress, Temporary National Economic Committee, *Investigation of Concentration of Economic Power*, 76th Cong. 2d sess., pt. 21 (Washington, 1940), 11181–224, for testimony of Hoffman and Vance, 6 Dec. 1939.

22 Minutes of the Board of Directors of Studebaker, 27 Oct. 1939, III:396, Studebaker Papers; Smallzried and Roberts, *More Than You Promise*, 312–13.

23 Minutes of the Board of Directors of Studebaker, 28 June 1940, IV:448, and 26 July 1940, IV:451, Studebaker Papers; Paul Hoffman to M. T. Moore, 6 June 1940, Hoffman Papers, box 150.

24 *New York Times*, 24 Sept. 1940, 13 Oct. 1940, 16 Oct. 1940; *University of Chicago Round Table*, "Where Are Those 50,000 Planes," NBC "Red," 15 Dec. 1940, Hoffman Papers, box 103.

25 Barton J. Bernstein, "The Automobile Industry and the Coming of the Second World War," *Southwestern Social Science Quarterly* 47 (June 1966): 32; Eliot Janeway, *The Struggle for Survival* (New Haven, Conn., 1951), 228.

26 "Assembly Line . . . ," *Iron Age* 150 (22 Oct. 1942): 86.

27 Hoffman, "Cooperation Will Not Be Rationed," speech to National Association of Purchasing Agents, 25 May 1942, Hoffman Papers, box 103.

28 *New York Times*, 29 Nov. 1943.

29 *Babson Report 1942* and *Babson Report 1944*; U.S., Congress, Joint Com-

mittee on the Economic Report, Subcommittee on Profits, *Corporate Profits*, 80th Cong., 2d sess. (Washington, D.C., 1949), 247.

30 *New York Times*, 16 Dec. 1942; Kenneth B. Elliott to Board of Directors of Studebaker, 22 Jan. 1943, Studebaker Papers, box 10.

31 "Direct to Dealers," *Business Week*, 19 Aug. 1944, p. 90; Minutes of the Board of Directors of Studebaker, 28 Sept. 1945, Studebaker Papers, box 11.

32 "Studebaker: Model Termination," *Business Week*, 29 Dec. 1945, pp. 66–71.

33 *New York Times*, 25 July 1945; Robert T. Swaine, *The Cravath Firm and Its Predecessors, 1819–1948* (New York, 1948), II:618–19; *Babson Report 1945*; Katz, *The Decline of Competition in the Automobile Industry*, 189.

34 *South Bend Tribune*, 8 Jan. 1943; *New York Times*, 21 Sept. 1943.

35 Hoffman, speech to Executive Committee of R.H. Macy & Co., 6 Feb. 1946, Hoffman Papers, box 109; Harbison and Dubin, *Patterns of Union-Management Relations*, 138–42.

36 Robert M. MacDonald, *Collective Bargaining in the Automobile Industry* (New Haven, Conn., 1963), 259–84, 359–67.

37 *New York Times*, 9 Oct. 1946.

38 See Lawrence J. White, *The Automobile Industry Since 1945* (Cambridge, Mass., 1971), and Charles E. Edwards, *Dynamics of the United States Automobile Industry* (Columbia, S.C., 1965).

39 Hoffman, speech to sales meeting, 15 Apr. 1946, Hoffman Papers, box 109; "Going Its Way," *Business Week*, 6 April 1946, p. 20; Minutes of the Board of Directors of Studebaker, 27 Sept. 1946 and 14 Nov. 1946, Studebaker Papers, box 11; Hoffman, speech to New York Society of Security Analysts, 19 Nov. 1947, Hoffman Papers, box 112; Richard M. Langworth, *Studebaker: The Postwar Years* (Osceola, Wis., 1979), 21.

40 *South Bend Tribune*, 7 May 1946.

41 Langworth, *Studebaker*, 26; Virgil Exner, "Are Dangerous Curves Ahead?" *Automobile Industries* 99 (1 Dec. 1948): 45–46.

42 "Hoffman, Paul G[ray]," *Current Biography, 1946* (New York, 1946), 265.

43 "Studebaker," *Life* 21 (16 Sept. 1946): 66–75.

44 "Studebaker Cars for 1947," *Consumers Research Bulletin* 18 (July 1946): 9–10; "Additional Information on 1947 Studebaker Cars," ibid. 18 (Oct. 1946): 12–13; "Economy-Model Cars," *Consumer Reports* 11 (July 1946): 171–73; "The Kaiser-Frazer and Studebaker Cars," ibid. 12 (May 1947): 149–52; ibid. 14 (May 1949): 214; Floyd Clymer, *A Report and Investigation of Post-War Studebaker Automobiles* (Los Angeles, 1948), 46. Cf. Alfred P. Sloan, *My Life with General Motors* (New York, 1965), 436–44.

45 Minutes of the Board of Directors of Studebaker, 28 March 1947, VIII:945, and 23 May 1947, VIII:963, Studebaker Papers.

46 Hoffman, speech to Executive Committee of R. H. Macy & Co., 6 Feb. 1946.

47 R[alph] A. Vail to UAW Local 5, 2 May 1946, UAW Local 5 Collection, box 4, Wayne State University; Minutes of the Board of Directors of Studebaker, 26 Sept. 1947, VIII:986–87, and 24 Oct. 1947, VIII:989, Studebaker Papers.

48 Hoffman to Vance, 20 July 1948, Hoffman Papers, box 150; 9 May 1949, 25 Oct. 1949, 5 Dec. 1949, box 2.

49 U.S., Congress, Joint Committee on the Economic Report, Subcommittee on Profits, *Corporate Profits*, 242–60.

50 Langworth, *Studebaker*, 163–65.

51 Samuel C. Stearn, "The Financial History of the American Automobile In-

dustry Since 1928," M.A. thesis, Wayne [State] University, 1948, pp. 160–61; Langworth, *Studebaker*, 42, 163.
52 Hoffman to Harold Vance, 9 May 1949, Hoffman Papers, box 2.

4. The Search for Stability and Growth, 1933–48

1 See Ellis Hawley, "The Discovery and Study of a 'Corporate Liberalism,'" *Business History Review* 52 (Autumn 1978): 309–20, and Joan Hoff Wilson, *Herbert Hoover: Forgotten Progressive* (Boston, 1975).
2 See David Burner, *Herbert Hoover* (New York, 1979), 139–41.
3 Hoffman, "Business and Conscription," speech to Des Moines Chamber of Commerce, 13 Dec. 1940, in *Vital Speeches*, 7 (1 Jan. 1941): 189–92.
4 Hoffman, "Free Enterprise or Feudalism," speech to National Institute of Trade Association Executives, 18 Aug. 1939, Hoffman Papers, box 102, Harry S. Truman Library; Hoffman, "The Corporation as a Social Instrument," in Bronson Batchelor, ed., *The New Outlook in Business* (New York, 1940), 105–16.
5 Hoffman to Henry I. Harriman, July 1934, Hoffman Papers, box 28; Hoffman, "I Am a Liberal," ibid., box 146; Hoffman, "Preface to Recovery," speech to Pittsburgh Chamber of Commerce, 24 May 1939, ibid., box 102.
6 Hoffman, "Future of American Business," speech to Purchasing Agents' Association of New York, 15 Feb. 1938, ibid., box 101; speech to Bond Club of New York, 9 Dec. 1938, ibid.; Hoffman, "The Corporation as a Social Instrument," 112.
7 Hoffman, "The Collective Responsibility of Business for Free Enterprise," speech to University of Chicago, 26 May 1938, Hoffman Papers, box 101.
8 Hoffman to James G. Blaine, 23 Oct. 1936, ibid., box 29.
9 Hoffman, speech to Lyons Township High School, 30 June 1937, ibid., box 100; Hoffman, "Free Enterprise vs. Feudalism," speech to National Association of Sales Finance Companies, 15 Sept. 1939, and American Petroleum Institute, 15 Nov. 1939, in *Vital Speeches* 6 (1 Dec. 1939): 102–05; Hoffman to Thomas E. Dewey, 12 Jan. 1940, Thomas E. Dewey Papers, Box 1:27, University of Rochester Library. On the opposition of automobile producers to government efforts to curb competition and "overproduction," see Herman Krooss and Charles Gilbert, *American Business History* (Englewood Cliffs, N.J., 1972), 284.
10 Earl Carpenter to Hoffman, 5 March 1936, Hoffman Papers, box 53.
11 Randolph E. Paul, *Taxation in the United States* (Boston, 1954), 210, 213–14; John Morton Blum, *From the Morgenthau Diaries* (Boston, 1959), I:441.
12 Hoffman to Earl Carpenter, 15 Nov. 1937, Hoffman Papers, box 53.
13 Hoffman, "Preface to Recovery." Cf. Jordan A. Schwarz, *The Speculator: Bernard M. Baruch in Washington, 1917–1965* (Chapel Hill, N.C., 1981), 315–18.
14 *Literary Digest*, 29 Jan. 1938, p. 4; Hoffman, "Preface to Recovery"; Hoffman, speech to University of Southern California, 3 May 1940, Hoffman Papers, box 102.
15 Hoffman, "Future of American Business."
16 Hoffman, "How to Save Democracy in U.S.," *Printers' Ink* 192 (5 July 1940): 9–11, 67–69; Hoffman, "Let's Live for America," speech to American Trade

Association Executives, 26 Sept. 1940, in *Congressional Record,* 76th Cong., 3d sess., 1940, 86, pt. 18: A6754–55.

17 Hoffman, "Business and Conscription"; *New York Times,* 27 March 1941.
18 See Morrell Heald, *The Social Responsibilities of Business* (Cleveland, 1970), 270–72, and Richard S. Tedlow, *Keeping the Corporate Image* (Greenwich, Conn., 1979), 76; Hoffman, "Dual Date with Destiny," speech to Tulsa Chamber of Commerce, 14 Jan. 1942, in *Vital Speeches* 8 (1 Feb. 1942): 232–34.
19 Hoffman to Norman Chandler, 18 Jan. 1940, Thomas E. Dewey Papers, box 1:27.
20 Hoffman to Chandler, 18 Jan. 1940; Hoffman to Thomas E. Dewey, 29 Aug. 1939 and 11 Dec. 1939, ibid.
21 Hoffman to Thomas E. Dewey, 11 Dec. 1939, 12 Jan. 1940, and 18 Jan. 1940, ibid.
22 Hoffman to James G. Blaine, 3 July 1940, Hoffman Papers, box 29; Hoffman to Russell Davenport, 12 Nov. 1940, ibid.
23 Hoffman to Henry Luce, 4 June 1940 and 21 Sept. 1940, Henry Luce Papers, Time Archives, New York.
24 Karl Schriftgiesser, *Business Comes of Age* (New York, 1960), 9–11; Sidney Hyman, *The Lives of William Benton* (Chicago, 1969), 231–34; Robert M. Collins, *The Business Response to Keynes, 1929–1964* (New York, 1981), 72–73.
25 Hoffman to Benton, 12 May 1941 and 2 Aug. 1941, Hoffman Papers, box 40.
26 William Benton to Thomas E. Dewey, 9 Nov. 1942, Thomas E. Dewey Papers, box 4:15.
27 *Time* 4 (6 Sept. 1943): 75–78.
28 *New York Times,* 12 Oct. 1945; Hoffman, "Employment and Private Industry," *Survey Graphic* 32 (May 1943): 176–77.
29 See Collins, *The Business Response to Keynes,* and Kim McQuaid, *Big Business and Presidential Power* (New York, 1982).
30 *New York Times,* 14 May 1947; Hoffman, book MSS, 27 Jan. 1948, Hoffman Papers, box 144; Hoffman to Paul Russell, 10 Oct. 1949, ibid., box 115; Hoffman, speech to National Association of Securities Commissioners, 16 Nov. 1945, and Hoffman, speech to American Bankers Association, 23 Sept. 1946, in *Congressional Record,* 80th Cong., 2d sess., 1948, 94, pt. 4:5253.
31 Hoffman, "The Recovery Program Builds European Unity," speech to National Planning Association, 31 Jan. 1949, Hoffman Papers, box 115; Hoffman, "How a Job Is Born," *New York Times,* 20 Aug. 1944; U.S., Congress, Joint Committee on the Economic Report, *Current Price Developments and the Problem of Economic Stabilization,* 80th Cong., 1st sess. (Washington, D.C., 1947), 62–63, 71 (hereafter cited as *Current Price Developments*).
32 Hoffman, "Private Enterprise at 39–1 Is Good Enough for Me," *Factory Management and Maintenance,* 104 (July 1946): 102–04; Hoffman, "A Blueprint for Business Stability," *American Business,* 16 (July 1946): 8–10; Hoffman, "The Great Challenge to Capitalism," *New York Times Magazine,* 8 Sept. 1946.
33 U.S., Congress, Senate, Subcommittee of the Committee on Banking and Currency, *Full Employment Act of 1945,* 79th Cong., 1st sess. (1945), 705–19 (hereafter cited as *Full Employment Act of 1945*).

34 *Full Employment Act of 1945*, 705–14; *New York Times*, 23 Oct. 1945; Hoffman to Henry Luce, 3 Feb. 1945, Henry Luce Papers.

35 Hoffman, "Winning the Peace," speech to American Road Builders' Association, 2 Feb. 1944, in *Congressional Record*, 78th Cong., 2d sess., 1944, 90, pt. 8:A861–63; U.S., Congress, House, Special Committee on Post-War Economic Policy and Planning, *Hearings*, 78th Cong., 2d sess., pt. 1 (1944), 193–216.

36 *Full Employment Act of 1945*, 714; Samuel H. Thompson to Henry A. Wallace, 6 Sept. 1945, in Henry A. Wallace, Oral History, Columbia University, 4072. See Stephen K. Bailey, *Congress Makes a Law* (New York, 1950), 132, 156, and 165.

37 *Full Employment Act of 1945*, 718; Schriftgiesser, *Business Comes of Age*, 71–75; *New York Times*, 19 Oct. 1946, 25 Feb. 1947, 22 March 1947; Howell John Harris, *The Right to Manage* (Madison, Wis., 1982), 110.

38 Hoffman, speech to Poor Richard Club, 1 Jan. 1950, in *Congressional Record*, 81st Cong., 1st sess., 1950, 96, pt. 13:A911–12.

39 *New York Times*, 1 July 1943; *Full Employment Act of 1945*, 714.

40 Collins, *The Business Response to Keynes*, 130; *Full Employment Act of 1945*, 714, 718.

41 Ibid., 709–14; Karl Schriftgiesser, *Business and Public Policy* (Englewood Cliffs, N.J., 1967), 5.

42 Collins, *Business Response to Keynes*, 134; *Current Price Developments*, 64; Hoffman, "Private Enterprise at 39–1 Is Good Enough for Me," 102–04.

43 *Current Price Developments*, 68.

44 U.S., Congress, Senate, Committee on Appropriations, *Foreign Aid Appropriation Bill, 1950*, 81st Cong., 1st sess. (1949), 109, 113; Hoffman to Frank Main, 29 July 1952, Hoffman Papers, box 62.

45 *New York Times*, 15 May 1947; Hoffman, "A Three-Way Program for Helping Small Business," *Dun's Review* 55 (Oct. 1947): 11–13.

46 Hoffman, *Peace Can Be Won* (Garden City, N.Y., 1951), 25.

47 Hoffman to William Benton, 12 May 1941, Hoffman Papers, box 40; *New York Times*, 16 Feb. 1942; Minutes of the Board of Directors of Studebaker, 23 May 1941, IV:504, Studebaker Papers; "China's Day," *Business Week*, 25 Aug. 1945, p. 119.

48 Calvin B. Hoover, *Memoirs of Capitalism, Communism, and Nazism* (Durham, N.C., 1965), 214, 221–22; Thomas G. Paterson, *On Every Front* (New York, 1979), 78–79.

49 U.S., Congress, House, Special Committee on Post-War Economic Policy and Planning, *Hearings*, 78th Cong., 2d sess., pt. 1 (1944), 211; *New York Times*, 5 July 1944.

50 Alfred E. Eckes, Jr., *A Search for Solvency: Bretton Woods and the International Monetary System, 1941–1971* (Austin, Tex., 1975), 168, 185, 191–92.

51 Hoffman to Beardsley Ruml, 2 April 1945, William Benton Papers, box 52:27, University of Chicago Library; Hoffman, "The Bretton Woods Plan," *American Druggist*, July 1945, p. 58.

52 Hoffman, "The Expansion of Private Enterprise and World Markets," speech to International Chamber of Commerce, 17 Aug. 1945, Hoffman Papers, box 108; Hoffman, "U.S. Business *Needs* Peace," *United Nations World* 1 (Nov. 1947): 25–27.

53 *New York Times*, 9 Aug. 1945; John Morton Blum, ed., *The Price of Vision: The Diary of Henry A. Wallace 1942–1946* (Boston, 1973), 560, 13 Mar. 1946; Hoffman to Blair Moody, 16 Dec. 1946, Blair Moody Papers, box 3, Michigan Historical Collections.

54 *New York Times*, 15 May 1947; U.S., Congress, Joint Committee on the Economic Report, *Current Price Developments*, 65; Hoffman to Walter Harnischfeger, 19 Jan. 1948, Hoffman Papers, box 113; U.S., Congress, Senate, Committee on Foreign Relations, *European Recovery Program*, 80th Cong., 2d sess., pt. 2 (1948), 847–53 (hereafter cited as *ERP* [1948]).

55 Hoffman to Lottie and Dewey Smith, 19 April 1948, Hoffman Papers, box 1; *Foreign Relations of the United States, 1949*, VII, pt. 2:634. (These volumes, hereafter cited as *FRUS* with the appropriate year, were published in Washington, D.C., 1973–1979.)

56 Arthur H. Vandenberg, Jr., ed., *The Private Papers of Senator Vandenberg* (Boston, 1952), 394, cited Hoffman interview, 9 Oct. 1951; Hoffman, "European Recovery Program," Oral History, Jan. 1966, Harry S. Truman Library.

57 *ERP* (1948).

58 *New York Times*, 22 May 1946; *Private Papers of Senator Vandenberg*, 394; Harry B. Price, *The Marshall Plan and Its Meaning* (Ithaca, N.Y., 1955), 71–74; Dean Acheson, *Present at the Creation* (New York, 1969), 242.

59 *New York Times*, 6 April 1948; *Congressional Record*, 80th Cong., 2d sess., 1948, 94, pt. 3:4149.

60 Henry Luce to Hoffman, 8 April 1948, Henry Luce Papers; "Noah," *Time* 51 (12 April 1948): 19; "Paul Hoffman," *Life* 24 (19 April 1948): 48, 53.

61 "Men for the ECA," *Fortune* 37 (June, 1948): 3; *Congressional Record*, 80th Cong., 2d sess., 1948, 94, pt. 3:4181–82.

62 Hoffman to C.K. Whittaker, 26 April 1948, Hoffman Papers, box 1.

63 Cf. Thomas J. McCormick, "Drift or Mastery? A Corporatist Synthesis for American Diplomatic History," *Reviews in American History* 10 (Dec. 1982): 318–330; Michael J. Hogan, "Revival and Reform: America's Twentieth-Century Search for a New Economic Order Abroad," *Diplomatic History* 8 (Autumn 1984): 287–310.

5. Administering the Marshall Plan, 1948–50

1 Joyce and Gabriel Kolko, *The Limits of Power* (New York, 1972), 359–60, 382–83, 462; Lloyd C. Gardner, *A Covenant with Power* (New York, 1984), 83.

2 Hoffman, "European Recovery Program," Oral History, Jan. 1966, p. 6, Harry S. Truman Library.

3 Hoffman to Lawrence F. Cuthbert, 19 June 1948, Hoffman Papers, box 60, Harry S. Truman Library.

4 Hoffman to Paul Helms, 19 April 1948, ibid., box 1; Hoffman to William Benton, 5 June 1948, ibid.

5 Hoffman to Earl Carpenter, 28 April 1948, ibid.; Hoffman, "European Recovery Program," Oral History, Truman Library, p. 16; Pres. Harry S. Truman to Hoffman, 9 Aug. 1948, Harry S. Truman Papers, box 1281, Harry S. Truman Library.

6 Hoffman to Paul Helms, 19 April 1948; U.S., Congress, House, Appropria-

tions Committee, *Foreign Aid Appropriation Bill for 1949*, 80th Cong., 2d sess. (1948), 5.

7 *ERP* (1948), 847–53; Harlan Cleveland, "The Future of Public Administration," *Bureaucrat* 11 (Autumn 1982): 7–8; Lincoln Gordon, Oral History, 17 July 1975, pp. 95–96, 98, 110, Harry S. Truman Library.

8 Paul F. Douglass, *Six Upon the World* (Boston, 1954), 42.

9 Hadley Arkes, *Bureaucracy, the Marshall Plan, and the National Interest* (Princeton, N.J., 1972), 237; Harry B. Price, *The Marshall Plan and Its Meaning* (Ithaca, N.Y., 1955), 228; Hoffman to Peter Hoffman, 4 April 1949, Hoffman Papers, box 2.

10 Robert H. Ferrell, ed., *Dear Bess: The Letters from Harry Truman to Bess Truman, 1910–1959* (New York, 1983), 549; "Hatchets at Hoffman," *Newsweek* 33 (20 June 1949): 22; Hoffman to Paul Helms, 16 Feb. 1949, Hoffman Papers, box 2.

11 U.S., Congress, House, Foreign Affairs Committee, *Extension of European Recovery Program*, 81st Cong., 1st sess., pt. 1 (1949), 350–51; U.S., Congress, House, Foreign Affairs Committee, *To Amend the Economic Cooperation Act of 1948, As Amended*, 81st Cong., 2d sess. (1950), 377–79.

12 U.S., Congress, Senate, Appropriations Committee, *Foreign Aid Appropriation Bill, 1950*, 81st Cong., 1st sess. (1949), 38.

13 House, Foreign Affairs Committee, *To Amend the Economic Cooperation Act of 1948, As Amended*, 379; Hoffman to Sen. Theodore Green, 21 Oct. 1949, Hoffman Papers, box 22.

14 Hoffman, "On With the Job," speech to Harvard University, 10 June 1948, in *Congressional Record*, 80th Cong., 2d sess., 1948, 94, pt. 11:A3901; U.S., Congress, House, Select Committee on Small Business, *Impact of the European Recovery Program on American Small Business*, 80th Cong., 2d sess. (1948), 12.

15 Hoffman, speech to University of Notre Dame, 6 June 1948, in *Congressional Record*, 80th Cong., 2d sess., 1948, 94, pt. 11:A3937–38; House, Foreign Affairs Committee, *To Amend the Economic Cooperation Act of 1948, As Amended*, 102; *New York Times*, 17 Feb. 1950.

16 U.S., Congress, House, Appropriations Committee, *Foreign Aid Appropriation Bill for 1949*, 80th Cong., 2d sess. (1948), 55; Hoffman to B. E. Hutchinson, 8 May 1948, Hoffman Papers, box 60.

17 Hoffman, "The Effect of the European Recovery Program on Marketing Management," speech to American Management Association, 18 Mar. 1949, Hoffman Papers, box 115; Hoffman, "European Recovery," *American Magazine* 147 (April 1949): 24–25; Hoffman, "ECA's New Strategy for a New Europe," *This Week*, 2 April 1950, in *Congressional Record*, 81st Cong., 2d sess., 1950, 96, pt. 14:A2697–98.

18 U.S., Congress, House, Merchant Marine and Fisheries Committee, *Sale, Charter, and Operation of Vessels*, 81st Cong., 1st sess. (1949), 217; U.S., Congress, Senate, Foreign Relations Committee, *Extension of European Recovery—1950*, 81st Cong., 2d sess. (1950), 40.

19 *New York Times*, 26 Aug. 1949; ECA, British Press Response, 26 Aug. 1949, Hoffman Papers, box 116. See William F. Sanford, Jr., "The American Business Community and the European Recovery Program, 1947–1952," Ph.D. diss., University of Texas, 1980, vi–vii and 157; David S. Painter, "Oil and the Marshall Plan," *Business History Review* 58 (Autumn 1984): 359–83.

20 House, Appropriations Committee, *Foreign Aid Appropriation Bill for 1949*, 33; Senate, Foreign Relations Committee, *Extension of European Recovery—1950*, 88.

21 U.S., Congress, Senate, Foreign Relations Committee, Hearings in Executive Session, *Reviews of the World Situation: 1949–1950*, 81st Cong., 1st and 2d sess. (1974), 60, 63; *Congressional Record*, 81st Cong., 2d sess., 1950, 96, pt. 11:15113–14.

22 Hoffman, speech to Textile Workers Union, CIO, 3 May 1950, in *Congressional Record*, 81st Cong., 2d sess., 1950, 96, pt. 15:A3566; Hoffman, speech to United Textile Workers of America, 22 June 1950, ibid., pt. 16:A4753–55.

23 Hoffman to Sen. H. Alexander Smith, 21 March 1950, Hoffman Papers, box 22.

24 Hoffman, "European Recovery Program," Oral History, Truman Library; Senate, Foreign Relations Committee, *European Recovery Program* (1948).

25 U.S., Congress, Senate, Appropriations Committee, *Economic Cooperation Administration*, 80th Cong., 2d sess. (1948), 575.

26 *New York Times*, 28 July 1948; Hoffman to James Carey, 5 Aug. 1948, CIO Papers, box 126, Walter P. Reuther Library, Wayne State University.

27 Hoffman, Report to Staff, 1 Nov. 1948, Hoffman Papers, box 22; Hoffman to Theodore Yntema, Apr. 25, 1951, ibid., box 4.

28 Arkes, *Bureaucracy, the Marshall Plan, and the National Interest*, 309–14.

29 *FRUS, 1948*, III:476–77, August 20, 1948.

30 Hoffman quoted in Demaree Bess, "Does the ERP Mean War or Peace?" *Saturday Evening Post* 221 (29 Jan. 1949): 15–17.

31 U.S., Congress, Senate, Appropriations Committee, *Foreign Aid Appropriation Bill, 1950*, 81st Cong., 1st sess. (1949), 656–58; U.S., Congress, House, Appropriations Committee, *Foreign Aid Appropriations for 1951*, 81st Cong., 2d sess. (1950), 57; *FRUS, 1949*, III:608–11, 3 Oct. 1949; *FRUS, 1948*, II:792, 16 Aug. 1948; ibid., 797, 26 Aug. 1948; ibid., 802, 3 Sept. 1948; ibid., 804, 7 Sept. 1948; ibid., 809, 16 Sept. 1948.

32 Ibid., 811, 24 Sept. 1948; ibid., 813–14, 29 Sept. 1948; ibid., 816–18, 11 Oct. 1948; *FRUS, 1949*, III:559, 4 March 1949; ibid., 608–11, 3 Oct. 1949.

33 Dean Acheson, *Present at the Creation* (New York, 1969), 324.

34 "Whip-Cracking Time for the ECA," *Newsweek* 34 (7 Nov. 1949): 31–32; John Osborne, "Paul Hoffman Puts It Up to Europe," *Life* 27 (5 Dec. 1949): 63–66.

35 Hoffman, "An Expanding Economy through Economic Integration," in *Vital Speeches* 16 (15 Nov. 1949): 68–70.

36 David S. McLellan, *Dean Acheson* (New York, 1976), 242–44; Robert Marjolin, "European Recovery Program," Oral History, 30 May 1964, p. 33, Harry S. Truman Library.

37 *FRUS, 1950*, V:10, 9 Jan. 1950; House, Foreign Affairs Committee, *To Amend the Economic Cooperation Act of 1948, As Amended*, 71–72.

38 Ernest H. van der Beugel, *From Marshall Aid to Atlantic Partnership* (Amsterdam, 1966), 264; Hoffman to Stafford Cripps, 15 March 1950, Hoffman Papers, box 26; Hoffman, "Toward Integration: France Points the Way," *New York Times Magazine*, 21 May 1950.

39 Hoffman, statement on China Aid Program, House Appropriations Committee, 18 May 1948, Hoffman Papers, box 113; *New York Times*, 12 December 1948; Hoffman, press conference statement, Shanghai, 13 Dec. 1948, Hoffman Papers, box 114.

NOTES TO PAGES 75–81   179

40 *FRUS, 1949,* IX:614, 14 Jan. 1949; ibid., 616, 25 Jan. 1949; ibid., V:872–73, 19 Feb. 1949.
41 Hoffman to Chiang Kai-shek, handwritten draft, Dec. 1949, Hoffman Papers, box 26; Hoffman to Bishop Herbert Welch, 22 April 1950, ibid., box 2.
42 U.S., Congress, House, Foreign Affairs Committee, *International Technical Cooperation Act of 1949,* 81st Cong., 1st sess. (1950), 429; "The Kremlin Will Crumble," *U.S. News & World Report* 28 (12 May 1950): 26–29.
43 *New York Times,* 17 Dec. 1948; U.S., Congress, House, Foreign Affairs Committee, *Korean Aid,* 81st Cong., 1st sess. (1949), 10–18; House, Appropriations Committee, *Foreign Aid Appropriation for 1950,* 809–11; Hoffman to Sen. Arthur H. Vandenberg, 7 Oct. 1949, Hoffman Papers, box 29; Senate, Foreign Relations Committee, *Extension of European Recovery—1950,* 365; House, Foreign Affairs Committee, *International Technical Cooperation Act of 1949,* 430; *FRUS, 1950,* VII:8, 18 Jan. 1950; ibid., 36–37, 27 March 1950; ibid., 91, 27 May 1950; Hoffman to John Cowles, 3 Feb. 1951, Hoffman Papers, box 19.
44 House, Foreign Affairs Committee, *To Amend the Economic Cooperation Act of 1948, As Amended,* 88; U.S., Congress, Senate, Appropriations Committee, *Foreign Aid Appropriations for 1951,* 81st Cong., 2d sess. (1950), 298.
45 Hoffman to Robert M. Hutchins, 16 June 1950, Robert M. Hutchins Papers, box 68:4, University of Chicago Library; Hoffman to William H. Draper, Jr., 7 Aug. 1950, Hoffman Papers, box 3.
46 *FRUS, 1950,* III:653, 4 May 1950; ibid., VI:811, 6 May 1950; U.S., Congress, Senate, Foreign Relations Committee and Armed Services Committee, *Mutual Defense Assistance Program, 1950,* 81st Cong., 2d sess. (1950), 91–104.
47 Hoffman to Robert Huse, 9 Aug. 1950, Hoffman Papers, box 3; U.S., Congress, Senate, Appropriations Committee, *Supplemental Appropriations for 1951,* 81st Cong., 2d sess. (1950), 274–76.
48 Imanuel Wexler, *The Marshall Plan Revisited* (Westport, Conn., 1983), 114; *New York Times,* 28 Sept. 1950 and 20 Oct. 1950; "Hoffman's Farewell," *Life* 29 (13 Nov. 1950): 51–54.
49 *New York Times,* 26 Sept. 1950; Arthur H. Vandenberg, Jr., ed., *The Private Papers of Senator Vandenberg* (Boston, 1952), 395, 29 Sept. 1950; Sen. Kenneth Wherry to Hoffman, 17 Nov. 1950, Hoffman Papers, box 21; Sen. Robert A. Taft to Hoffman, 24 Nov. 1950, ibid.
50 Alfred E. Eckes, Jr., *A Search for Solvency: Bretton Woods and the International Monetary System, 1941–1971* (Austin, Tex., 1975), 216–18; Wexler, *The Marshall Plan Revisited,* ix.
51 Theodore H. White, *In Search of History* (New York, 1978), 304.
52 Hoffman, *Peace Can Be Won* (Garden City, N.Y., 1951), 20–22, 25–26, 40, 44, 47–51.
53 Ibid., 65.
54 Price, *The Marshall Plan and Its Meaning,* 242–44.

6. President of the Ford Foundation, 1951–53

1 Edward H. Berman, *The Influence of the Carnegie, Ford, and Rockefeller Foundations on American Foreign Policy* (Albany, N.Y., 1983), 4–9.
2 Dwight Macdonald, *The Ford Foundation* (New York, 1956), and William

Greenleaf, "The Ford Foundation: The Formative Years," July 1958 (unpublished), Ford Foundation Archives, New York, and Henry Ford Museum, Dearborn, Michigan.

3 "Report of the Study for the Ford Foundation on Policy and Program," Nov. 1949 (unpublished), Hoffman Papers, box 43, Harry S. Truman Library.

4 *New York Times*, 18 Dec. 1949; Sidney Hyman, *The Lives of William Benton* (Chicago, 1969), 425; Hoffman to William Benton, 15 Aug. 1950, Hoffman Papers, box 3; Hoffman to Ernest Breech, 30 Oct. 1950, ibid.; Hoffman to William R. Keast, 18 Aug. 1950, ibid.

5 U.S., Congress, House, Select Committee to Investigate Tax-Exempt Foundations and Comparable Organizations, *Tax-Exempt Foundations*, 82d Cong., 2d sess. (1953), 228 (hereafter cited as Cox Committee).

6 Hoffman to Mrs. Roger Lapham, 25 April 1951, Hoffman Papers, box 19. The Ford Foundation later raised his salary to $100,000.

7 *New York Times*, 7 Nov. 1950; Hoffman to Henry Ford II, 10 Mar. 1951, Hoffman Papers, box 4; Frank K. Kelly, *Court of Reason: Robert Hutchins and the Fund for the Republic* (New York, 1981), 14.

8 Greenleaf, "The Ford Foundation," ch. II, p. 36; Bela Kornitzer, *American Fathers and Sons* (New York, 1952), 147–166.

9 Kelly, *Court of Reason*, 13–14; Robert Hutchins, Oral History, 23–24 May 1972, p. 1, Ford Foundation Archives, New York.

10 Hoffman to Chester Barnard, 9 Dec. 1950, Hoffman Papers, box 3; Hoffman to Edward Posniak, 15 Dec. 1950, ibid.; Rowan Gaither to Hoffman, 2 Jan. 1951, ibid., box 43.

11 Greenleaf, "The Ford Foundation," ch. II, p. 34, and ch. V, p. 45.

12 Agenda for Conference with President of the Ford Foundation, Oct. 1950, Hoffman Papers, box 43.

13 W. H. Ferry, Oral History, 13 July 1972, p. 15, Ford Foundation Archives; Kelly, *Court of Reason*, 36–37, 72–73, 323; Hoffman to W. H. Ferry, 26 Feb. 1953, Hoffman Papers, box 62.

14 Hoffman, speech to ECA, 2 April 1951, Hoffman Papers, box 25.

15 U.S., Congress, House, Foreign Affairs Committee, *Mutual Security Program*, 82d Cong., 1st sess. (1951), 317–53; *FRUS, 1951*, I:339, 21 July 1951; Hoffman to Thomas Cabot, 25 July 1951, Hoffman Papers, box 5; Hoffman to Arthur Krock, 23 Aug. 1951, ibid.

16 Rowan Gaither to Hoffman, 2 Jan. 1951; Hoffman to Ford Foundation trustees, 29 Jan. 1951, Hoffman Papers, box 44.

17 Hoffman to George Kennan, 12 Mar. 1951, ibid., box 4; George Kennan, Oral History, 29 March 1972, Ford Foundation Archives; Hoffman to John J. McCloy, 19 March 1951, Hoffman Papers, box 44; Greenleaf, "The Ford Foundation," ch. II, pp. 47–48.

18 Hoffman to Gardner Cowles, 22 Aug. 1951, Hoffman Papers, box 5; Hoffman to Henry Ford II, 31 Dec. 1952, ibid., box 5; Cox Committee, 258. Cf. Don K. Price, Oral History, 22 June 1972, pp. 57–59, Ford Foundation Archives; Hutchins, Oral History, 45.

19 Hoffman to Volney Hurd, 9 Jan. 1951, Hoffman Papers, box 61; Hoffman to Barbara Lucas, 7 Sept. 1951, ibid., box 5; House, Foreign Affairs Committee, *Mutual Security Program*, 319, 326, 341.

20 John B. Howard, Oral History, 13 Feb. 1973, p. 6, Ford Foundation Archives; Ford Foundation press release, 24 Aug. 1951, ibid.

21 Hoffman to Gen. Dwight Eisenhower, 23 Aug. 1951, Hoffman Papers, box 26; Hoffman to Arthur Krock, 23 Aug. 1951, ibid., box 5.
22 Cox Committee, 233; Carl Spaeth, Oral History, 24 April 1972, p. 29, Ford Foundation Archives; Hoffman to Amb. Chester Bowles, 13 Sept. 1952, Hoffman Papers, box 20, and 8 Jan. 1953, ibid., box 8; Frank Ninkovich, "The Rockefeller Foundation, China, and Cultural Change," *Journal of American History* 70 (March 1984): 799–820.
23 Milton Katz, Oral History, 22 June 1972, pp. 6–7, 13–14, Ford Foundation Archives.
24 Hoffman to Ralph Reynolds, 26 July 1951, Hoffman Papers, box 5.
25 Hoffman to Sen. William Benton, 5 Sept. 1951, ibid.
26 Hoffman, Freedom Award Address, 7 Oct. 1951, in *Congressional Record*, 82d Cong., 1st sess., 1951, 97, pt. 15:A6466–68. See Thomas C. Reeves, *The Life and Times of Joe McCarthy* (New York, 1982), 423.
27 Macdonald, *The Ford Foundation*, 25, 48; Hoffman to George Pepperdine, 15 Oct. 1951, Hoffman Papers, box 43.
28 W.H. Ferry to Hoffman, 16 Aug. 1951, Hoffman Papers, box 43; Milton Katz, Oral History, 3.
29 Hoffman to Rep. Donald L. Jackson, 4 Feb. 1951, Hoffman Papers, box 6.
30 Thomas C. Reeves, *Freedom and the Foundation: The Fund for the Republic* (New York, 1969), 16; Hoffman to Sydney Weinberg, 5 April 1952, Hoffman Papers, box 7.
31 Hoffman to Henry Ford II, 29 May 1952, Hoffman Papers, box 19.
32 George Romney to Pyke Johnson, 2 May 1949, ibid., box 29; Noble Parker to Hoffman, 22 Dec. 1948 and 6 Dec. 1951, ibid.; *New York Times*, 12 Aug. 1951; *Washington Post*, 11 Sept. 1951; George Gallup, "What the GOP Needs to Win in '52," *Look* 15 (25 Sept. 1951): 37–40; William Lowe, "Why NOT Paul Hoffman?" ibid. 15 (9 Oct. 1951): 103–05.
33 Hoffman to Averell Broughton, 16 Nov. 1948, Hoffman Papers, box 60; Hoffman to Sen. Henry Cabot Lodge, 10 April 1950, ibid., box 2.
34 Hoffman to Sen. Ralph Flanders, 28 Feb. 1952, ibid., box 19; Hoffman to Gen. Dwight Eisenhower, 29 March 1952, ibid., box 26; Hoffman to V.W. Johnson, 14 Dec. 1951, ibid., box 29.
35 Robert H. Ferrell, ed., *The Eisenhower Diaries* (New York, 1981), 194, 4 June 1951; Dwight D. Eisenhower to Hoffman, 4 Oct. 1951, Hoffman Papers, box 26.
36 Hoffman to Dwight D. Eisenhower, 26 Sept. 1951, 29 Oct. 1951, and 5 Dec. 1951, ibid.
37 Gen. Dwight Eisenhower to Lucius Clay, 8 Jan. 1952 and 9 Feb. 1952, Dwight D. Eisenhower, Pre-Presidential Papers, box 24:3, Dwight D. Eisenhower Library; Gen. Dwight Eisenhower to Hoffman, 9 Feb. 1952, Hoffman Papers, box 26.
38 Richard Bissell to Hoffman, 7 March 1952, Hoffman Papers, box 30.
39 Henry Cabot Lodge, *The Storm Has Many Eyes* (New York, 1973), 102, 106.
40 Lucius Clay to Gen. Dwight Eisenhower, 14 April 1952, Dwight D. Eisenhower, Pre-Presidential Papers, box 24:3.
41 Hoffman to Douglas Fairbanks, Jr., 28 May 1952, Hoffman Papers, box 31; Hoffman to Herbert Cramer, 21 June 1952, ibid.; Hoffman to W.M. Hart, 27 June 1952, ibid., box 32.
42 *New York Times*, 8 Feb. 1952 and 9 May 1952; Hoffman to Mrs. Jack Hardy,

17 June 1952, Hoffman Papers, box 30; Hoffman to E. Stanley Goldman, 27 June 1952, ibid., box 31; Hoffman, "Why Eisenhower Is Needed As President," speech to University of New Hampshire, 5 March 1952, ibid., box 125; Hoffman to Calvin Verity, 26 May 1952, ibid., box 34.

43 Henry D. Spaulding, *The Nixon Nobody Knows* (Middle Village, N.Y., 1972), 296–97.

44 Hoffman to Mrs. Douglas Horton, 30 July 1952, Hoffman Papers, box 32; Hoffman to Rev. F.E. Davison, 7 Aug. 1952, ibid., box 31; Hoffman to Mrs. M.R. Oliver, 13 Sept. 1952, ibid., box 33; Hoffman to Sen. Richard Nixon, 20 Aug. 1952, ibid., box 7, and 19 Aug. 1952, ibid., box 28.

45 Earl Mazo to Hoffman, 20 April 1958, ibid., box 28, contains text of Mazo's interview with Hoffman; Herbert S. Parmet, *Eisenhower and the American Crusades* (New York, 1972), 134–35; Richard M. Nixon, *Six Crises* (New York, 1962), 108; Hoffman to James G. Blaine, 29 Sept. 1952, Hoffman Papers, box 20; Hoffman to Robert Heller, 29 Sept. 1952, ibid., box 32.

46 *New York Times*, 18 Nov. 1952 and 24 Nov. 1952; Ellis Slater, *The Ike I Knew* (n.p., 1980), 40.

47 Hoffman to Harry S. Bishop, 10 Nov. 1952, Hoffman Papers, box 61; Hoffman to Sherman Adams, 5 Nov. 1952, ibid., box 30; Hoffman to Herbert Brownell, 5 Nov. 1952, ibid.; Hoffman to Clemens Frank, 3 Dec. 1952, ibid., box 31; Hoffman to Ed Wimmer, 23 Jan. 1953, ibid., box 63.

48 Hoffman to Harold Stassen, 9 Dec. 1952, ibid., box 22; Hoffman to W. John Kenney, 13 Nov. 1952, ibid., box 61; Hoffman to Sen. Ralph Flanders, 30 Jan. 1952, ibid., box 6; Hoffman to Dwight Eisenhower, 29 Dec. 1952, ibid., box 26; and 31 Dec. 1952, ibid., box 27; Hoffman to Henry Ford II, 31 Dec. 1952, ibid., box 8; Hoffman to Harry A. Bullis, 20 Nov. 1952, ibid., box 61.

49 Hoffman to Henry Ford II, 29 May 1952, ibid.; Hoffman to Sen. William Benton, 25 July 1952, ibid., box 20; Hoffman to Douglas Fairbanks, Jr., 29 July 1952, ibid., box 31; Ford Foundation, meeting of trustees, 15–16 July 1952, ibid., box 44; Hoffman to Henry Ford II, 22 Aug. 1952, ibid., box 20.

50 Hoffman to F.J. Radwick, 21 Aug. 1952, ibid., box 28; Hoffman to Paul Burke, 26 Aug. 1952, ibid., box 80.

51 William G. Moore, "Ford Foundation, a Big Owner, May Want One Day to Diversify," *Wall Street Journal*, 22 Sept. 1952; Hoffman to Henry Ford II, 23 Sept. 1952, Hoffman Papers, box 7; Henry Ford II to Hoffman, 23 Sept. 1952, ibid.; Agenda for Conference with President of the Ford Foundation, 23 Sept. 1952, ibid.; Ferry, Oral History, 17–18; Hutchins, Oral History, 19.

52 Cox Committee, 226–62.

53 Hoffman to Henry Ford II, 31 Dec. 1952, Hoffman Papers, box 8.

54 Henry Cabot Lodge, *As It Was* (New York, 1976), 22, 14 Nov. 1952; Richard Bissell to Hoffman, 3 Dec. 1952, Hoffman Papers, box 22; Hoffman to Henry Ford II, 31 Dec. 1952, ibid., box 8.

55 Reeves, *Freedom and the Foundation*, 19; Chester Davis, Oral History, 21 April 1972, Ford Foundation Archives; Ferry, Oral History, 18–19.

56 *Time*, 69 (10 June 1957): 60–68; Donald K. David, Oral History, 14 and 23 March 1972, pp. 54–55, Ford Foundation Archives.

57 *New York Times*, 5 Feb. 1953 and 7 Feb. 1953; *Time*, 61 (16 Feb. 1953): 27; *Newsweek* 41 (16 Feb. 1953): 67–68; Slater, *The Ike I Knew*, 40.

58 Hoffman to Dwight Macdonald, 26 Nov. 1954, Hoffman Papers, box 43; Hoffman to Christy Borth, 5 Dec. 1960, ibid., box 26.

7. *Studebaker Strikes Out, 1953–56*

1 Eric Sevareid, script, CBS, 25 Sept. 1950, Hoffman Papers, box 21, Harry S. Truman Library.
2 Floyd Hunter, "The Decision Makers," *Nation* 179 (21 Aug. 1954): 148–50, 159; Hunter, *Top Leadership, U.S.A.* (Chapel Hill, N.C., 1959), 22, 30, 197.
3 See Thomas C. Reeves, *Freedom and the Foundation: The Fund for the Republic* (New York, 1969), and Frank K. Kelly, *Court of Reason: Robert Hutchins and the Fund for the Republic* (New York, 1981).
4 Hoffman to Vice Pres. Richard M. Nixon, 24 March 1953, Fund for the Republic Papers, Princeton University Library; Hoffman to Dwight Eisenhower, 18 April 1952, Hoffman Papers, box 26; U.S., Congress, House, Special Committee to Investigate Tax-Exempt Foundations and Comparable Organizations, *Tax-Exempt Foundations*, 83rd Cong., 2d sess. (1954), 25–26 and 1053–55 (hereafter cited as Reece Committee).
5 Reece Committee, 379–85, 1053–55; Hoffman to Arthur Motley, 14 Jan. 1955, Hoffman Papers, box 13; Edgar Bergen Show script, CBS, 20 Feb. 1955, ibid., box 131.
6 Hoffman to James Laughlin, 3 April 1953, ibid., box 43; Hoffman to Martin Dickinson, 6 Aug. 1954, ibid., box 11; *New York Times*, 6 Jan. 1954.
7 Hoffman to Martin Dickinson, 14 June 1954 and 6 Aug. 1954, Hoffman Papers, box 11.
8 Hoffman to Pres. Dwight Eisenhower, 25 Mar. 1954, ibid., box 10; Hoffman to Sherman Adams, 26 Nov. 1954, ibid., box 84. See David M. Oshinsky, *A Conspiracy So Immense: The World of Joe McCarthy* (New York, 1983), 357–59.
9 Robert Griffith, *The Politics of Fear* (Lexington, Ky., 1970), 279–81; Hoffman to Raymond Cheseldine, 29 July 1954, Hoffman Papers, box 11; Hoffman to Sen. Homer Ferguson, 26 July 1954, ibid., box 84; Hoffman to Sherman Adams, 26 Nov. and 27 Nov. 1954, ibid.; Maurice Rosenblatt to Hoffman, 17 Dec. 1954, ibid., box 75.
10 Hoffman to Z. David Zellerbach, 1 Nov. 1955, Hoffman Papers, box 14; Hoffman to Carey Orr, 23 Aug. 1954, ibid., box 84.
11 W. H. Ferry to Hoffman, 24 Aug. 1955, Fund for the Republic Papers; Henry Ford II to Hoffman, 27 Oct. 1955, ibid.; Hoffman to Henry Ford II, 1 Nov. and 17 Nov. 1955, ibid. See Kelly, *Court of Reason*, 54–70.
12 Gaither quoted in Kelly, *Court of Reason*, 93.
13 Hoffman to Dana Wier, 12 Aug. 1954, Hoffman Papers, box 11; Dana Wier to Hoffman, 17 March 1956, ibid., box 52.
14 Raymond Loewy to Hoffman, 21 Sept. 1955, Hoffman Papers, box 52.
15 Richard Langworth, *Studebaker: The Postwar Years* (Osceola, Wis., 1979), 40–42, 165.
16 Harold Vance to Hoffman, 6 Feb. 1953, Hoffman Papers, box 150; *Newsweek* 41 (16 Feb. 1953): 67–68; *Dictionary of American Biography, Supplement VI, 1956–60* (New York, 1980), 649–50.
17 Harold Vance to Hoffman, 6 Feb. 1953, 20 Feb. 1953, and 27 Feb. 1953, Hoffman Papers, box 150.
18 Langworth, *Studebaker*, 62–64.
19 Hoffman to Kenneth B. Elliott, 27 June 1953, Hoffman Papers, box 150.

20 Hoffman to Paul Helms, 17 July 1953, and Hoffman to Dewey Smith, 10 Aug. 1953, ibid., box 9.

21 Robert M. MacDonald, *Collective Bargaining in the Automobile Industry* (New Haven, Conn., 1963), 259–84, 359–67; Hoffman, Oral History, Columbia University, 27 July 1963, p. 85; Nelson Lichtenstein, "Auto Worker Militancy and the Structure of Factory Life, 1937–1955," *Journal of American History* 67 (Sept. 1980): 335; William Ogden, Oral History by Prof. Loren Pennington, 15 May 1972, Walter P. Reuther Library, Wayne State University.

22 Hoffman to Frederick Warburg, 17 July 1953, and Hoffman to Dewey Smith, 10 Aug. 1953, Hoffman Papers, box 9.

23 Hoffman to John K. Jessup, 31 Aug. 1953, Hoffman Papers, box 128; Hoffman, "How to Avoid a Psycho-Recession," *New York Times Magazine*, 15 Nov. 1953; Hoffman quoted in *Sales Management* 71 (15 Dec. 1953): 26.

24 *New York Times*, 12 Jan. 1954, 24 Jan. 1954, 6 March 1954; Robert Griffith, "The Selling of America: The Advertising Council and American Politics, 1942–1960," *Business History Review* 57 (Autumn 1983): 406–07.

25 Hoffman, speech to Federation of Automobile Dealer Associations, Toronto, 15 Oct. 1953, Hoffman Papers, box 128; George Romney to Hoffman, 21 Oct. 1953, and Hoffman to Romney, 27 Oct. 1953, ibid., box 81.

26 Hoffman, speech to Studebaker Dealer Meeting, Nov. 1953, ibid., box 128; Hoffman to Philip Salisbury, 14 Nov. 1953, ibid., box 10; Robert S. Armacost to Hoffman, 28 Mar. 1953, ibid., box 6; Lathrop Hoffman to James J. Nance, 17 Nov. 1955, ibid., box 52.

27 "Anna M. Rosenberg—She Sells Intuitions," *Fortune* 50 (Nov. 1954): 73.

28 Anna M. Rosenberg Associates, "The Studebaker Quality Code Program," 8 Dec. 1953, and Anna M. Rosenberg to Hoffman, 7 Jan. 1954, ibid., box 151.

29 Hoffman to Lottie and Dewey Smith, 19 March 1954, ibid., box 10.

30 Hoffman to L.E. Belcourt, 4 Nov. 1953, ibid.; Howard A. Darrin to Hoffman, 24 March 1954, ibid., box 45; Hoffman to H. J. Ketchum, 25 March 1954, ibid., box 10; Hoffman to Richard L. Simon, 30 Aug. 1955, ibid., box 46; Hoffman to John E. Kearns, 4 Feb. 1954, ibid., box 45.

31 Hoffman to R.W. Newman, 14 Dec. 1953, ibid., box 10; Editors of Consumer Guide, *Cars of the 50s* (New York, 1978), 7.

32 Hoffman to Ed Wimmer, 14 Nov. 1953 and 24 Nov. 1953, Hoffman Papers, box 63, and 19 Jan. 1954, ibid., box 45.

33 Hoffman to Dewey Smith, 28 Dec. 1953, ibid., box 10; Hoffman to Lottie and Dewey Smith, 30 April 1954, ibid., box 11; Hoffman to G. Herbert McCracken, 25 Jan. 1954, and Hoffman to Joseph Cain, 4 Feb. 1954, ibid, box 45.

34 Hoffman to Hugh J. Ferry, 2 Sept. 1953, ibid., box 9; James J. Nance to Hoffman, 7 Oct. 1953, ibid., box 62; *New York Times*, 30 Dec. 1953.

35 Hoffman to Dewey Smith, 23 June 1954, Hoffman Papers, box 11; Hoffman to George Romney, 28 June 1954, ibid., box 64; Hoffman to Barbara Ward Jackson, 7 Oct. 1954, and Hoffman to Peter Hoffman, 27 Nov. 1954, ibid., box 12; George Romney, speech to Press Conference, 12–19[?] Oct. 1954, ibid., box 64.

36 Hoffman to Lester Bermant, 21 Aug. 1954, ibid., box 11.

37 Hoffman to Paul Helms, 24 July 1954, and Hoffman to Louis Horvath, 29 July 1954, ibid.

38 Hoffman to Paul Helms, 19 Aug. 1954, and Hoffman to Elizabeth Webster, 21 Aug. 1954, ibid.

39 Hoffman to Walter Reuther, 13 Aug. 1954, ibid.; "A Vote for Life," *Time* 64 (23 Aug. 1954): 66.

40 Hoffman, speech to Industrial Relations Center, University of Minnesota, 14 Oct. 1954, Hoffman Papers, box 130; Hoffman to Milton Katz, 1 Sept. 1954, ibid., box 64; Hoffman to M.T. Moore, 25 Sept. 1954, ibid., box 12.

41 Hoffman to Walter Lippmann, 5 Oct. 1954, Hoffman Papers, box 12; Hoffman to Barbara Ward Jackson, 7 Oct. 1954, ibid.; Hoffman to Pres. Dwight D. Eisenhower, 15 Oct. 1954, ibid., box 27; Hoffman to William B. Harris, 22 Oct. 1954, ibid., box 46.

42 Hoffman to D. L. Patten, 6 Oct. 1954, ibid.

43 Langworth, *Studebaker*, 71, 75–76.

44 Anna M. Rosenberg Associates, "Studebaker Management Development Program Status Report," 1 March 1955, Hoffman Papers, box 47.

45 *Newsweek* 47 (16 Jan. 1956): 60.

46 Hoffman to Neil Clark, 24 Nov. 1953, Hoffman Papers, box 10; Hoffman to Harry Ferguson, 7 Sept. 1956 and 21 Sept. 1956, ibid., box 65; Raymond Loewy to Hoffman, 21 Sept. 1955, ibid., box 46.

47 *Time* 67 (23 April 1956): 103.

48 Langworth, *Studebaker*, 75–76.

49 Hoffman to James J. Nance, 20 Jan. 1955, Hoffman Papers, box 46, and 22 March 1955, ibid., box 13.

50 Hoffman to Dewey Smith, 27 Aug. 1953, ibid., box 9.

51 Hoffman to Dewey Smith, 12 April 1955 and 7 Dec. 1955, ibid., box 14. Robert Ferrell, ed., *The Eisenhower Diaries* (New York, 1981), 325–26, 20 April 1956.

52 *New York Times*, 17 April 1956; *Newsweek* 47 (30 April 1956): 90; Ferrell, ed., *The Eisenhower Diaries*, 325–26; Hoffman to Lottie Smith, 26 June 1956, and Hoffman to Peter Hoffman, 26 June 1956, Hoffman Papers, box 15.

53 Hoffman to Barbara Ward Jackson, 18 June 1956, ibid.; Hoffman to Dewey Smith, 7 Aug. 1956, ibid., box 16, and 19 Aug. 1956, ibid., box 17.

54 Hoffman to Harold Churchill, 13 Aug. 1956, ibid., box 16.

55 MacDonald, *Collective Bargaining in the Automobile Industry*, 259–84 and 359–67. Lester Fox, Oral History by Prof. Loren Pennington, 21 and 23 June 1971; T. Forrest Hanna, Oral History by Prof. Loren Pennington, Spring 1971; George Hupp, Oral History by Prof. Loren Pennington, 19 May 1972, Walter P. Reuther Library, Wayne State University.

56 Hoffman, Oral History, 92–93; Hoffman to Chester K. Whittaker, 17 Aug. 1956, Hoffman Papers, box 16; William B. Harris, "The Breakdown of Studebaker-Packard," *Fortune* 54 (Oct. 1956): 139–41, 222–32; Edward C. Mendler to Hoffman, 13 Nov. 1956, and Hoffman to Edward C. Mendler, 22 Nov. 1956, Hoffman Papers, box 47.

57 See Charles E. Edwards, *Dynamics of the United States Automobile Industry* (Columbia, S.C., 1965), and Lawrence J. White, *The Automobile Industry Since 1945* (Cambridge, Mass., 1971).

58 Hoffman to Peter Hoffman, 26 June 1956, Hoffman Papers, box 15; Hoffman to Dewey Smith, 7 Aug. 1956, ibid., box 16, and 18 April 1958, ibid., box 17.

8. *"Waging Peace" with Trade and Aid*

1 Max F. Millikan and W.W. Rostow, *A Proposal: Key to an Effective Foreign Policy* (New York, 1957), 1, 4, 7.
2 *Public Papers of the Presidents of the United States: Dwight D. Eisenhower, 1954* (Washington, D.C., 1954), 666, no. 172, 28 July 1954.
3 Burton I. Kaufman, *Trade and Aid: Eisenhower's Foreign Economic Policy, 1953–1961* (Baltimore, Md., 1982), 6–7.
4 Sec. John Foster Dulles to Hoffman, 24 Aug. 1954, Hoffman Papers, box 26, Harry S. Truman Library; Hoffman to Peter Hoffman, 27 Nov. 1954, ibid., box 12.
5 Hoffman to Sherman Adams, 3 July 1956, ibid., box 16.
6 Hoffman to Robert Wacker, 13 March 1956, ibid., box 92.
7 Hoffman to Barbara Ward Jackson, 18 June 1956, ibid., box 15.
8 Hoffman to Peter Hoffman, 26 June 1956, ibid.; *Congressional Record*, 84th Cong., 2d sess., 1956, 102, pt. 1:480 and pt. 9:12291–94; *New York Times*, 14 July 1956 and 18 July 1956.
9 John T. Flynn, script, 22 July 1956, Fund for the Republic Papers, Princeton University Library; Frank S. McNeal to Hoffman, 20 July 1956, Hoffman Papers, box 52.
10 Hoffman to Sen. William Knowland, 16 July 1956, ibid., box 66; Sen. A.S. Monroney to Hoffman, 21 July 1956, ibid., box 28; Hoffman to Pres. Dwight D. Eisenhower, 3 Aug. 1956, ibid., box 27; Hoffman to Courtney Johnson, 1 Aug. 1956, ibid., box 93.
11 Hoffman to Claude Geyer, 8 March 1957, ibid., box 16.
12 Hoffman to Amb. John L. Tappin, 12 July 1957, ibid., box 67.
13 Henry Cabot Lodge, *As It Was* (New York, 1976), 196–98; Seymour Maxwell Finger, *Your Man at the U.N.* (New York, 1980), 86; Hoffman to Pres. Dwight D. Eisenhower, 17 Dec. 1956, Hoffman Papers, box 27; Hoffman, "Reply," *Christian Century*, 74 (3 April 1957): 427.
14 Hoffman to Pres. Dwight D. Eisenhower, 17 Dec. 1956 and 22 March 1957, Hoffman Papers, box 16; Hoffman to C. D. Jackson, 15 March 1957, ibid., box 73; Hoffman to Sec. George Humphrey, 22 March 1957, ibid.; Hoffman to Sec. John Foster Dulles, 24 Jan. 1957, ibid., box 26.
15 Pres. Dwight D. Eisenhower to Hoffman, 8 March 1957, ibid., box 73; Sec. George Humphrey to Hoffman, 26 March 1957, ibid. See Kaufman, *Trade and Aid*, 30, 103–04.
16 Hoffman to Sec. George Humphrey, 8 April 1957, Hoffman Papers, box 73; Hoffman to Atherton Lee, 7 Feb. 1957, ibid., box 67.
17 Hoffman to C.D. Jackson, 15 March 1957, ibid., box 73.
18 Amb. Henry Cabot Lodge to Hoffman, 25 March 1957, and 11 March 1957, ibid., box 28.
19 Finger, *Your Man at the U.N.*, 86.
20 Hoffman to Dewey Smith, 18 April 1958, Hoffman Papers, box 17.
21 Hoffman to Dewey Smith, 19 Aug. 1957, ibid.; Hoffman to Harry B. Price, 20 Dec. 1957, ibid., box 67.
22 Hoffman to William J. Donovan, 26 Aug. 1957, ibid., box 26; Hoffman to David Lilienthal, 22 April 1958, ibid., box 17; *New York Times*, 17 Oct. 1957; Hoffman, "The New European Market," *Business Horizons* 1 (Winter 1958): 17–23.

23 Pres. Dwight D. Eisenhower to Hallock Hoffman, 7 Feb. 1955, and Pres. Dwight D. Eisenhower to Paul G. Hoffman, 18 Jan. 1958, Dwight D. Eisenhower Papers, Administrative Series, box 21, Dwight D. Eisenhower Library.

24 Hoffman to Sen. Ralph Flanders, 12 Feb. 1958, Hoffman Papers, box 17; U.S., Congress, House, Ways and Means Committee, *Renewal of Trade Agreements Act*, 85th Cong., 2d sess., pt. 1 (1958), 350–62; U.S., Congress, Senate, Finance Committee, *Trade Agreements Act Extension*, 85th Cong., 2d sess., pt. 1 (1958), 543.

25 U.S., Congress, Senate, Banking and Currency Committee, *International Development Association*, 85th Cong., 2d sess. (1958), 68–91; Hoffman to Kenneth Maxwell, 7 Aug. 1958, Hoffman Papers, box 18.

26 Hoffman to Seymour Maxwell Finger, 21 July 1958, ibid., box 83; Hoffman to Sen. A.S. Monroney, 24 July 1958 and 16 Sept. 1958, ibid.; Sen. A.S. Monroney to Hoffman, 22 Dec. 1958, ibid., box 28.

27 Hoffman, "Capitalism," *Western World* (May 1958); Hoffman, Memorandum for American Committee on United Europe, n.d., Fund for the Republic Papers; Hoffman to A. Crawford Greene, 1 Aug. 1958, Hoffman Papers, box 84.

28 Hoffman to Amb. David K. E. Bruce, 29 Oct. 1958, ibid., box 78; Hoffman to Sen. A. S. Monroney, 16 Sept. 1958, ibid., box 83.

29 Hoffman to Elizabeth Webster, 16 Sept. 1958, ibid., box 18; Hoffman to Pres. Dwight D. Eisenhower, 29 Oct. 1958, ibid., box 28.

30 Walter Johnson et al., eds., *The Papers of Adlai E. Stevenson* (Boston, 1977), VII:283, 14–18 Aug. 1958; John Bartlow Martin, *Adlai Stevenson and the World* (Garden City, N.Y., 1977), 437.

31 Hoffman to Arthur Krock, 22 Sept. 1958, Hoffman Papers, box 78; Hoffman to G. L. Mehta, 5 Sept. 1958, ibid.

32 Hoffman to Maxwell Rabb, 26 March 1958, ibid., box 17.

33 Amb. Henry Cabot Lodge to Pres. Dwight D. Eisenhower, 2 April 1958, Eisenhower Papers, Administrative Series, box 27.

34 Lodge, *As It Was*, 113–14, 2 April 1958.

35 *Congressional Record*, 85th Cong., 1st sess., 1957, 103, pt 2:2335–36, and 2d sess., 1958, 104, pt. 11:14205; Fulton Lewis, Jr., script, 14 May 1958, Fund for the Republic Papers.

36 Finger, *Your Man at the U.N.*, 89–90.

37 Hoffman to Arthur Compton, 26 Sept. 1958, Hoffman Papers, box 78; Hoffman, UNDP memorandum, 5 Jan. 1972, ibid., box 146.

38 Hoffman to Pres. Dwight D. Eisenhower, 29 Oct. 1958, ibid., box 28; Hoffman to Jawaharlal Nehru, 12 Nov. 1958, ibid., box 18.

39 Hoffman to Dag Hammarskjold, 1 Dec. 1958, ibid.

40 Johnson et al., eds., *The Papers of Adlai E. Stevenson*, VII:312, 10 Dec. 1958; Hoffman to J. Nielsen-Lange, 31 Dec. 1958, Hoffman Papers, box 76; Hoffman to Pres. Dwight Eisenhower, 31 Dec. 1958, ibid., box 28.

41 Pres. Dwight D. Eisenhower to Hoffman, 11 Jan. 1961, ibid.

9. The U.N.'s Development Programs, 1959–71

1 *New York Times*, 25 April 1971; Hoffman, speech to General Assembly, Committee II, 13 Nov. 1969, Hoffman Papers, box 144, Harry S. Truman Library.

2 Hoffman, "The Two-Way Benefits of Foreign Aid," *Fortune* 85 (Mar. 1972): 118.

3 *New York Times*, 12 Oct. 1971.

4 Hoffman to Pres. Dwight D. Eisenhower, 4 Sept. 1959 and 30 Nov. 1959, Hoffman Papers, box 28; Dwight Eisenhower to Hoffman, 9 Sept. 1959, in Robert L. Branyan and Lawrence H. Larson, eds., *The Eisenhower Administration 1953–1961* (New York, 1971), II:1179.

5 *Congressional Record*, 86th Cong., 1st sess., 1959, 105, pt. 2:1811–12, and pt. 8:1117–19; Hoffman to Rep. Omar Burleson, 7 July 1959, Hoffman Papers, box 76.

6 Hoffman to John F. Kennedy, 3 Jan. 1961, ibid., box 28.

7 David A. Baldwin, *Economic Development and American Foreign Policy, 1943–62* (Chicago, 1966), 195; Frank M. Coffin, *Witness for Aid* (Boston, 1964), 39; U.S., Congress, House, Foreign Affairs Committee, Subcommittee on International Organizations and Movements, *Winning the Cold War*, 88th Cong., 2d sess., pt. VIII (1964), 953.

8 *New York Times*, 26 Sept. 1961.

9 Crane Haussamen, *The Story of Paul G. Hoffman* (Santa Barbara, Calif., 1966), 63.

10 Andrew Shonfield, *The Attack on World Poverty* (New York, 1960), 26; *New York Times*, 6 March 1960; C. V. Narasihman, Oral History, 18 April 1962, Columbia University.

11 Hoffman, "Operation Breakthrough," *Foreign Affairs* 38 (Oct. 1959): 31–45; Hoffman to Dwight D. Eisenhower, 31 March 1967, Hoffman Papers, box 28; Hoffman, speech to General Assembly, Committee II, 11 Nov. 1968, ibid., box 144.

12 Hoffman, "Development and Growth," *Saturday Review* 43 (16 Jan. 1960): 32–35, 37; *New York Times*, 7 Dec. 1960; Hoffman, *One Hundred Countries* (Washington, D.C., 1960), 44.

13 Hoffman, *World without Want* (New York, 1962), 139; Hoffman, speech to UNDP Governing Council, 5th Sess., 5 Jan. 1968, UN doc. DP/L.65.

14 Hoffman to Pres. Dwight D. Eisenhower, 30 Nov. 1959, Hoffman Papers, box 28; Hoffman to William Henry, 12 Oct. 1961, ibid., box 76.

15 Hoffman, *The Greatest Challenge of All* (New York, 1961), 12; Arthur Herzog, "A Visit With Paul Hoffman," *Think* 28 (Feb. 1962): 20–23.

16 Hoffman, *World without Want*, 24–33, 119; Hoffman, *One Hundred Countries*, 44.

17 Ibid., 23.

18 Hoffman, "The Six Imperatives of Economic and Social Progress," in Francis O. Wilcox and H. Field Haviland, Jr., eds., *The United States and the United Nations* (Baltimore, Md., 1961), 43; Council on World Tensions, *Restless Nations* (New York, 1962), 92–98, 175–79.

19 Hoffman, "No Time like the Future," speech to General Assembly, Committee II, 13 Oct. 1971, in *Congressional Record*, 92d Cong., 1st sess., 1971, 117, pt. 30:38739–42, 39665–68.

20 Hoffman to William L. Clayton, 25 March 1960, William L. Clayton Papers, box 126, Harry S. Truman Library; Hoffman, *One Hundred Countries*, 61; Hoffman, "Food and Population," *War on Hunger* 3, no. 7 (July 1969).

21 Hoffman, *World without Want*, 142; James Daniel, "Foreign Aid That Works," *Reader's Digest* 89 (Sept. 1966): 203–10.

22 U.S., Congress, Senate, Foreign Relations Committee, Subcommittee on International Organization Affairs, *United Nations Special Fund*, 88th Cong., 1st sess. (1963), 41.

23 Andrew W. Cordier and Max Harrelson, eds., *Public Papers of Secretaries-General of the United Nations, Vol. VI: U Thant, 1961–1964* (New York, 1976), 316–17, 19 Feb. 1963.

24 John G. Stoessinger, *The United Nations and the Superpowers* (New York, 1965), 152–63; Philip Klutznick to author, 18 Jan. 1983.

25 *Congressional Record*, 88th Cong., 1st sess., 1963, 109, pt. 2:2273–74, 2456; Senate, Foreign Relations Committee, Subcommittee on International Organization Affairs, *United Nations Special Fund*, 3, 17; *New York Times*, 21 Feb. 1963; Richard N. Gardner, *In Pursuit of World Order* (New York, 1964), 119–20.

26 Hoffman to Pres. Lyndon Johnson, 6 June 1966, Hoffman Papers, box 142; "Paul Hoffman and UN Aid Programs," *The United Nations in Action* 1 (Sept.-Oct. 1963): 21–23.

27 Lathrop Hoffman to author, 5 April 1983; *Pasadena Star-News*, 18 May 1961.

28 "Anna M. Rosenberg—She Sells Intuitions," *Fortune* 50 (Nov. 1954): 73; *Detroit News*, 3 June 1962; *New York Times*, 20 July 1962 and 10 May 1983.

29 Hoffman to Peter Hoffman, 16 June 1962, Hoffman Papers, box 19.

30 Hoffman, "A War on Want," *UN Monthly Chronicle* 1 (June 1964): 92–98; *New York Times*, 15 Jan. 1965 and 23 Nov. 1965.

31 Mahdi Elmandjra, *The United Nations System* (London, 1973), 62, 245–50.

32 Hoffman to Bruce Barton, 28 June 1951, Hoffman Papers, box 5; *New York Times*, 11 Dec. 1959 and 21 Dec. 1959.

33 *New York Times*, 3 Dec. 1959; Hoffman to Richard Fagley, 4 Jan. 1960, Hoffman Papers, box 18; Hoffman to Andrew Shonfield, 5 July 1960, ibid., box 76.

34 Hoffman, speech to UNDP Governing Council, 21 May 1968, UN doc. DP/L.84.

35 Hoffman, "Ecumenism and Global Development," *Ecumenical Review* 19 (April 1967): 154–57.

36 *New York Times*, 6 June 1967, 16 Nov. 1967, 24 Jan. 1968.

37 Hoffman to Dwight D. Eisenhower, 5 Jan. 1962, Hoffman Papers, box 28.

38 Hoffman, confidential memorandum to the Inter-Agency Consultative Board, 13 Oct. 1966, ibid., box 142.

39 Report by the Administrator to the Governing Council of the UNDP, 15 Nov. 1967, UN doc. DP/L.57.

40 *A Study of the Capacity of the United Nations Development System* (Geneva, 1969), UN doc. DP/5, II:427, 430 (hereafter cited as Jackson Report); Robert G.A. Jackson, "Postface," Elmandjra, *The United Nations System*, 330–34.

41 *New York Times*, 22 March 1970; Shirley Hazzard, *Defeat of an Ideal* (Boston, 1973), 217.

42 Jackson Report, I:iii.

43 Ibid., 13.

44 Ibid., 9, 10, 16, 29, 41, 49.

45 *New York Times*, 28 Feb. 1971; Myer Cohen, interview, 14 March 1983; Arthur E. Goldschmidt, interview, 16 March 1983.

46 UNDP Governing Council, 9th sess., 19–30 Jan. 1970, UN doc. DP/SR, 183,

p. 98; Hoffman, speech to Columbia University Conference on International Economic Development, 20 Feb. 1970, Hoffman Papers, box 145.

47 *New York Times*, 30 Oct. 1970, 27 Dec. 1970.

48 Ibid., 28 Feb. 1971, 26 Oct. 1971.

49 Hoffman, "No Time Like the Future."

50 Ibid.; Hoffman, speech to U.N. Special Fund Governing Council, 15 June 1964, 12th Sess., UN doc. SF/L.108; Hoffman, "The Rich and the Poor: 1966," *Saturday Review* 49 (17 Sept. 1966): 22–25; Hoffman, "Development Co-operation," *Virginia Quarterly Review* 47 (Summer 1971): 321–35.

51 *Congressional Record*, 92d Cong., 1st sess., 1971, 117, pt. 30:38742; Andrew W. Cordier and Max Harrelson, eds., *Public Papers of Secretaries-General of the United Nations, Vol. VIII: U Thant, 1968–1971* (New York, 1977), 575.

52 Myer Cohen, interview; Hoffman, speech to UNDP Pledging Conference, 29 Oct. 1970, Hoffman Papers, box 145.

53 *Christian Science Monitor*, 12 June 1973.

54 Robert S. McNamara, *One Hundred Countries, Two Billion People* (New York, 1973), 113.

55 Robert Heilbroner, "Innocence Abroad," *Commentary* 35 (Feb. 1963): 174–76.

56 Denis Goulet, *The Cruel Choice* (New York, 1971), 16, 68, 85, 104, 244. See also Michael Harrington, *The Vast Majority* (New York, 1977), 254.

57 Goulet, *The Cruel Choice*, x, 235, 246, 279, 317; Denis Goulet, "Domesticating the Third World," in Denis Goulet and Michael Hudson, *The Myth of Aid* (New York, 1971), 28, 56.

58 Hoffman, draft foreword to Denis Goulet's *The Cruel Choice*, 16 April 1970, Hoffman Papers, box 145.

59 Hoffman, "Letter to the Editor," *Center Magazine* 1 (Nov. 1968): 95–97.

60 Hoffman, "The Six Imperatives of Economic and Social Progress," in Wilcox and Haviland, eds., *The United States and the United Nations*, 30; Hoffman, speech to University of Ottawa, 11 Oct. 1968, Hoffman Papers, box 144; Hoffman, speech to Foreign Service Institute, 9 Dec. 1969, ibid.

61 Hoffman to Henry Luce, 4 Feb. 1965, Henry Luce Papers, Time Archives, New York.

62 *New York Times*, 16 Nov. 1967; Hoffman, "What's Good for the World Is Good for the U.S.A.," in Clarence C. Walton, ed., *Business and Social Progress* (New York, 1970), 85–89; Clinton Rehling, interview, 5 June 1981.

63 Hoffman, "Ecumenism and Global Development"; Hoffman, "No Time like the Future."

Conclusion

1 E.g., Robert Griffith, "Dwight D. Eisenhower and the Corporate Commonwealth," *American Historical Review* 87 (Feb. 1982): 87–122.

2 Michael J. Hogan, "Revival and Reform: America's Twentieth-Century Search for a New Economic Order Abroad," *Diplomatic History* 8 (Fall 1984): 287–310, portrayed Hoffman, the CED, and the ECA pursuing an ideologically inspired "technocorporatism."

3 Robert A. Packenham, *Liberal America and the Third World* (Princeton,

N.J., 1973), 163, 303–09, makes a sharp critique of the liberal consensus among social scientists.

4 Allen J. Matusow, *The Unraveling of America: A History of Liberalism in the 1960s* (New York, 1984), chs. 8, 9, critically analyzes the War on Poverty.
5 See Robert W. Tucker, *The Inequality of Nations* (New York, 1977), 53–59, 67–68, 91, 108, 195.

Essay on Sources

During Hoffman's lifetime many biographical articles, often based on interviews with him, appeared in newspapers and magazines. Besides those accounts, Bela Kornitzer, *American Fathers and Sons* (New York, 1952), and Paul F. Douglass, *Six upon the World* (Boston, 1954), each devoted an admiring chapter to Hoffman based on information supplied by him. Crane Haussamen, *The Story of Paul G. Hoffman* (Santa Barbara, Calif., 1966), an uncritical tribute compiled by the Center for the Study of Democratic Institutions primarily to raise money for itself, contains material not available elsewhere. Theodore H. White, *In Search of History* (New York, 1978), included a sentimental personal account by a friend and former collaborator. Short essays about Hoffman have recently appeared in John Ingham, *Biographical Dictionary of American Business Leaders* (Westport, Conn., 1983), and Warren Kuehl, ed., *Biographical Dictionary of Internationalists* (Westport, Conn., 1983).

Hoffman did not write a memoir, but he did participate in two oral history projects. His interview at the Columbia Oral History Office repeated information and anecdotes about his early life and career largely available in journalistic accounts. Unfortunately, that interview did not carry the story beyond the reorganization of Studebaker in the mid-1930s. His oral history at the Harry S. Truman Library focused exclusively on the Marshall Plan.

The single best source of primary material about Hoffman is the collection of his papers at the Truman Library. Besides copies of hundreds of articles and speeches by him, the collection contains most of his correspondence from the mid-1920s through the 1960s. Missing, regrettably, is correspondence with his wife Dorothy. According to Anna Rosenberg, his second wife, Hoffman requested that she destroy such letters after his death, and she complied with his wishes.

Although a large collection, the Hoffman Papers at the Truman Library lack some important correspondence. Additional materials relevant to Hoffman's career are located in the following collections: William Benton Papers, Robert Hutchins Papers, and Harold Swift Papers, all at University of Chicago; Thomas E. Dewey Papers, University of Rochester; Henry Luce Papers, Time Archives, New York; Harry S. Truman Papers and William L. Clayton Papers, Truman Library; Dwight D. Eisenhower Papers, Dwight D. Eisenhower Library.

Studebaker and the Automotive Industry

The role of the automobile in American society and culture is favorably assessed in John B. Rae, *The Road and the Car in American Life* (Cambridge, Mass., 1971) and B. Bruce-Briggs, *The War against the Automobile* (New York, 1977). James J. Flink, *The Car Culture* (Cambridge, Mass., 1975) provides a more critical view. Joel W. Eastman, "Styling vs. Safety: The Development of Automotive Styling, 1900–1960" (Ph.D. dissertation, University of Florida, 1973), published as *Styling vs. Safety: The American Automobile Industry and the Development of Automotive Safety, 1900–1966* (Boston, 1984), presents useful information, including an interview with Hoffman, within an interpretive scheme hostile to the automotive industry. Mark S. Foster, "The Model T, the Hard Sell, and Los Angeles's Urban Growth: The Decentralization of Los Angeles during the 1920s," *Pacific Historical Review* 44 (Nov. 1975): 459–84, discussed Hoffman's first venture into public affairs. Foster, *From Streetcar to Superhighway* (Philadelphia, 1981), and Paul Barrett, *The Automobile and Urban Transit* (Philadelphia, 1983), provide sensible explanations for the growing popularity of automobiles and the decline of mass transit. Mark Rose, *Interstate* (Lawrence, Kan., 1979), is the standard work on the efforts that led to the nation's interstate highway system.

Several good studies have examined the economics of the automotive industry. Robert P. Thomas, "Style Change and the Automobile Industry during the Roaring Twenties," in Louis P. Cain and Paul J. Uselding, eds., *Business Enterprise and Economic Change* (Kent, Ohio, 1973), emphasized the economic consequences of technological and design innovations. E.D. Kennedy, *The Automobile Industry* (New York, 1941) presented the case against corporate concentration within the oligopolistic industry. The difficulties of small automakers competing against the Big Three are discussed in Samuel C. Stearn, "The Financial History of the American Automobile Industry since 1928" (M.A. thesis, Wayne [State] University, 1948); Charles E. Edwards, *Dynamics of the United States Automobile Industry* (Columbia, S.C., 1965); Lawrence J. White, *The Automobile Industry since 1945* (Cambridge, Mass., 1971); and Harold Katz, *The Decline of Competition in the Automobile Industry, 1920–1940* (New York, 1977).

The conversion of the automotive industry to war production is celebrated in Christy Borth, *Masters of Mass Production* (Indianapolis, 1945), and in the Automobile Manufacturers Association, *Freedom's Arsenal: The Story of the Automotive Council for War Production* (Detroit, 1950). Barton J. Bernstein, "The Automobile Industry and the Coming of the Second World War," *Southwestern Social Science Quarterly* 47 (June 1966): 22–33, challenged that view and indicted the automakers for their willingness to profit from the economic expansion after 1939 while resisting complete conversion to military production.

Studebaker's own version of its history appears in the following works: Albert Russel Erskine, *History of the Studebaker Corporation* (South Bend, Ind., 1924); Charles A. Lippincott, "Promoting Employee Team Work and Welfare without Paternalism," *Industrial Management* 71 (March 1926): 146–50; Glenn Griswold, "Humanized Employee Relations: Studebaker an Example," *Public Opinion Quarterly* 4 (Sept. 1940): 487–96; Kathleen Smallzried and Dorothy Roberts, *More Than You Promise* (New York, 1942); and Stephen Longstreet, *A Century on Wheels* (New York, 1952). Robert T. Swaine, *The Cravath Firm and Its Predecessors, 1819–1948*, II (New York, 1948), an inhouse history of the legal firm employed by Studebaker, contains some useful information about financial dealings during the period of Hoffman's management.

No comprehensive scholarly history of Studebaker has yet been published. Richard M. Langworth, *Studebaker: The Postwar Years* (Osceola, Wis., 1979) provides a useful summary by a competent automotive historian critical of Hoffman's management; regarding the fate of Studebaker-Packard, Langworth followed too closely the self-serving claims of James J. Nance. The Studebaker Papers at Discovery Hall Museum in South Bend were uncatalogued and difficult to use, but the collection contained valuable information not available elsewhere. The South Bend Public Library provided a useful clipping file. For more general information, the Detroit Public Library's automotive history collection proved particularly helpful.

Opinions about Studebaker's labor policies have been sharply divided. Frederick H. Harbison and Robert Dubin, *Patterns of Union-Management Relations* (Chicago, 1947), written during the postwar boom, favorably contrasted Studebaker with General Motors. Robert M. MacDonald, *Collective Bargaining in the Automobile Industry* (New Haven, Conn., 1963), written after Studebaker collapsed, sharply criticized its management for laxity; though MacDonald blamed that collapse almost exclusively on labor policies without adequately considering other market forces, his book is a valuable corrective to the argument of Harbison and Dubin. Nelson Lichtenstein, "Auto Worker Militancy and the Structure of Factory Life, 1937–1955," *Journal of American History* 67 (Sept. 1980): 335–53, explains the relationship of technological change, shop stewards, and worker resistance to management.

The accounts of Studebaker's labor policies left by officials of the United Auto Workers, Local 5, did not prove enlightening. James D. Hill, *A Brief History of the Labor Movement of Studebaker* (South Bend, Ind., 1953), written when the company needed favorable publicity, resembles publicity for Studebaker's centennial celebration. On the other hand, oral histories at the Walter P. Reuther Library, Wayne State University, including copies of interviews conducted independently by Loren Pennington, generally share MacDonald's critical stance and often bitterly denounce Hoffman and Harold Vance for laxity; in some cases those interviews also reveal serious errors or misunderstanding about Studebaker's policies and the economics of the automotive industry. The UAW-Local 5 Papers at the Reuther Library provided disappointing. The American Federation of Labor (AFL) Papers at the State Historical Society of Wisconsin provided some material about the establishment of the union at Studebaker.

Hoffman's leadership in the automotive safety campaign and related matters of car design are discussed in my own article, "Paul G. Hoffman, Studebaker, and the Car Culture," *Indiana Magazine of History* 79 (Sept. 1983): 209–30. Some useful correspondence not in Hoffman's papers at the Truman Library is in the Roy D. Chapin Papers and the Blair Moody Papers at the Michigan Historical Collections and the Abbott L. Lowell Papers at Harvard University. Jeffrey L. Meickle, *Twentieth Century Limited* (Philadelphia, 1979), discusses the career of Studebaker's chief industrial designer, Raymond Loewy.

Business and Government: The CED

The best study of how corporate leaders viewed the role of management in society is Morrell Heald, *The Social Responsibilities of Business* (Cleveland, 1970). Richard S. Tedlow, *Keeping the Corporate Image* (Greenwich, Conn., 1979), explores the growth of corporate public relations, including lobbying. Robert Griffith, "The Selling of America: The Advertising Council and American Politics, 1942–1960," *Business History Review* 57 (Autumn 1983): 388–412, an account of one organization's public relations campaign, sensibly avoids exaggerating the influence of business. Howell John Harris, *The Right to Manage* (Madison, Wis., 1982), is an excellent study of industrial relations during the 1940s. Randolph E. Paul, *Taxation in the United States* (Boston, 1954), is an important study that considers business influence on public policy.

The emergence of the Committee for Economic Development is most fully discussed by Karl Schriftgiesser, *Business Comes of Age* (New York, 1960), and *Business and Public Policy* (Englewood Cliffs, N.J., 1967). Sidney Hyman, *The Lives of William Benton* (Chicago, 1969), is a biography of

Hoffman's friend and cofounder of the CED. William Steinert Hill, Jr., "The Business Community and National Defense: Corporate Leaders and the Military, 1943–1950" (Ph.D. dissertation, Stanford University, 1980), includes the CED in a discussion of business-government relations. Calvin B. Hoover, *Memoirs of Capitalism, Communism, and Nazism* (Durham, N.C., 1965), contains useful information about the CED.

Several historians have linked Hoffman and the CED with a business ideology categorized as "corporatism." *Business History Review* 52 (Autumn 1978) was devoted entirely to this interpretive scheme; for a sophisticated and subtle treatment of the semantics, see in particular Ellis Hawley, "The Discovery and Study of a 'Corporate Liberalism,'" 309–20. Joan Hoff Wilson, *Herbert Hoover: Forgotten Progressive* (Boston, 1975), and Jordan A. Schwarz, *The Speculator: Bernard M. Baruch in Washington, 1917–1965* (Chapel Hill, N.C., 1981), portray their subjects, often similar in thinking, as advocates of a variant of corporatism. Robert M. Collins, in *The Business Response to Keynes, 1929–1964* (New York, 1981), and in his articles identified the CED with that business ideology. A similar perspective is advanced by Kim McQuaid in *Big Business and Presidential Power* (New York, 1982), and his other works.

The Marshall Plan and Foreign Relations

Historians who emphasize the corporatist ideology often link it with business leaders' interests in international trade policies. Without actually referring to "corporatism," William A. Williams, *The Contours of American History* (Cleveland, 1961) does discuss Hoffman, the CED, and American corporate "syndicalism." David W. Eakins, "Business Planners and America's Postwar Expansion," in David Horowitz, ed., *Corporations and the Cold War* (New York, 1969), 143–71 and "Policy-Planning for the Establishment," in Ronald Radosh and Murray N. Rothbard, eds., *A New History of Leviathan* (New York, 1972), 188–205, follow that interpretive scheme and provide fuller discussion. Alfred E. Eckes, Jr., "Open Door Expansionism Reconsidered: The World War II Experience," *Journal of American History* 59 (Mar. 1973): 909–24, provides a sensible rebuttal to those scholars who exaggerate business fears of a postwar depression and the need for foreign markets.

On postwar American foreign policy, Lloyd C. Gardner, *Architects of Illusion* (New York, 1970), and Gabriel and Joyce Kolko, *The Limits of Power* (New York, 1972), provide a revisionist perspective emphasizing the search for markets. Thomas G. Paterson, *Soviet-American Confrontation* (Baltimore, Md., 1973), discusses the American goal of peace and prosperity. Alfred E. Eckes, Jr., *A Search for Solvency: Bretton Woods and the International Monetary System, 1941–1971* (Austin, Tex., 1975) focuses on the technical economic issues of international trade.

For the history of the Marshall Plan, Harry B. Price, *The Marshall Plan and Its Meaning* (Ithaca, 1955) comes close to being the official version, emphasizing its role in the Truman administration's containment policy. Ernest H. van der Beugel, *From Marshall Aid to Atlantic Partnership* (Amsterdam, Netherlands, 1966), explores the diplomacy of containment. Hadley Arkes, *Bureaucracy, the Marshall Plan, and the National Interest* (Princeton, N.J., 1972), critically assesses the administration of the aid program. Imanuel Wexler, *The Marshall Plan Revisited* (Westport, Conn., 1973), is an assessment by an economist that does not challenge prevailing views. William F. Sanford, Jr., "The American Business Community and the European Recovery Program, 1947–1952" (Ph.D. dissertation, University of Texas, 1980), includes a sensible discussion of the CED. Michael J. Hogan, "Revival and Reform: America's Twentieth-Century Search for a New Economic Order Abroad," *Diplomatic History* 8 (Fall 1984): 287–310 and "American Marshall Planners and the Search for a European Neocapitalism," *American Historical Review* 90: 44–72 (Feb. 1985), link Hoffman, the CED, and the ECA with the business ideology of "technocorporatism." David S. Painter, "Oil and the Marshall Plan," *Business History Review* 58 (Autumn 1984): 359–383 shows that the ECA refused to support the pricing policies of American oil companies but faced limited options.

Among published works by those connected with the Marshall Plan, Arthur H. Vandenberg, Jr., ed., *The Private Papers of Senator Vandenberg* (Boston, 1952), is most useful about the circumstances of Hoffman's selection. Dean Acheson, *Present at the Creation* (New York, 1969), should be supplemented by David S. McLellan, *Dean Acheson* (New York, 1976). E.A.J. Johnson, *American Imperialism in the Image of Peer Gynt* (Minneapolis, 1971), is a thoughtful and broad ranging memoir by the director of the ECA's Korean Program.

Several of the participants in the Marshall Plan have left oral histories. At the Truman Library, the most valuable oral histories, besides Hoffman's, were those of William H. Draper, Jr., Lincoln Gordon, Milton Katz, Robert Marjolin, and Lord Oliver Franks. The oral histories of Richard M. Bissell and David K. E. Bruce did not contain useful information or insights not available elsewhere. At the Columbia Oral History Office, interviews with Arthur A. Kimball and James J. Wadsworth provide interesting accounts of Hoffman as an administrator and policy-maker; Averell Harriman's interview does not add much.

Besides the files of his correspondence and speeches at the Truman Library, Hoffman's views while head of the ECA are best followed through his many appearances before congressional committees. The volumes of the *Foreign Relations of the United States, 1948–1951* (Washington, D.C., 1973–1979), though incomplete, are also useful. The Harry S. Truman Papers at the Truman Library contain surprisingly little. The papers of the Economic Cooperation Administration are located at the National Archives. Contemporary journalistic accounts are still useful, but many merely reveal the success of the ECA's publicity apparatus.

The Ford Foundation and the Fund for the Republic

Hoffman's experiences with the Ford Foundation and its spinoff, the Fund for the Republic, have been examined in several studies. Dwight Macdonald, *The Ford Foundation* (New York, 1956), without the benefit of cooperation from Hoffman and other important insiders, emphasized substantive issues dividing Hoffman the activist and Henry Ford II, a more cautious businessman. Partly to answer Macdonald, the foundation commissioned William Greenleaf, "The Ford Foundation: The Formative Years," completed in July 1958 and deposited at the Ford Foundation Archives in New York and at the Henry Ford Museum in Dearborn, Michigan. Greenleaf's unpublished manuscript is indispensable. Thomas C. Reeves, *Freedom and the Foundation: The Fund for the Republic* (New York, 1969), based on the Fund's papers (which have been partially destroyed since his research), remains the standard work. Frank K. Kelly, *Court of Reason: Robert Hutchins and the Fund for the Republic* (New York, 1981), provides an insider's view especially strong on personal disputes within the organization. Edward H. Berman, *The Influence of the Carnegie, Ford, and Rockefeller Foundations on American Foreign Policy: The Ideology of Philanthropy* (Albany, N.Y., 1983) is a revisionist work short on research and heavy with predictable criticism of the foundations as class institutions that promote American cultural imperialism. A more sensible critique of the activities of foundations appears in Frank Ninkovich, "The Rockefeller Foundation, China, and Cultural Change," *Journal of American History* 70 (March 1984): 799–820.

Although it did not make its files available, the Ford Foundation did grant access to its excellent and extensive oral history collection, directed during the early 1970s by Charles T. Morrissey. The interview with Henry Ford II remains closed, but Morrissey personally assured me that Ford said nothing not available elsewhere. Bernard Gladieux's interview is also closed; however, he provided a personal account of his perspective as Hoffman's assistant in New York, and his interview at the Columbia Oral History Office also proved useful. Because the interviewees so often used their oral histories to continue personal rivalries and disputes, I decided not to quote directly their unsubstantiated statements. In particular, I discounted W.H. Ferry's interview, though pungent in expression, because of his falling-out with Robert Hutchins shortly before the oral history was conducted. The files of the Fund for the Republic, originally located in Santa Barbara but now at Princeton University, were partially destroyed well after Thomas Reeves had used them and contain little about Hoffman. U.S., House of Representatives, Select Committee to Investigate Tax-Exempt Foundations and Comparable Organizations, *Tax-Exempt Foundations,* 82d Cong., 2d sess. (1953) and 83rd Cong., 2d sess. (1954), are standard sources for understanding how right-wingers assaulted the foundations.

The Eisenhower Administration

On the Eisenhower administration, Herbert S. Parmet, *Eisenhower and the American Crusade* (New York, 1972), is an excellent overview. Also valuable is the much briefer work, Charles C. Alexander, *Holding the Line* (Bloomington, Ind., 1975). An important study of Eisenhower's world view is Robert Griffith, "Dwight Eisenhower and the Corporate Commonwealth," *American Historical Review* 87 (Feb. 1982): 87–122, though it strains to find a consistent pattern of corporatist ideology.

Eisenhower's *Mandate for Change, 1953–1956* (Garden City, N.Y., 1963), discusses the 1952 election campaign. *Public Papers of the Presidents of the United States: Dwight D. Eisenhower, 1954, 1956* (Washington, 1954, 1956) must be supplemented by other works. Robert L. Branyan and Lawrence H. Larson, eds., *The Eisenhower Administration 1953–1961,* II (New York, 1971), and Robert Ferrell, ed., *The Eisenhower Diaries* (New York, 1981), are important collections. Both Eisenhower's papers at the Dwight D. Eisenhower Library and Hoffman's papers at the Truman Library contain correspondence not published elsewhere.

Of the other published memoirs, the most useful regarding Hoffman's relationship with Eisenhower were Sherman Adams, *Firsthand Report* (New York, 1961); Henry Cabot Lodge, *The Storm Has Many Eyes* (New York, 1973) and *As It Was* (New York, 1976); Richard M. Nixon, *Six Crises* (New York, 1962); Ellis D. Slater, *The Ike I Knew* (n.p., 1980); C. L. Sulzberger, *A Long Row of Candles* (New York, 1969). At the Columbia Oral History Office, the following interviews shed light on Hoffman's activities: Sherman Adams, Chester Bowles, Herbert Brownell, Lucius Clay, Roscoe Drummond, Percy M. Lee, Kevin McCann, and Irving Salomon.

Several works examine the campaign against Senator Joseph McCarthy. Harry M. Scoble, *Ideology and Electoral Action* (San Francisco, 1967), focuses on the National Committee for an Effective Congress. Robert Griffith, *The Politics of Fear* (Lexington, Ky., 1970) is useful for identifying the leaders of the CED as among the strongest critics of McCarthy. Richard M. Fried, *Men against McCarthy* (New York, 1976), focuses more closely on Congress. David M. Oshinsky, *A Conspiracy So Immense: The World of Joe McCarthy* (New York, 1983), amplifies Griffith's explanation of why businessmen like Hoffman opposed McCarthy.

Besides the works already mentioned, Eisenhower's foreign policy is the subject of Robert A. Divine, *Eisenhower and the Cold War* (New York, 1981). More useful for understanding Hoffman's role are Blanche Wiesen Cook, *The Declassified Eisenhower* (Garden City, N.Y., 1981), and especially Burton I. Kaufman, *Trade and Aid: Eisenhower's Foreign Economic Policy, 1953–1961* (Baltimore, Md., 1982).

The U.N. and Economic Development

The best way to understand American views on economic development is through David A. Baldwin, *Economic Development and American Foreign Policy, 1943–62* (Chicago, 1966), and Robert A. Packenham, *Liberal America and the Third World: Political Development in Foreign Aid and Social Science* (Princeton, N.J., 1973). Burton I. Kaufman's *Trade and Aid* also discusses how American leaders dealt with that theme during the late 1950s, a critically important period. Alfred E. Eckes, Jr., *A Search for Solvency*, answers critics of American trade policies with the undeveloped countries. Robert W. Tucker, *The Inequality of Nations* (New York, 1977) is a philosophical rebuttal of radical critics of inequality.

Of the many works on the structure and operations of the U.N., the most useful are: John G. Hadwen and Johan Kaufman, *How United Nations Decisions Are Made* (Leyden, Netherlands, 1960); Ernest B. Haas, *Tangle of Hopes* (Englewood Cliffs, N.J., 1968); Mahdi Elmandjro, *The United Nations System* (London, 1973); Martin Hill, *The United Nations System* (Cambridge, Eng., 1978).

Hoffman's experiences as a member of the U.S. Mission to the U.N. are discussed in Henry Cabot Lodge's diary, *As It Was*, and Harrison Brody's *U.N. Diary* (New York, 1957). Another insider's account, Seymour Maxwell Finger, *Your Man at the U.N.* (New York, 1980), offers a broader perspective on those events. The U.S. State Department, *Bulletin* (1957) published Hoffman's speeches to the U.N.

For the critical period when the U.N. launched the Special Fund, biographies of Dag Hammarskjold are useful. Brian Urquhart, *Hammarskjold* (New York, 1972), is a comprehensive work by a U.N. official who had access to private papers. Joseph P. Lash, *Dag Hammarskjold* (Garden City, N.Y., 1961), and Mark W. Zacher, *Dag Hammarskjold's United Nations* (New York, 1970), provide valuable insights. Andrew Cordier's "Recollections of Dag Hammarskjold and the United Nations" and C. V. Narasihman's oral history at the Columbia Oral History Office are disappointing.

The affairs of the U.N. leadership can also be followed in Andrew Cordier and Wilder Foote, eds., *Public Papers of Secretaries-General of the United Nations: U Thant* (New York, 1976). The activities of the Governing Councils of the Special Fund and of the Development Program can be followed through the U.N. document series.

On the Special Fund, Andrew Shonfield, *The Attack on World Poverty* (New York, 1960), is a favorable account by a British journalist. Richard N. Gardner, *In Pursuit of World Order* (New York, 1964), presents the Kennedy administration's view of the Cuban controversy. John G. Stoessinger, *The*

United Nations and the Superpowers (New York, 1965), also examines that issue. U.S., Senate, Foreign Relations Committee, *United Nations Special Fund*, 88th Cong., 1st sess. (1963), provides information on that controversy.

Shirley Hazzard, *Defeat of an Ideal* (Boston, 1973), criticizes the U.N. and its development program even more sharply than does her novel, *People in Glass Houses* (New York, 1967). Hazzard relied very heavily on the Jackson Report, *A Study of the Capacity of the United Nations Development System* (Geneva, 1969), a two-volume work of enormous significance.

Hoffman's papers at the Truman Library, usually a rich source for his correspondence, prove disappointing for the 1960s, when he headed the Special Fund and the Development Program. I did gain insights about Hoffman's activities at the U.N. from interviews with Anna Rosenberg Hoffman, Myer Cohen, Arthur Goldschmidt, Clinton Rehling, and John von Arnold. Sir Robert Jackson, between trips abroad, consented to a telephone interview.

Index

Gray, John (Paul Hoffman's great-grandfather), 2, 4
Gross, H. R., 135
Guffey-Vinson Act, 46
Gwinn, Ralph Waldo, 62

Hammarskjold, Dag, 130, 131, 135, 143
Harriman, Averell, x, 60, 66, 77, 100
Harriman Committee, 60-61, 70
Heilbroner, Robert, 151
Henry, Paul-Marc, 143
Hill & Knowlton, 111
Hoffman, Anna (second wife), *See* Rosenberg, Anna
Hoffman, Clare, 130
Hoffman, Dorothy Brown (first wife), 10, 11, 36, 65, 111, 122, 141, 142
Hoffman, Eleanor Lott (mother), 3
Hoffman, George Delos (father), 2-3, 4-5
Hoffman, Hallock (son), 89, 101
Hoffman, Lathrop (son), 107, 109, 143
Hoffman, Paul G.
—personality and character, ix-x, xi, 5, 42, 44, 133, 148, 154, 158
—family background, 1-5
—education, 3-4
—and Studebaker: early connection with, 5-6, 9; vice-president, 13-21, 155-56; receiver, 22-24; president, 24, 28-41, 65, 156; leave from (1948), 39, 40; chairman, 98, 100, 107-17, 156; Studebaker-Packard chairman, 112, 114, 116, 117-19, 156-57; career assessed, 155-58
—and traffic safety, 8, 17, 28, 49, 157-58
—and Republican politics, 9, 49, 50, 61, 91-95, 130
—life in South Bend, 10-11
—on labor relations, 25-26, 27, 35, 36, 44, 55, 119
—managerial philosophy, 26-27, 30-31, 55-56
—on New Deal and Franklin D. Roosevelt, 43, 44, 45, 46-47, 48, 49, 50, 56, 159
—and CED, 52-54, 126, 159-60
—on government economic policies, 53-58, 108-09, 158-61
—on foreign affairs, 58-59, 60, 63; China, 58, 75-76, 121, 138; Cold War mentality, 59, 61, 63, 121, 138, 162; Soviet Union, 59-60, 68-69, 70, 78-79; trade and aid, 67, 68, 79, 120, 125,

132, 162; Indo-China, 76; Korea, 76, 77; *Peace Can Be Won*, 78; India, 87, 88, 121, 131
—and Harriman Committee, 60-61, 70
—and Johnston-Hoffman report, 61
—and ECA: administration, 61, 62, 66-70, 74, 77, 82, 83; policies, 63, 64-65, 69, 70-76, 79, 162-63; consultant, 86
—and Truman, 64-65, 92, 94
—on militarization, 76-77, 86
—and Ford Foundation: affairs within, 77, 82-86, 93-94, 96-98, 180 n. 6; foreign programs of, 79, 86-88, 163; congressional investigations of, 90-91, 97
—on economic development, 79, 120, 127, 133-134, 137-40, 145, 151-53, 164-65
—and Joseph McCarthy, 89, 90, 94, 96, 102, 103, 161
—attacks on, 90, 102, 103, 104, 113, 122-23, 130, 135
—and Eisenhower: political support for, 92-94, 95, 96; career problems discussed with, 98, 121, 122, 129, 130; automobile industry discussed with, 108, 117-18; foreign affairs discussed with, 120, 121, 124-25, 126, 127, 132, 135, 138
—and Henry Ford II, 96, 97, 98
—and Fund for the Republic, 98, 100-01, 102, 104, 119, 126
—career dilemma in 1950s, 121-22, 126, 129
—and United Nations: U. S. Mission, role in, 122, 123-26, 134; UNSF managing director, 130, 131, 132, 133-40; personal life while at, 141-42; UNDP administrator, 143, 144, 146, 148-50, 153
—and John F. Kennedy, 135-36
—and Lyndon Johnson, 141
—and Anna Rosenberg Hoffman, 142-43, 148, 154
—on population control, 144
—retirement and death, 153-54
—awarded Medal of Freedom, 154
Hoffman, Paul G., Company, 7, 8, 9, 34, 46
Hoffman, William Delos (grandfather), 2
Hoffman Specialty Manufacturing Corp., 5, 119, 126, 143, 167-68 n. 12
Holcombe, Arthur, 58